Peace Education

PEACE
EDUCATION

by
Ian M. Harris

McFarland & Company, Inc., Publishers
Jefferson, North Carolina, and London

Library of Congress Cataloguing-in-Publication Data

Harris, Ian M., 1943–
  Peace education.

  Bibliography: p. 221.
  Includes index.
  1. Peace—Study and teaching. I. Title.
JX1904.5.H39   1988   327.1′72′07   88-42509

ISBN 0-89950-354-3 (60# acid-free natural paper) ∞

Manufactured in the United States of America.

McFarland & Company, Inc., Publishers
  Box 611, Jefferson, North Carolina 28640

Acknowledgments

This work has had many contributors — people who have helped in its preparation, as well as people who have been spiritual guides and supporters of the author in his quest for peace and justice. In this latter category the author would like to acknowledge the important contribution of his wife, Sara Spence, whose deep commitment to social justice has been an inspiration. He would also like to acknowledge the important contribution that Quakers have made to his awareness of the role of love and nonviolence in the affairs of human beings. Without the courage and conviction of the millions of individuals involved in various peace movements throughout the world, this book would never have been written. The author is indebted to these people for the hope they have provided him.

In terms of preparing this manuscript, the author would like to thank Phil Smith and the staff of the Office of Research at the School of Education at the University of Wisconsin–Milwaukee who have helped with typing, reduplicating, and various data analyses connected with this study. Cathy Nelson from the Word Processing Office at the same institution has struggled with many different drafts of this manuscript.

The author would like to thank Sam Yarger, Dean of Education at the University of Wisconsin–Milwaukee, for a sabbatical leave during the academic year 1986–87. This leave enabled him to finish this manuscript. Delbert Clear and Diane Pollard deserve thanks for their support during the author's application for tenure. The tenured position which he received has made possible the extensive research that went into the preparation of this manuscript. Ken Wodtke from the Department of Educational Psychology has been a constant source of support and professional challenges. This book was first conceived at his cabin in Madelaine Island.

Clint Fink has carefully read this manuscript, making important corrections that have sharpened both the style and accuracy of this book. A graduate student, Karen Gerrity, prepared a first draft of Chapter Eight. Kate Jolin, a community educator from Waukesha, Wisconsin, has read the manuscript, helping the author sharpen its style and content.

The author would also like to thank all the students who have taken his class on peace education. They have dared to open themselves up to exploring the terrifying issues of violence in their lives and have in many important ways supported their teacher's quest for peace and justice.

Table of Contents

Preface

Many adults currently active in the peace movement see their lives as journeys towards justice, a gradual awakening to the terrors of violence. Adults have important stories to tell about their life histories—how they have responded to violence and developed alternative nonviolent ways of dealing with conflict. These stories should be incorporated within peace education efforts to help focus interest on the various topics of peace education. Consequently, this book will begin with the journey of this author, telling how he became aware of the war and peace dilemmas that face his world and how he has responded to those dilemmas. This story will tell how one person has overcome violent social conditioning and dedicated his life to peace.

Ian M. Harris is a professor of community education at the University of Wisconsin–Milwaukee, where he teaches adult courses on peace education, conflict and change, and male identity. He has for three years chaired a faculty network that promotes peace studies on this urban campus of about 25,000 students. This group has recently created on that campus a peace studies certificate: an undergraduate student can earn a certificate in the study of War, Peace and Conflict by completing eighteen credits in prescribed courses that have an emphasis on peace and war issues. He has consulted with teachers and school systems in the Milwaukee area interested in peace education. Recently he has helped organize a statewide consortium of twenty public and private colleges for the study of war, peace and global conflict. He has presented papers on peace education at the American Educational Studies Association, at the American Educational Research Association, at the International Peace Research Association, at the annual Educators for Social Responsibility conference, and at scholarly meetings sponsored by COPRED, the Consortium on Peace, Research, Education, and Development. In the fall of 1987 he helped host a COPRED conference whose theme was "Peace Studies at the Crossroads." He serves on an advisory committee of the Wisconsin chapter of Educators for Social Responsibility which has been training teachers to run in-services on nuclear age education throughout the state of Wisconsin. He started to write this book when he realized there was no good introductory text for people interested in peace education.

He grew up on the East Coast on a small farm in northern New Jersey.

His father was English, a retired military officer from the Royal Air Force. His mother came from Indianapolis. His family was proud of its war traditions. His uncle, Sir Arthur Harris, headed bomber command for the Royal Air Force, and perfected the "art" of saturation bombing of civilian populations during the Second World War. In his family war was a glorious occupation. After all, he was born in 1943 when the Allies were busy defeating the Nazis.

As a young lad, he dreamed about becoming an airplane pilot. He participated in competitive sports, supported Barry Goldwater, and went hunting with his friends. His first association with nonviolence was when his father questioned the shooting of small animals — squirrels, rabbits, and chipmunks. Otherwise, he grew up adapting to the violent culture and norms of the 1950s.

The first questioning of the role of violence in his life came from the Vietnam War. At age eighteen he faced being drafted. He was able to avoid the draft by remaining in school at St. John's College in Annapolis, Maryland. While an undergraduate he often participated in anti-war demonstrations in Washington, D.C., which was only one hour from Annapolis. Upon graduating from college, he became a teacher, which in 1967 was a draft-deferrable occupation. In college he became close to a Quaker family in Bucks County and roomed with the oldest son from this family in 1968 in Philadelphia, where he became involved in anti-draft work. He volunteered for Eugene McCarthy's candidacy for president, and helped establish a public alternative inner-city high school in West Philadelphia, a part of the city dominated by youth gangs and crimes, where he had first-hand experience with the role of violence in young people's lives. This school had an affective education curriculum designed to help young people get in touch with their feelings and deal with conflicts in their lives.

Upon finishing his doctoral degree at Temple University in 1975 in Foundations of Education, Ian Harris received a position as an assistant professor at the University of Wisconsin in Milwaukee, where he teaches and advises older adults completing their undergraduate degree. In 1983 Dr. Harris first taught his course on peace education in response to concerns and interests expressed by students about the threats of nuclear weapons and the horrors of domestic abuse. At the same time a citizens' task force was being established in Milwaukee to promote peace education in the public schools. Harris has since that time taught that course to undergraduates and graduate students. He hopes through the course to have people become aware of the tremendous efforts that exist in the world to bring about peace and contribute to those efforts. A final paper for this course requires students to develop a peace curriculum. He has found that teachers who take this course initiate many different peace activities and lessons in their classrooms. Other students, if they aren't already involved in peace activities when they take this course, don't work for peace unless they are supported in these efforts by their peers. Most students, as a result of these classes, tend to adopt a more peaceful lifestyle.

In the process of preparing for this class he read extensively on the topics of violence and the arms race. He found such discussions about weapons, war, and destructive human behavior so deeply disturbing that he was having nightmares and feeling anxious. He felt the need for support for the insights he received about the depth of the problems of violence in contemporary life and sought a group that both understood the terror of violence and strongly opposed it. Consequently, he joined the local Friends Meeting in Milwaukee and has become spiritually enmeshed in seeking answers to questions about the dark side of human existence. Belonging to a Quaker community that for three hundred years has challenged violence on this planet gives him the strength and hope to continue on his quest to solve the problems of why human beings treat each other so cruelly. Although Dr. Harris is proud to be a Quaker, he doesn't think of himself as a pacifist. He feels that social change will come about through struggle. As a Quaker he does not believe in physical fighting, but rather nonviolent struggle for peace and justice. Peace education — attempting to convince people about the horrors of violence and instructing them about alternatives to violent behavior — makes an important contribution to that struggle.

Introduction

An art professor at a large Midwest university asked his students to draw pictures depicting peace. His students were bewildered by this request. Many thought for a while, but had a hard time imagining peaceful images. After a while a few students drew pictures of rainbows, doves, or other natural scenes. These students had a hard time responding to this simple request because the concepts associated with peace are not prevalent in contemporary culture. On the contrary, images of violence, destruction, and death dominate popular culture.

In 1910 William James, a distinguished American philosopher, wrote "The Moral Equivalent of War," an essay stating that educators and leaders should wage a campaign against militaristic thinking that was perverting civilization. Such a campaign would galvanize popular opinion, capturing the imagination of citizens heretofore influenced by war, which sparks heroism, bravery, and glory. The struggle for peace, if it is to be successful, must also provoke courage, must be understood as a heroic task, and must recruit thousands if not millions of converts willing to renounce violent means to settle disputes. Educators have an important role to play in this struggle because they help determine the values and beliefs of people throughout the world.

Since the nineteenth century social reformers have looked to schools to provide changes in society. Those opposed to the horrors of war have hoped that education could help create a more peaceful society by raising young people with an aversion to violence, an international awareness, a desire to settle disputes in nonviolent ways, an ability to resolve social conflicts peacefully, and an understanding of the calamity of war.

Most recently, fear of war has grown because nuclear weapons threaten the very existence of human civilization. Forty years after the development of the first atomic weapons, masses of citizens around the world are coming to grips with the horrifying consequences of unleashing the fundamental power that holds the universe together. An awareness of the terribly destructive nature of these weapons has initiated a growing fear about whether or not there will be a future.

Concerns about the impending nuclear holocaust have generated a new interest in teaching citizens to settle their conflicts nonviolently. Educators and citizens are discovering great ignorance about the complex

1

forces that promote violence in this world. To remedy this, peace education is becoming a more widely heralded field, where national and local
organizations provide conferences, courses, curricula, public events, and
seminars that enhance public awareness about the problems of war and
peace. School districts are adopting resolutions requiring teachers to address the threat of warfare. Churches are conducting forums, workshops, retreats, and study groups to inform their congregations about
the consequences of current military strategy. Colleges are teaching courses
and funding research institutes that concentrate on war, peace, and
conflict. Scholars are publishing research on the problems associated with
violence. Concerned citizens are conducting community education forums
to draw attention to policies that promote violence. A large peace movement with millions of members in countries throughout the world is
demanding the abolition of war. These organizations, by using educational means to promote knowledge about peace and militarism, are
discovering the richness of peace education as a strategy to deal with
violence.

Peace education involves students and educators in a commitment to
create a more just and peaceful world order. This type of education provides citizens with information about current policies, sharpens their ability
to analyze current states of affairs, encourages commitment in various
spheres of individual concern and endeavor—politics, public affairs, trade
union activities, social and cultural life—and strives to promote the free
will necessary to make personal choices about public policy. Students of
peace education study current defense policies so they can either support
or challenge them. Peace educators point citizens and future citizens
towards practical steps they can take to resolve conflicts in their own lives
as well as to become more effective actors in political systems. Although
schools provide an ideal forum for dealing with the issues of violence, these
public institutions are not the only arena for programs dealing with peace
and war. Because adults need to be informed about these critical issues,
church groups, neighborhood organizations, civic clubs, and volunteer
associations are becoming actively involved in peace education.

Peace education enhances the purpose of education, which is to reveal
and tap those energies that make possible the full human enjoyment of a
meaningful and productive existence. Educators try to create a healthy
growth and development in children and adults, but violent threats
challenge educational endeavors. The nature of human consciousness, as
Camus wrote, requires a belief in the future. Thus, as modern nations produce weapons systems that can annihilate human existence, they may be
altering the structure of human consciousness, which will in turn affect
pedagogical relationships between teachers and students. Students who
don't believe in the future will give up in school. The gravity of this impending crisis will make many educational activities meaningless.

Teachers at all levels can contribute to the efforts to make the world more peaceful both by helping their students understand and deal creatively with the consequences of violent human behavior and by teaching them how to be peacemakers. Securing peace will require knowledge, changing attitudes, new ways of behaving, skills for managing conflict, and political change.

This book, *Peace Education,* introduces a relatively new area of educational reform. It defines peace education, discusses current activities, presents key issues and topics, describes obstacles, suggests educational approaches for different age groups, discusses new ways of thinking, explains how to construct educational programs that will provide information about the impact of violence upon human communities, addresses fears generated by the arms race, and presents alternatives for resolving conflict nonviolently. This book has been written for a broad audience that includes school personnel, university professors, scholars, church leaders, and peace movement activists. Many different types of people are currently concerned with peace, and the issues of violence that spark their interest cover many different realms — from domestic abuse to international terrorism. Such diversity requires a book with many different foci. The first three chapters, written for the general reader, provide the goals, theory and practice of peace education. Chapter Four presents key topics that should be understood by those who want to become peace educators. Chapter Five describes how teachers and concerned citizens can develop peace education programs for their classes, communities, or churches. Chapter Six emphasizes obstacles to teaching about war and peace. Chapter Seven, "The Peaceful Classroom," presents the principles of peace pedagogy, how teachers can provide experiences with the techniques of nonviolence while students are learning about the problems of war and peace. The principles of pedagogy introduced here should be applicable both for classes in formal schools and in community settings — churches, homes, storefront offices, neighborhood recreation sites, and community-based organizations — where so much adult education for peace takes place. Chapter Eight, "Developmental Issues," describes how to teach peace to pupils of different age groups. The ninth chapter evaluates various educational issues that peace educators need to be aware of while teaching about war, peace and conflict. This chapter might be of most interest to teachers and other school personnel in formal educational settings. The final chapter, "What Difference Does It Make," evaluates the effectiveness of peace education.

1. Goals of Peace Education

Since wars begin in the minds of men, it is in the minds of men that the defenses of peace must be constructed. — Preamble of the Constitution of the United Nations Educational, Scientific and Cultural Organization (UNESCO)

The creation of peace is one of the great unsolved human problems. Since the advent of organized society, human beings have prayed for, dreamed about, and strived to achieve peace. In recent years human warlike propensities have reached new heights. Large majorities of the populations of the most technologically advanced countries in the world are held hostage by nuclear stockpiles. The creation of the atomic bomb, the development of biological and chemical warfare, and the manufacture of high-tech weaponry have elevated the dangers of war to a point where the future can no longer be taken for granted. The scientific modes of thinking developed in Europe in the eighteenth century have created an industrial society that has brought the human race to a point where it can no longer rely on militaristic ways to resolve differences but must adopt nonviolent solutions to problems.

Most human societies have waged war, educated their youth into the traditions of war, and spent large portions of their wealth building armaments. When both vast profits and individual careers depend on the perpetuation of warlike policies, militaristic behavior will not disappear simply because people pray for an end to war. This emphasis on military might will change only if it is rejected and replaced with peaceful behavior. As Albert Einstein said fifty years ago:

> We stand, therefore, at the parting of the ways. Whether we find the way of peace or continue along the road of brute force, so unworthy of our civilization, depends on ourselves. On the one side the freedom of the individual and the security of society beckon to us; on the other, slavery for the individual and the annihilation of our civilization threaten us. Our fate will be according to our deserts.[1]

People learn warlike behavior from parents, friends, teachers, cultural norms, social institutions, and the mass media. Violent images promoted in the culture reinforce violent behavior and instill the belief that aggression must be regulated through violent means. This need not be true. Indeed, Margaret Mead and other anthropologists have discovered supportive, caring cultures that practice nonviolence. For example, the Inuits, commonly known as Eskimos, do not fight among each other but rather channel aggressive impulses to overcome the harsh vicissitudes of an arctic existence. If some cultures exist peacefully, why can't all of them?

To a large extent cultural norms and messages determine behavior in a given society. If individuals receive messages that describe social reality as violent, they will be fearful. People who believe that the only way to preserve their lives, liberties, and properties is through physical violence will turn to weapons to protect themselves. Because they are afraid, they arm themselves. In this way physical force and the use of violence rest upon human insecurity. In order to overcome this reliance upon force individuals have to be educated about how nonviolent alternatives can provide security.

Even within current social arrangements that teem with violence, the ways of peace have successfully altered aggressive behavior. Gandhi's nonviolent principles liberated India from one of the world's largest empires. United States citizens, organizing for peace in the 1960s and 1970s, contributed to the end of the Vietnam War. Neighborhood block clubs where individuals organize against crime have been shown to decrease urban vandalism. In the United States Dr. Martin Luther King, Jr., and other civil rights leaders dedicated to the principles of nonviolence, helped minority people gain dignity and civil rights. In the 1950s and 1960s citizen protest against atmospheric testing of nuclear weapons led to a partial test ban treaty. In 1986 the Philippine people used nonviolent tactics to depose their ruler, Ferdinand Marcos. It has also been demonstrated that domestic violence can be reduced through improved communication.

In order to eliminate war and violence humans must understand, desire, and struggle to achieve peace. If and when the desire for peace becomes strongly rooted in human consciousness, people will demand new social structures that reduce risks of violence. Peace education not only promotes such a desire for peace within the human mind, but also teaches peacemaking skills so that human beings can learn nonviolent ways to deal with each other.

Peace education confronts directly the forms of violence that dominate society by creating a commitment to the ways of peace. Just as a doctor learns in medical school how to minister to the sick, students in peace education classes learn how to solve problems caused by violence.

Social violence and warfare can be described as a form of pathology, a disease. Few people would be satisfied with simply treating the symptoms of a severely debilitating or life-threatening disease. Yet, we continue to respond to most forms of violence by preparing for the continued incidence of social violence and the repeated outbreak of warfare, rather than by trying to eliminate their causes.[2]

Societies spend money and resources training doctors to heal the ill. Why shouldn't they also educate their citizens to conduct affairs nonviolently?

The Concept of "Peace"

The concept of peace has changed throughout recorded history as different groups and individuals have struggled to realize a harmonious state of existence. Many people think of peace as tranquility or the absence of war. Peace is a positive concept which implies much more than the absence of war.[3] Peace is the practice of love. As a necessary condition for human survival, it implies that human beings resolve conflicts without using force. "Peace" has been defined as a state of existence where:

> Neither the overt violence of war nor the covert violence of unjust systems is used as an instrument for extending the interests of a particular nation or group. It is a world where basic human needs are met, and in which justice can be obtained and conflict resolved through nonviolent processes and human and material resources are shared for the benefit of all people.[4]

"Peace," a concept which motivates the imagination, connotes more than the cessation of war. It implies human beings working together to resolve conflicts, respect standards of justice, satisfy basic needs, and honor human rights.

While the absence of war can be understood as peace, and the absence of peace can be war, peace and war are not correlatives. A state not at war may not be peaceful. Its citizens may reside in neighborhoods with high crime rates or live in families where they are beaten. They may exist in conditions where they are oppressed economically, starved or in miserable health. Violence can imply more than a direct, physical confrontation. It is expressed not only on battlefields but also through circumstances which limit life, civil rights, health, personal freedom, and self-fulfillment. This type of violence, referred to as *structural violence,* occurs when wealth and power exploit or oppress others, and standards of justice are not upheld. It is created by the deprivation of basic human needs and creates suffering for individuals throughout the world. Structural violence implies that those situations where an individual's survival is threatened are not peaceful.

Since societies will always have hostilities, disagreements, and arguments, the pursuit of peace does not strive for an idealized state of human existence with no aggression or conflict. It strives, rather, for the means to resolve disagreements without resort to warfare or physical force, and for justice where human beings are treated with dignity. Peace has an individual context which implies peace of mind and the absence of fear. For an individual to live peacefully he or she must be able to satisfy basic needs and resolve conflicts within friendships, work-places, families, and communities in a way that promotes the well-being of all.

Peacemaking is a skill that can be taught. Individuals can learn how to arbitrate conflicts and negotiate agreements. Societies provide peace for their citizens by developing a collective security with laws that govern human behavior. In this social context peace implies law and order, self control, a respect for others, and the guarantee of human rights. Much concern about peace relates to nations and their ability to settle disagreements without resorting to war. Internationally, peace implies that governments will respect the sovereignty of nations and will use methods other than force to manage conflicts.

Strategies for Peace

Although most people desire peace, there exists considerable disagreement about how to achieve it. During war a strategy for peace addresses ways to terminate the violence of battles. In times when a country is not waging war a strategy for peace might involve constructing elaborate defenses against perceived enemies, or a literacy campaign to relieve the oppression of citizens unable to satisfy basic needs. What particular approach to peace a given society uses depends upon the traditions and values of that society. There are five major strategies for a lasting state of peace. They are (1) peace through strength, (2) pacifism, (3) peace with justice, (4) institution building, and (5) peace education. Peace educators need to become familiar with these different approaches so they can present their strengths and weaknesses to students who can, in turn, decide for themselves the best ways to achieve peace.

• **Peace Through Strength.** The concept of "peace through strength" is credited to the Roman Empire: "Si vis parem, para bellum" (if you desire peace, prepare for war). In modern terms peace through strength requires massive armaments, and it is often discussed in terms of *balance of power.* Under this approach to peace, a state, an individual, or group of individuals is dissuaded from going to war because the opposition is so well armed that a state, individual, or group of individuals cannot be sure that it (they) will win. A balance of power depends upon approximate equality of military force. If one country has military superiority over another, the weaker nation may feel threatened.

For modern industrial nations peace through strength involves *nuclear deterrence,* where the element of dissuasion lies not so much in the possibility of losing, but in fear of the catastrophic consequences of going to war. Deterrence and peace through strength currently dominate the thinking of the superpowers, so that attempts to promote other strategies for peace are often considered subversive. This desire to be stronger than potential enemies so stimulates the cultures of nations that they devote large portions of their budgets to support the military expenses which are "justified" because they maintain peace by deterring aggression. Peace through strength, the current policy endorsed by those in power in many of the nations of the world, is credited for deterring a war between the United States and the Soviet Union.

In order to increase their power and hence secure the safety of their citizens, nation states support strong militaries, which in turn create a set of values referred to as *militarism* — "the result of a process whereby military values, ideology and patterns of behavior achieve a dominating influence over the political, social, economic and foreign affairs of the state."[5] Militarism comes from values, opinions and social organizations which support war and violence as legitimate ways to manage human affairs. Military traditions — salutes, orders, parades, war movies, paramilitary societies, and other militaristic rituals — are deeply rooted in minds throughout the world and contribute to a global predicament where nuclear warheads imperil human civilization, where arms races gobble up precious resources, and where political elites use military means to protect their privileges.

Arguments against peace through strength include its tremendous cost. Economists have done numerous studies which indicate that an increase in military expenditure is inversely correlated with the growth of a civilian economy.[6] Money spent on defense comes from general revenue, so that an increase in military spending often means a decrease in social services and a lowered standard of living for many citizens. This approach to peace presents severe difficulties for countries in the underdeveloped world, where scarce resources are directed away from human needs towards human destruction. The total amount of money spent on arms each year in the world is fast approaching one trillion dollars — a huge sum of money that diverts resources from solving many of the problems that cause war in the first place.

Peace through strength relies upon technological solutions to social problems, as researchers and defense experts spend time and money developing sophisticated weapon systems. The conflicts that cause wars are human, and their resolution requires the energy, talents, and creativity of human beings, not relying on machines, but rather on trusting human instincts to bridge and resolve the gaps inherent in conflict. More sophisticated weaponry creates a situation where civilizations could be annihilated through some technical error. The irony of peace through strength is that the invention of modern weapons has created a destabilizing world climate where many citizens feel insecure because of the tremendous threats posed by weapons that have been created to enhance their security. The use of these weapons would kill millions of people and severely alter the earth's ecosystem. This scenario has been detailed by scientists, who describe a "nuclear winter," where the use of nuclear, chemical and biological weapons relied upon by deterrence theory could destroy human civilization.[7] Concern about this threat has stimulated large peace movements in industrialized societies and has created a desire on the part of many people to live in a world that no longer relies on war to solve its problems. Indeed, deterrence theory, because it depends on such destructive weapons, may make war obsolete.

- **Pacifism.** The pacifist road to peace implies the total absence of warmaking and the use of violence in daily affairs. Under this approach peace comes from setting a peaceful example and eschewing physical violence to settle disagreements. To pacifists all forms of life are sacred, and hence, they only use physical force to defend themselves. Killing any form of life is immoral. They employ nonviolent conflict resolution strategies to deal with human aggression. On an international scale this approach to peace suggests that if all nations disarm, they will have to adopt nonviolent resistance as a means to counteract a hostile invasion. However, with the majority of countries unarmed, the threat of war would be greatly reduced.

Pacifism has a moral and spiritual strength. Major religions have promoted pacifism as a goal for human enterprise. Buddhists renounce the use of violence as a part of a spirituality that finds all forms of life sacred. Early Christians opposed conscription in the Roman army. Quakers in England in the seventeenth century resisted Cromwell's forced conscription in the British countryside. By using civil disobedience tactics, pacifists mobilize support for alternatives to physical force. Although in most societies pacifists represent a very small minority, they have in determined ways provided a moral force against the wholesale use of violence endorsed by nation-states.

Human societies are so structured that pacifist policies create insecurities. People who live in violent or potentially violent areas feel that they have to arm in order to protect themselves. If a particular nation were to disarm, it could be vulnerable to attack from armed states that desire its resources, and hence a pacifist strategy allows nations with strong militaries to dominate the world. Pacifists, if they are to reduce the wholesale adoption of military strategy as a means of defense, must teach the ways of nonviolent resistance as an alternative to reliance upon armaments.

● **Peace Through Justice.** Peace through justice implies that peace can be attained by eliminating social oppression and economic exploitation. Peace through justice is concerned with poverty, disease, starvation, human misery, and the violation of human rights. People who promote peace through justice take an active stand against structural violence by demonstrating to rally public opinion, and by discrediting the violence of those they oppose.

Peace through justice addresses suffering and misery. As important as it may seem to many people to reduce nuclear stockpiles and promote arms control agreements, 41,000 people a day starve to death in this world. Millions suffer from disease, lack of sanitary conditions, racial injustice, inadequate health care, and malnutrition. People living under such conditions suffer or even face death because they cannot meet basic survival needs. Addressing these needs is a way to eradicate violence on this planet.

Championing justice involves this approach to peace in ideological controversy. Capitalists claim that socialist societies practice political repression, while socialists attack capitalism for exploiting the mass of humankind to generate profits. The banner of peace through justice is carried by many combatants, each side claiming that it stands for justice while the opposition stands for tyranny and oppression. Because peace through justice identifies with oppressed people, it is practiced outside the circles of traditional politics in many nations. The independent peace movement is repressed in Russia, as the radical Catholic Worker movement in the United States is treated with suspicion. Peace through justice, currently championed by a liberation theology that has grown up in South and Central America, points toward an emancipatory theology that threatens power elites. Thus, the struggle for justice is highly political.

● **Institution Building.** The development of effective international institutions hopes to avoid war by creating legal and political alternatives for resolving international conflicts. Known as *peace through politics,* which emphasizes working through political channels, this method for achieving peace is best typified by the United Nations, whose charter enumerates measures for the prevention of war and removal of threats to peace. The primary purpose of the establishment of the United Nations Educational, Scientific, and Cultural Organization (UNESCO), a branch of the United Nations, is

> to contribute to peace and security by promoting collaboration among the nations through education, science and culture in order to further universal respect for justice, for the rule of the law and for the human rights and fundamental freedoms which are affirmed for the peoples of the world, without distinction of race, sex, language or religion, by the Charter of the United Nations.[8]

Another example of a kind of institution that promotes peace between nations is the International Law of the Sea. Arms control treaties also fall under this heading. Such institutions use political processes, laws, and traditions to provide alternatives to armed conflict.

Developing institutions to resolve disagreements represents the rational solution to resolving conflicts between groups of human beings. Diplomats and heads of state negotiate and bargain to reduce hostilities on a global scale. They look to international law to settle disputes. Advocates of this position hope to create institutions that can be appealed to in seeking to resolve disputes. This strategy is limited, however, by the same pressures that cause disputes to rise in the first place. Countries go to war because they disagree strongly with the actions of another country and use military means to gain advantage. War is a gamble, and they hope to win. Generally, those same countries are not interested in resolving their disputes through arbitration. They fight to impose their will and enjoy the fruits of victory. Arbitration and diplomatic resolution of conflicts might be invoked if a military strategy has become stalled, but seldom are they the first avenues that nations use to resolve their differences. Another problem of peace through politics is the question of sanctions—what exactly can be done to punish a country that violates international treaties and obligations? If there are no effective nonmilitary means to punish aggressive states, there may be no way to enforce international agreements, thus weakening peace through institution building.

• **Peace Education.** Our last approach, peace education, attempts to teach people about peaceful conditions and the process of creating them. Peace education hopes not only to inform people about the various aspects of human conflict but also to teach skills of conflict resolution. The assumption behind peace education is that if citizens have more information about alternatives to the use of force that they will abjure the ways of violence. This assumption was tested in California by members of Physicians for Social Responsibility in the San Francisco area, who distributed a two-part questionnaire at a series of fifty-seven separate educational events.[9] The first part, distributed prior to presentations on the medical effects of nuclear war, asked among other questions, "Are there causes worth fighting a nuclear war for?" Ten percent of the 1,355 people who completed the survey responded "yes" to this item. After the presentation, half of the people who originally said they thought there were causes worth fighting a nuclear war for changed their minds and answered "false" to this item. Although this study represents only a brief attitude change, it indicates that education can develop an aversion to war.

Peace education, as a strategy for lasting peace, relies on educating enough people to establish within a given population widespread support for peaceful policies. Support for this strategy is provided by Everett

Rogers, a professor at Stanford University,[10] in his studies of how an idea or innovation spreads through society. The six stages of adoption that he has defined are (1) attention, (2) interest, (3) evaluation, (4) trial, (5) adoption, and (6) confirmation. An individual has to first become aware of a new idea, for example, through media exposure. Interest is developed, and a favorable or unfavorable attitude forms. The pros and cons of the idea are compared and the idea is tried out. A decision is then made to adopt or reject the idea. Finally, the individual seeks confirmation for a particular decision concerning this idea. The rate of adoption is influenced by the degree to which the new idea is perceived as offering an advantage over the presently held idea and the degree to which the new idea is compatible with an individual's present beliefs. This research is most applicable to peace education when it discusses how a new idea, such as a freeze in production of nuclear weapons, becomes adopted by a society. His research has shown that the adoption of a new idea follows an s-shaped curve as illustrated in Table 1.[11] This s-shaped curve of adoption rises slowly at first when there are few people who adopt a new idea. It then accelerates to a maximum until half of the individuals in a society accept that idea. The curve increases at a slower rate as remaining individuals finally adopt the idea. The shaded area marks the time period during which the adoption process takes off. As Rogers points out, after a new idea is adopted by 20 percent of the population, it is virtually unstoppable. An important goal of peace education, then, is to have 20 percent of the population of any given country renounce the use of force to settle disagreements. This theory implies that a concern for peace would sweep thrugh society and become a norm guiding human conduct. This approach to peace was typified by President Dwight D. Eisenhower, one of the great modern warriors, in a comment he made in a radio interview with Prime Minister Harold MacMillan on August 31, 1959:

> The people in the long run are going to do more to promote peace than our government. Indeed, I think that people want peace so much that one of these days governments had better get out of their way and let them have it.

Peace education attempts to transform society by creating a peaceful consciousness that condemns violent behavior. Peace education offers a long-term solution to immediate threats of war. For peace education to be effective, it must transform ways of thinking that have been developed over the millenia of human history. At best peace education represents an indirect solution to the problems of violence. As a strategy it depends upon educating millions of students, who must in turn work to change violent behavior. A teacher who teaches the topics of peace education has no guarantee that his or her students will either embrace peace or work to

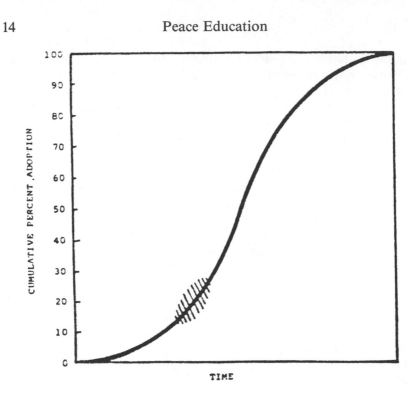

Table 1. S-Shaped Cumulative Curve for Adopter Distribution.

reduce violence. Education influences culture slowly. Teachers use their skills and knowledge to transmit certain messages to their pupils, who may ultimately develop behaviors and attitudes that shape cultural norms, creating a transformation that does not take place overnight. Many fear that in the perilous situation the world finds itself in today a quicker remedy is required to reduce the threat of war.

"Peace Education"

The word "education" comes from the Latin word *educare,* to draw or lead out. "Peace education" implies drawing out from people their instincts to live peacefully with others and emphasizes peaceful values upon which society should be based. Human beings will always have aggressive impulses. They project their feelings of anger out onto the world and categorize others as good or bad, friends or enemies. Human beings have within them destructive and aggressive forces that need to be controlled through a civilizing process. Peace education deals with both internal conflicts within the human psyche and violent situations in the world.

Traditionally, peace education has focused on the causes of war. More recently, with the inclusion of structural violence, peace education has expanded to include the study of all the causes of human conflict. A European peace educator has defined peace education as "the initiation of learning processes aiming at the actualization and rational resolution of conflicts regarding man as subject of action."[12] According to this definition, peace education teaches the skills of peacemaking. A Japanese peace educator states that peace education is concerned with peaceless situations.[13] These include struggles for power and resources, the nuclear race among superpowers, ethical conflicts in local communities, threats of violence, and wars. In this way peace education studies structures which support peacelessness as well as the values that give credibility to those structures. An American peace educator, Betty Reardon, defines peace education as "learning intended to prepare the learners to contribute toward the achievement of peace."[14] She goes on to state that peace education "might be education for authentic security,"[15] where a need for security motivates humans to form communities and nations. Because individuals disagree about how to achieve security, there are many different paths to peace. Peace education teaches about the various ways to provide security so that students can select which paths to follow. Peace education has a moral thrust where, through education, human beings work together to create a better social order.[16] The attempt of teachers to use their professional skills to address the problems associated with a commitment to militarism responds to a moral imperative to work for the well-being of others.

Although most of the current effort to educate about peace comes as a response to the impending nuclear threat, peace education in both formal schools and informal community settings implies much more than awareness of nuclear weapons. It implies teaching people how to manage violence and conflict without physical force. The study of peace attempts to nourish those energies and impulses that make possible a meaningful and life enhancing existence:

> The advantage of peace education and peace research is that it enables us to keep criticizing the structure and using brains and imaginations on alternatives, so that when the opportunities come — and they do come — we can use them.[17]

Peace education addresses the violent nature of society, and asks: Must it be this way? Aren't there other ways human beings can solve their conflicts? How do we get to these other ways? Just as war has its adherents and its schools, peace needs to be taught and promoted so that it becomes active in the minds of citizens and world leaders.

Throughout history many educational efforts have supported and promoted war:

> It is obvious that a warfare curriculum for human beings has been
> developed and refined over the entire course of man's history. Its
> teachings have been part of man's education in almost all societies in each
> succeeding generation.[18]

Traditional education glorifies established political power that uses brute
force to oppress people and legitimize its authority. History books praise
military heroes and ignore the contributions of peacemakers. Violence is
carried on by governments oppressing weaker nations and exhibited in
homes where physical assault, is used in situations of conflict, disobedience, anger, and frustration. Structural violence condemns people to
substandard levels of existence, while educational systems support those
structures which contribute to the militarization of social life. Peace education questions the structures of violence that dominate everyday life and
tries to create a peaceful disposition to counteract the omnipotent values
of militarism.

The Goals of Peace Education

Educational activity is purposeful. Teachers try, through instructional
activities, to achieve certain goals that help structure and evaluate learning.
As Douglas Sloan has pointed out, peace education has short- and long-
term goals.[19] The short-term goals are to turn things around so that life will
be more stable. At this level peace educators respond to immediate situations that threaten life on this planet. The longer term goals are to create
in human consciousness concepts and beliefs that desire peaceful existence
and hence transform human values to promote nonviolence.

A good illustration of the short-term goals of peace education has been
provided by a Romanian peace educator, Adrian Nastase.[20] Quoting the
French philosopher Pascal, he observed that human beings are "running
carelessly towards a precipice after having put something in front of us to
hinder us from seeing it."[21] Drawing from this analogy he suggests that the
goals of peace education are to discover the "precipice" and to understand
the irrational state of the present world, where the development of
technology contains the tremendous contradictions of both improving the
human condition and threatening its destruction. Peace education alerts
people to the danger of their own destructive fantasies and demonstrates
the obstacles that keep us from focusing on our suicidal behavior. Once this
awareness has been achieved, peace education develops alternatives that
could become the basis for gradually braking and finally stopping this mad
rush towards the "precipice." Another way of stating the urgency of peace
education is the famous statement by H.G. Wells that human beings are
embarked upon "a race between education and catastrophe."[22]

The field of peace studies varies from studying the causes of human violence to studying the causes of war. The study of human violence involves the human psyche and aspects of aggression, while the study of war focuses on the behavior of armies and nation-states. In between these two poles lies a vast academic domain that includes the study of conditions of survival, problems of communication, international relations, legal theory, and environmental awareness.

Whether working to achieve immediate or long-range objectives, peace education has ten main goals: (1) To appreciate the richness of the concept of peace; (2) to address fears; (3) to provide information about defense systems; (4) to understand war behavior; (5) to develop intercultural understanding; (6) to provide a future orientation; (7) to teach peace as a process; (8) to promote a concept of peace accompanied by social justice; (9) to stimulate a respect for life; and (10) to end violence. These ten goals describe the sorts of things taught in peace education classes. They are neither exhaustive nor exclusive. Peace education is a broad field that includes many different academic disciplines. These ten goals do not necessarily incorporate all the various academic topics of peace studies, but they do provide a framework for planning educational activities and constitute a set of learning objectives for peace classes. Optimally, peace education students will be exposed to the various concepts implied within all ten of these goals.

(1) Peace education provides in students' minds a dynamic vision of peace to counteract the violent images that dominate culture. Peace implies love and respect for all forms of life. Many examples of the richness of the concept "peace" come from arts and literature — the film *Gandhi,* the novels *War and Peace* and *Fail Safe,* and sections from the Bible. Throughout history peace has stimulated human imagination. Every major religion values peace. Peace education teaches about past, present and proposed future efforts to achieve justice.

(2) Peace educators address people's fears. Children are abused at home. Citizens fear being attacked on streets. Violence permeates schools. Increases in teenage suicide have been linked to despair about the future. Recent research indicates profound psychological effects of growing up in the nuclear age.[23] People fear for their own security, as they realize that stockpiling nuclear weapons does not necessarily achieve world stability but rather threatens mass destruction. As Jonathan Schell has said:

> The Hiroshima people's experience, accordingly, is of much more than historical interest. It is a picture of what our whole world is always poised to become — a backdrop of scarcely imaginable horror lying just behind the surface of our normal life, and capable of breaking through into that normal life at any second. Whether we choose to think about it or not, it is an imnipresent, inescapable truth about our lives today.[24]

Studies indicate that the majority of children in the United States fear for their future, and that children can be reassured when parents and adults face these fears by doing something to avert war.[25]

People upset about violent situations often have strong emotions. Those who have been physically abused have deep-seated resentments and insecurities. Citizens grieve about violence and fear conflict. Because powerful emotions about violent experiences can interfere with pedagogical efforts, peace educators enter the affective domain to become aware of the tensions and problems created by living in a violent world. Understanding these problems can help address student concerns and make relevant the study of tensions that threaten human existence.

(3) Citizens of all countries need information about defense systems. The notion of collective security implies that nations build weapons and create armies, navies, and air forces because they provide protection from attack. Citizens need to know what goes into these systems, the implications of developing and depending upon them, and their cost. Because a citizenry ignorant of what these weapons represent cannot make informed decisions about them, peace educators need to teach about the causes, nature, and consequences of the arms race. At the same time that each nation develops a war apparatus, often referred to as "the national security state," to defend itself, many nations shroud their security operations in secrecy. Peace education demystifies the public structures created to provide national security, so citizens can make enlightened choices about the best security systems for their circumstances. Leaving these decisions in the hands of the military guarantees the perpetuation of militaristic policies. Peace educators discuss the modern ramifications of peace through strength and encourage students to draw their own conclusions about defense policies.

(4) Students in peace education classes study the major causes of injustice, violence, and war. In the 3000 years of recorded history there have been only 250 years wherein war or armed conflict did not occur. Human societies try to control destructive impulses. Is aggression a natural part of human nature or is it learned through socialization? Individuals such as Alexander the Great, Napoleon Bonaparte, and Adolf Hitler have played a strong role in promoting wars, but we all have destructive fantasies. Because human groupings have different values and differing security needs, peace education includes the psychology, sociology and anthropology of human aggression. Peace educators provide their students with an understanding of how different individuals, cultures and political systems respond to conflict.

(5) Since wars occur as a result of conflicts between individuals, cultures, religions, and nations, peace education promotes respect for different cultures. Awareness of the role of the United Nations and other world systems is crucial to understanding what institutions human beings

can create to bridge different cultures and guarantee survival on "spaceship earth." International studies, where students learn about different values of human communities, have always been a part of peace education. Peace studies focus on how human institutions manage large-scale conflicts on the international level, as well as learning about how those conflicts originated.

(6) Peace education, by providing students with a future orientation, strives to recreate society as it should be. Students and teachers in peace studies classes imagine what the future will be like and then discuss what can be done to achieve peace. Peace studies include courses about the future that stimulate students to think about less violent ways of managing human behavior.

(7) As important as it is to emphasize knowledge, peace education also teaches skills. To move the world away from violence will require change. How can we bring peace to the world if we can't even create it in our own personal lives? Peace education focuses on strategies to achieve both individual and societal change. Peacemaking is a process that must be taught if human beings are to alter their violent behavior. People wishing to achieve peace understand that peace is a process that transforms their own lives as they start personifying their visions of the future. In peace education classes students examine how their daily actions and beliefs contribute to the perpetration of injustice and the development of war. They learn strategies to deal with aggressive behaviors and concrete skills that will help them become effective peacemakers.

(8) Because the struggle for peace embraces justice, peace education students learn about the problems of human rights and justice. Since the absence of war does not necessarily bring peace or harmony, peace studies programs do not focus only on national security issues but also include the study of social justice, human rights, development, feminism, racism, non-violence, and strategies for social change.

> To facilitate education for justice and peace, one must, above all, believe: believe that justice and peace are possible, believe that each and every one of us can do something to bring justice and peace into being.[26]

Peace educators teach about the problems brought about by injustice and use this knowledge to empower others.

(9) The achievement of peace represents a humanizing process whereby individuals overcome their violent tendencies. Peace education teaches a respect for life. Peace education students need to develop positive self images, a sense of responsibility for self and others, and a capacity to trust others. Peace education contributes to the social growth of all children if it helps them develop characteristics essential for the attainment of peace—a sense of dignity and self-worth, a confidence to question their values, communication skills, an ethical awareness, and an empathy for others:

> To prevent future upheavals human beings must be lifted from their selfish natural state to the social and finally to the moral state. Education must help the people regain their sense of moral independence and inner security. This training should be extended to all children, and should be rooted in love.[27]

Peace educators teach caring and a spirit of empathy, not just a rational understanding of the problems faced by others. This caring applies not just to other human beings but also to the planet with an appreciation of the ecological balances that support life. We have to hear within ourselves the sound of the earth crying, the pain of people who suffer in war, and the agony of people repressed by militarism. In this way peace education emphasizes the spiritual and moral development of human beings.

(10) The ultimate goal of peace education is to redress the problems created in a world consumed with violent behavior. Street crime, war, domestic quarrels, and poverty result in millions of people having to live in violent conditions where they have little or no security and struggle to survive. Peace education can't directly halt violence, but it does teach about violent situations, the effects of violence, and alternatives to violent behavior. Peace education students learn how to resolve disputes nonviolently and how to make the world a more secure place. Until violence is curtailed, human beings will not be able to achieve their full potential.

To achieve these goals will not be easy. The task is heroic, energizing, and crucial. Violent crimes are increasing. Wars are occurring throughout the world. Weapons are growing more awesome, and a frightened populace seems compliant in the face of ever-increasing defense budgets. Most members of modern nation-states believe that military institutions are a necessary component of contemporary life. The repeated failure of arms negotiations and a continuing worldwide arms race paint a picture of civilization heading towards oblivion with little respect for the citizens of the earth or the fragile ecosystems that support life. Unless something is done to control the spread of violence, citizens of the world face at best terror, mass poverty and starvation; at worst nuclear annihilation.

Educators help ward off such disasters by teaching about the nature of violence and developing in their classes strong visions of peace that provide alternatives to violent behavior. In order to create a less violent world, human beings must delegitimize the basic premises underlying the current global order and reassess fundamental assumptions regarding human motivations, essential values, and ultimate goals. Educators, whether they teach in community centers or formal classrooms, can play an important role in achieving global peace by challenging the old ways of thinking that rely on the inevitability of human aggression. They need to ask their students what kind of world they really want, and help them achieve a vision that will motivate a fundamental change in the way humans conduct their affairs.

2. Empowerment Education

*Peace education has to that extent to be an empowering process —
whether in a classroom or in the community; those who press for peace
education have the responsibility of showing that ordinary people,
children or adults, can do something effective about the problems that are
raised — that they are problems created by human beings and can now be
solved by them.*

Nigel Young

An informed public provides the basis of democracy. The strength of
an open society rests on independent, thinking citizens who are free to talk,
to meet, to think, to seek truth, to be different, to try something new, and
to make the best of their lives according to their ideals. In a dynamic
society, debate and controversy are signs of health. Peace education can
contribute to the health of modern societies by empowering citizens to contribute to the public debate about how to best defend their country. "Empower" in this sense implies enabling people to develop their own
democratic capacities to become effective citizens, shaping public policy.
Empowerment, by encouraging people to take charge of their own
destinies, allows them to discover within themselves the capacity to bring
about change.

A citizenry that passively contemplates the threat of nuclear annihilation awaits its own destruction. Likewise, a woman locked within the terror
of a physically violent home can't see how to escape her repressive situation. Peace education seeks to empower people by helping them envision
a less violent world that eschews the use of force. "The main task of peace
education is to strengthen confidence in democracy and its capacity of solving problems."[1] Peace education adheres to democratic traditions which
have relied on schools to train people to shape society on the basis of ac-
cumulated wisdom from the past and stressed creative approaches to a new
social order.

This raises a key question: Is peace education *about* peace, or is it
education *for* peace? The answer to this question is not an either-or; peace
education incorporates both. Peace education teaches *about* peace because
many citizens are ignorant about the problems associated with militarism
and violence; but it also stands *for* peace, where teachers and students ex-

21

plore together solutions to violent social realities. Peace education involves a three-part strategy—formation, information, and transformation. At the personal level peace education should challenge individual attitudes about war, peace and conflict by helping people understand how they formed their attitudes about violence and peace. In addition to understanding better their own reactions to peace and violence, individuals need to know more about the ways of peace, so peace education provides information about peace that will help transform an individual from someone who knows little about the problems of violence and the issues of peace to an active citizen working to make the world more peaceful. In this way peace education promotes peace. The capacity for peace education to involve people in creating a more peaceful world can be illustrated by the following diagram:

Decreasing of Action	Increasing of Action
apathy-seclusion-cynicism-ignorance//awareness-consciousness-engagement-ability	
Decreasing Power	Increasing Power

Peace education attempts to move people towards the right on this continuum, away from a condition of seclusion and despair to a condition of active involvement. The stage of "ability" at the farthest right on the scale implies that people have a positive self-image as socially responsible actors who know how to change the world.

This chapter will discuss the concept of education for liberation and describe how most traditional approaches to education do not empower students to either work for peace or understand the ways of peace. Within this framework empowerment education will be presented as a remedy to the violence of traditional educational practice. Finally, some questions will be raised as to the effects of peace education. How does it empower?

Education for Liberation

Using schools to address social problems comes from an academic tradition established by John Dewey in the early part of the twentieth century. In their laboratory school in Chicago the Deweys sought to develop in children "a habit of considering problems,"[2] an approach that encourages schools, colleges, and universities to allow students to shape informed opinions about the crucial dilemmas of their age. Under this orientation teachers encourage students to examine key social problems, most specifically in peace studies, coming to grips with the causes and effects of violence. According to Dewey, education aims to help people understand their environment so that they can control it rather than being controlled by it. In the classroom learners can select, organize, and direct their social experiences in order to create a better life:

> Education is that reconstruction or reorganization of experience which adds to the meaning of experience and which increases ability to direct the course of subsequent experience.[3]

Dewey believed that education reconstructs society by creating individuals with a capacity for reflective thinking who will build a more equitable social order. In considering social problems students must intelligently organize their own experiences. Action without thinking is as bad as thinking without action. Students who express concern about a social problem such as violence often desire to improve their own lives and the communities they inhabit. This desire provides an important motivation for learning that ought to be supplemented by gathering of relevant facts, the formulation of a plan of action, execution of the plan, and evaluation — all components of the scientific method which lead to intelligent action.

This approach to education, developed during the 1930s as a part of progressive education, has been labeled *reconstructionism* by educational historians and views the school as a chief means for building a new social order. George Counts typified reconstructionism in his book *Dare the Schools Build a New Social Order?* wherein he stated that unhealthy societies threaten individual survival, that something can be done to change the nature of social reality, and that education provides the means to build a better society.

A similar educational tradition has been carried forth in modern times by Jurgen Habermas[5] and other thinkers within the Frankfurt School, where the search for meaning comes from critically questioning the dominant ideologies that support social reality. This approach to education attempts to free the learner to adopt new modes of belief and operation. Similar to reconstructionism, this pedagogy challenges educators to question how social forces impact upon the beliefs and ideals that motivate individuals. Critical thinking empowers people to come up with their own concepts of social justice and provides conceptual tools (understanding of social reality, familiarity with political systems, knowledge of alternatives) to realize those concepts.

Just such a liberating education has been proposed and developed by the Brazilian educator Paulo Friere. Working with illiterate citizens, Friere developed a concept of *conscientization,* which helped oppressed people to think critically, to recognize themselves as dignified human beings, and to develop actions to transform their oppression. Friere criticized traditional education, which he said relied on what he calls a *banking concept:*

> In the banking concept of education, knowledge is a gift bestowed by those who consider themselves knowledgeable upon those whom they consider to know nothing.[6]

The banking metaphor contains the notion that teachers deposit knowledge in a pupil's mind for use some time in the future. Learning, as promoted by traditional education, neither promotes action nor has any immediate use for the learner. Within this metaphor learners are empty, passive receptacles who are tested to see how well the knowledge has been deposited. According to Friere, banking education adapts students to existing social structures by "domesticating" them.

Working in rural Brazil, Friere was able to teach illiterate peasants how to read by discussing basic concepts that affected their lives. He labeled traditional education "persuasion" or "propaganda," while liberating education "incarnates the search of people together with others for their becoming more fully human in the world in which they exist."[7] In this model the teacher and the students become "coinvestigators in dialogue,"[8] increasingly posing problems experienced in their daily lives. Pupils and teachers together name and transform the world through dialogue with each other. Friere suggests that liberating education should be put into practice and help the learner become a "subject rather than an object of history."[9] The key to this education is a dialogue between the learner and the teacher, where each respects the other and learns from the encounter. Knowledge gained through this dialogue is not something static but rather will help students become active in the struggle to build a better world.

> Dialogue cannot imprison itself in any antagonistic relationship. Dialogue is the loving encounter of people, who, mediated by the world, "proclaim" that world. They transform the world and in transforming it, humanize it for all people. This encounter in love cannot be an encounter of irreconcilables.[10]

In this type of education the teacher tries to understand the norms, values, beliefs, and fears of students. He or she then structures educational programs that provide hope, by valuing what students bring to the dialogue and teaching about how different social arrangements can improve their lives. Education used this way demystifies reality and becomes the practice of freedom. The steps involved in Frierian education are: (1) listening (choosing items to discuss); (2) dialogue (reflecting to resolve problems); and (3) action (doing something with the new understanding to resolve the problems discussed).

This educational approach to solving people's problems has been used successfully in places other than Brazil. Throughout Central America people are gathering in base communities to learn literacy skills and work on local projects that provide jobs and training. In the Philippines educators using the techniques of development education in poor communities involve people in a small group learning process of self-discovery based on their shared experiences. Underpinning these groups is the notion of the individual as a thinking, feeling and active subject who can, through communication with others, undertake, in Friere's terminology, "cultural action for freedom." In Tanzania, Julius Nyerere revamped the colonial British model of education towards a system that promoted self-reliance. Under this model pupils learned while working in villages to improve the standard of living of villagers. Teachers and pupils worked together on development projects that become the focus of educational curricula.[11]

In Sicily, Danilo Dolci has helped peasants plan their future in educational groups. A strong believer in nonviolence, he uses education in ways similar to Friere — to help people define and solve problems. He sees that the greatest impediment to peace is human misery:

> It goes without saying that there will never be peace — organic peace, so long as the world knows hunger, poverty, ignorance, exploitation, unemployment, and social systems that hinder man's fulfillment.[12]

To Dolci, underprivilege is itself a source of conflict. He teaches people who lack faith in their ability to alter the course of their existence to depend upon themselves to solve their own problems:

> Men must be taught self knowledge to cure their weaknesses and renew their being; and this calls for a great educational effort. An illness which is deep seated and long-standing calls for drastic, radical treatment.[13]

Dolci feels that people isolated from each other need to join together in what he calls *planning groups* to develop a collective consciousness of their own oppression. Within these groups peasants and ordinary citizens in Sicily have developed new social structures to address their problems and understand each other by exploring their common wishes:

> The basic problem is how to set in motion the collective creative experience; to liberate the power of creation which lies in every individual, group, area, and nation. People must be brought to believe in this personal creative power of theirs to join forces without delaying in the common task of creation.[14]

For Dolci, peace educators bring people together in planning communities to collectively develop plans to address common needs. Nonviolence as a way of life for Dolci has its own rewards, pointing to a new way of behaving that contrasts sharply with the violent and brutal tactics of those in power.

In the United States many different educational efforts have been advanced to empower people to work through positions of oppression and create better lives for themselves. Examples of this include workers education centers sponsored by labor unions, citizenship schools established during the civil rights movement to prepare people for literacy tests so they could vote, and settlement schools which provided immigrants with basic skills to keep and find work.[15] The most outstanding example of this type of education has taken place in Tennessee at the Highlander School, established during the 1930s. Early in its history Highlander worked with the Congress of Industrial Organizations (CIO) to help workers organize unions in the South. In the 1950s the staff at Highlander helped train civil rights workers who, in turn, provided literacy education for adults in rural southern communities. Currently Highlander is working with Appalachian people on ways to create jobs in poor areas of the South.[16] In discussing the educational principles that motivate Highlander's work, one of the staff members wrote:

> Highlander had to learn not to convert, but to bring forth; education not only had to serve the people, but, more importantly, had to be of the people.[17]

This principle requires educators to discover people's needs and to build with students educational programs that will address those needs.

The Violence of Traditional Education

Traditional education reinforces the status quo. Rather than orienting curricula towards student needs, most public schools teach existing social priorities and attempt to mold students to those priorities. Nations support school systems which raise young people to accept the policies of that nation. Young people are raised in educational institutions to accept uncritically the policies of their governments and to become patriots. By not learning to question authority in schools, students carry uncritical behavior forward in their adult lives. All this comes about because governments fund education to promote their own nationalist goals:

> Education has fundamental connections with the idea of human emancipation, though it is constantly in danger of being captured for other interests. In a society disfigured by class exploitation, sexual and racial oppression, and in chronic danger of war and environmental destruction, the only education worth its name is one that forms people capable of taking part in their own liberation. The business of school is not propaganda. It is equipping people with the knowledge and skills and concepts relevant to remaking a dangerous and disordered world. In the

most basic sense, the process of education and the proces of liberation are the same. They are aspects of the painful growth of the human species' collective wisdom and self-control. At the beginning of the 1980s it is plain that the forces opposed to that growth here and on the world scale are not only powerful but have become increasingly militant. In such circumstances, education becomes a risky enterprise. Teachers too have to decide whose side they are on![18]

Traditional education glorifies war and does not teach pupils alternatives to war and violence. Two countries with high education levels are the Soviet Union and the United States, but both these countries are spearheading an arms race that could obliterate life on this planet. Traditional education, as practiced in these countries and many others, supports the commonly accepted views of peace through strength.

A recent analysis of schools in advanced industrial societies has led to the conclusion that education helps perpetuate some of the inequities that lead to war. This analysis, called *reproduction theory,*[19] argues that societies are economically, socially, and politically stratified, and that schools reproduce that stratification; so that schools, rather than ameliorating the class divisions which cause structural violence, replicate and reinforce those divisions. Revisionist historians have debunked the myth of schools as providing opportunities for upward mobility and argued that schools allow a few people, mostly children of the upper and middle classes, to gain the rewards offered by society, while the vast majority of children experience failure, which leads to lives of poverty, misery, and substandard achievements.[20] Reproduction theory does not say that this is a conscious conspiracy of teachers, adult educators, school boards, curriculum developers, and state education departments to reproduce the inequality and structural violence that exist in society. Nor does it postulate a mechanistic, one-way determinism. Reproduction theory does posit that teachers, students, adult educators, and families can and do have effects upon their pupils, but at any given point in history, their efforts may be limited or shaped by broader social forces.

Children learn violence in school. In addition to studying a history that emphasizes the achievements of violent men and their armies, pupils learn violence in the streets and in the home. They also learn it from the media. Between his or her fifth and eighteenth birthdays, the average child in the United States watches 15,000 hours of television, 30 percent more time than they spend in school.[21] These same children will have seen on television an average of 18,000 violent deaths.[22] Peace educators are confronted by these violent messages that permeate society when they attempt to create a peaceful learning environment that will provide the motivation and skills to work for peace.

In the 1960s a great deal of attention was focused on the shortcomings of American schools.[23] Many critics at that time sought to humanize the schools through such reforms as open classrooms, Montessori education, individual guided instruction, credit-noncredit evaluations instead of grades, alternative schools, and open admissions policies. In spite of these efforts, many schools have continued to operate as they always have.

Through critical examination researchers and scholars uncovered a hidden curriculum of school life which, in turn, leads to oppression.[24] The hidden curriculum is not what is taught, but rather refers to the way things are taught and what students learn about life as a result of the way schools are run.

Schools are structured hierarchically, led by the school board, followed by the principals, department heads, and teachers. Students are at the bottom of this ladder. In such an environment students learn obedience and are punished if they disagree with those in authority. Students learn to be powerless and are prepared for the hierarchy of military organizations. They learn to take orders and not to challenge the status quo. They can't change things and are helpless to run their own lives. Students in schools are kept from making decisions that enable them to affect the reality of their daily lives:

> The process of instruction, regardless of subject area, usually places students in the passive role of receiving knowledge. For much of their school life they are supposed to absorb materials by attending to presentations of teachers; by using textbooks and other media; by answering orally and in writing questions posed by teachers or texts; and by observing other classmates' responses to those questions. In short, the student must usually assume an unassertive, inactive, almost docile role, allowing the environment to impinge upon oneself, rather than taking initiative to influence it.[25]

Having been taught not to question authority, students accept passively what teachers say. The need for control and discipline in the classroom teaches young people to pay attention to the clock and respect the limits set by authority figures. In this way schools reproduce conditions in the larger society conducive to the creation of an obedient work force that produces the economic goods that provide the basis for social wealth.

In addition to the hierarchy of the classroom which teaches obedience to authority, schools emphasize competition. The social relations established in the classroom become a microcosm for the larger society—with its divisions into winners and losers. Grades are meted out in a controlled way on a curve, so that some excel, some are mediocre, and others fail. Such distinctions brand some students with marks of failure, while others are rewarded with success. Students are taught to be aggressive in order to get ahead. Students learn early in the schools that there aren't enough rewards to go around, and that if they fail, it's their fault for not being "smart" enough or working hard enough. In classroom discussions students are pitted against one another, with teachers ignoring "wrong" answers, and reinforcing "brighter" students for their "correct" answers, which more often than not conform to what the teacher thinks is right. This same competitive classroom environment neither encourages cooperation, nor teaches pupils the skills of working together. School achievement is an individual accomplishment, and academic excellence is understood as individual brilliance, not collective enterprise.

Competition within the schools is emphasized by a battery of professional educators, counseling and testing officials who determine normal distributions and establish grading curves that condemn many students to mediocrity. The myth of schools is that they provide equal educational opportunities for all students. In reality, intelligence tests and other such standardized testing procedures support a society that needs a few select engineers, technocrats and scientists, while many others, as modern societies require more and more education for decent jobs, fall to the wayside and are banned from "the good life." Speaking about the ways schools help create structural violence in society, one educational critic has said:

> It was the schools as "the balance wheel of the social machinery" which triumphed—the balance being the imposition of controls for social stability in favor of the moneyed and powerful, and not the substance behind egalitarian rhetoric.[26]

Schools serve to justify the status quo because they set up a system that appears to be fair and just. If a person doesn't succeed in society, it is because he or she did not succeed in school. Since the schools allow all to participate, the individual, and not the larger social structure, is responsible for his or her own failure:

> The condition of growing disempowerment and domination afflicting millions of Americans in the closing decades of this century is rooted in the particular forms of domination and exploitation to be found in the economic, political, and cultural "instances" of the social formation. Education helps to provide the ideological "glue" sustaining this formation, providing the legitimations, rationalizations, and distorted consciousness necessary to support the forms of domination and oppression which permeate the society.[27]

Schools are supposed to provide preparation for mature citizenship and participation in society, but in the United States 40 percent of the high school students enrolled in urban systems drop out of school and, because of the increasing demands for educational credentials, cannot become effective members of the community. These educational practices condemn many citizens in modern nation-states to misery, poverty, and powerlessness — conditions that reinforce structural violence, which in turn creates violence as people express their outrage against such unjust social conditions.

Schools further disempower students through punishment. In the most extreme cases, corporal punishment is used, although many countries have outlawed it in public schools. Rules come down from on high with little or no pupil input. Even if students challenge a particular code their disagreements are often ignored or overruled by administrators. Teachers assume positions of authority not only in relation to the subject matter taught but also in relation to the way the classroom is run. Teachers set the rules and mete out the punishment. Rules aren't collectively negotiated, and pupils learn from their environment to be obedient and not question people in authority.

In addition to the way schools are administered and curricula are established, the actual material taught in classes promotes violence. History is presented as a succession of wars, and students are taught to revere the accomplishments of great warriors. The way to settle disagreements is to go to war, not to negotiate. A detailed examination of history books reveals that they are dominated by themes such as

> (1) an over-valuing of social harmony, social compromise and political consensus, with very little said about social struggle; (2) an intense nationalism and chauvinism; (3) an almost total exclusion of labor history; and (4) a number of myths regarding the nature of political, economic, and social life.[28]

Human beings have for a long time used nonviolent strategies to resist violent governments. This struggle has been well documented by Gene Sharp[29] and needs to be emphasized if students are going to learn alternatives to violent military ways of resolving conflict.

Schools worship power to the near exclusion of everyone and everything else. They glorify the actions and behaviors of the rich and powerful. A tacit assumption seems to prevail in education that the powerless don't count. History focuses on the activities of the wealthy and military leaders, ignoring the lives and contributions of ordinary citizens. The rich and powerful are glorified, while the brutality of their endeavors is overlooked. "Our educational system is committed to a scale of values which confers immortality on egomaniacs and punishes the thoughtful with oblivion."[30] Teachers and curricula promote a view that to have power is a superior attribute but ignore the corollary of power, that it oppresses others. Millions of people in this world face a survival crisis because the authorities who control them are either unable or unwilling to respond to their needs. Peace education must deal with these power relationships by encouraging the powerless to speak out so that their wishes become part of public debate. Ultimately, in order for there to be peace, the powerful themselves must be converted by pressure from "below." Millions of courageous people in many parts of the world have attempted this,[31] but their stories are excluded from most history books.

Empowerment Education

Peace education teaches about democratic uses of power. In most countries power benefits a few people who oppress others to reinforce their own privileges. Military hierarchies demand blind obedience to such arrangements. Peace education rests on these assumptions about power: Political power is a right. All people have political power by virtue of their citizenship and they have a right to exercise that power to promote peace and justice. Those governments and social institutions are least oppressive that allow for the maximum participation by those who depend upon them and do not use violent methods to further their own ends. Peace education promotes the power of cooperative action, where ordinary people by banding together can learn how to create institutions that respect the innate dignity in all human beings and resist those organizations and individuals that treat people violently.

Peace education, by providing knowledge about efforts to bring peace and justice to this world, aims to teach people how to overcome violence in their lives. Instead of education serving the interests of the relatively few members of the privileged classes who use military might to recreate colonial oppression throughout the world, peace educators use educational means to create a peace-loving culture:

> The task of the school and education cannot be simply to "see" and theorize about those things. The school must try, whenever practicable, to do something about them. We need a different kind of education orientation with its implied applicative emphasis.[32]

If education is to play a vital role in bringing peace to the world, it must cease as a vehicle that enables the privileged to strengthen their power and must help those without power learn how to become powerful. Peace education, by providing new information about nonviolent alternatives, helps people transform their lives from situations of powerlessness to situations where they are actively working to overcome violence. Empowerment education liberates the intellect to allow individuals to question even the most basic assumptions about the meanings of life and social arrangements. It encourages students to construct their own meanings and prepares them to be effective citizens in democratic states:

If experiments in real democracy are possible anywhere in our social order, they are possible in our academic communities, for in most of these communities the levels of articulation are relatively high and the levels of desperation relatively low.[33]

Empowerment education rests on the assumption that people can and will take control over their own lives. The key to this type of education is the process. Peace educators affirm learners' sense of competence by creating classrooms modeled upon democratic principles where students learn how to articulate concerns in group settings. In this model the teacher serves more as a midwife, helping students give birth to their own ideas and inclinations.[34] Peace education challenges traditional educational practice when it is based on a mutual dialogue where teachers and students participate as equals. Teachers may have more information than students, but together they can seek the answers to such thorny questions as "Why are humans violent?"

The first step in empowering people is to catch their imaginations.[35] Overcoming a feeling of powerlessness is often a question of motivation. Because people must believe that by working for peace they can, in fact, achieve it, peace education tries to get students to see themselves as causal agents capable of contributing to the effort to bring peace to the world. By learning how peacemakers have practiced nonviolence, students' imaginations can be inspired by visions of a peaceful world.

Part of capturing people's imagination is to dwell on the deep-seated fears related to violence. Many people may not acknowledge these fears, while most are paralyzed from acting on them because they are deeply embedded in subconscious minds. In the empowerment process, personal change begins to occur when people acknowledge their deep feelings about violence and the perilous nature of the world. Violent behavior originates in aggressive impulses. Each individual possesses unconscious ravings and deeply seated urges that can lead to violence. These deep psychological elements of the human personality need to be explored in order to understand attitudes and behaviors that both express deep urges and determine how individuals react to fearful situations. Accepting feelings of fear as normal human reactions frees people to share those feelings with others and explore common links that provide the basis for joining together to address these problems. People make connections with others based on fear for their own survival and concern for the future. Many see the relationships between the violence of every-day life—physical assault, rape, battering, child abuse, and the global violence of military conflict. The empowerment process builds a deep sense of commitment as people decide they want to realize profound moral feelings about the intrinsic worth of human life.

Empowerment education includes knowledge about public affairs. Peace education should sharpen people's abilities to make moral judgments and think clearly about world affairs. Addressing the problems of war and peace can heighten intellectual abilities by encouraging pupils to study some of the most pressing problems facing the human species. Empowerment education should move beyond traditional presentations of "civics" to let students understand the informal channels of influence—money, social affiliations, political debts, etc.—that support war policies. Citizens who are going to be able to change the deep patterns of militarism that characterize modern states need to understand the dynamics of power close to their lives so they can exercise their citizenship to influence existing power arrangements. Learning abstractly about the seats of power in remote capitals won't provide knowledge of what paths to take to influence public policy. Traditional civics boasts of the virtues of national governments. Empowerment education teaches the manipulations of the state apparatus in a way that will demystify the workings of government and transform people to become political decision makers. Ronald Remy has suggested that standard citizenship competencies include acquiring and using information, assessing involvement, forming decisions, making judgements, communicating, cooperating, and promoting interests.[36] In peace education classes students assess their own involvement in violent situations, issues, decisions, and policies, developing ethical and moral standards about people, institutions, policies, and decisions. They learn how to communicate with other citizens, decision makers, leaders, and officials and how to challenge bureaucratically organized institutions to promote peaceful alternatives.

Leadership training is another aspect of empowerment education. Peace educators need to know how to serve as animators or facilitators of small groups, how to reach consensual decisions, how to manage organizations, how to respond to conflict, how to work on problems collaboratively, how to develop open and experimental attitudes in groups, and how to motivate others. They should be able to train learners in group participation; in planning, conducting, and critiquing learning activities; and in sharing leadership. They will have to know how to encourage and support others interested in exploring the problems of violence. In order for an individual to be transformed from a passive victim of violence to an active citizen promoting peace, that individual will need access to resources that can be directed towards bringing peace to the world.

The final stage in empowerment education involves people taking action. As traditional education leads to knowledge, empowerment education should lead to knowledge and action. As John Dewey stated, a person's development is related to his or her ability to influence the environment.[37] Studies have indicated that an individual learns how to be effective by working on real problems. A sense of competence comes from the ability to affect reality.[38] James Coleman even found that environmental competence, finding a sense of control over one's environment and future, has a stronger relationship to school achievement than all other "school" factors influencing achievement.[39] Allowing people to express their concerns about the threat of war supports their psychological health, mental growth, and personality development. Mere reflection will not change the state of affairs that makes the world such a dangerous place.

All in all, empowerment education relies upon the model of education used in community development.[40] Community development brings people together at a local level to work on commonly perceived problems. The work of Dolci (discussed above) provides a prototype for this kind of activity, which encourages self-improvement through the study, planning, and action of concerned citizens. Community development involves a wide variety of people in decision-making and problem-solving of issues that face a whole community by drawing citizens into cooperative activities to focus on problems that directly touch their lives. As an educational process, community development teaches the skills of problem identification, data collection and analysis, decision-making, planning, carrying out appropriate action, and evaluating the results of that action. Empowerment education can use these processes to teach peace educators the social skills of working in collective settings.

Empowerment education relies on group settings to allow citizens to construct their own meaning of reality. Each individual interprets reality in a unique way. Working in a small community or group setting provides insights, allows participants to share concerns and question the role of violence in people's daily lives. Such groups of people working together to promote nonviolence have traditionally been called *affinity groups,*[41] which are primarily truth-seeking groups. In writing about affinity groups, one author has said:

> What is prefigurative here is the sense of being empowered, which arises as people begin to shake off their apathy and make the connection between the realities of everyday life — which they feel keenly enough, but in a limited way — and those of the nuclear order — which is felt insufficiently but places their whole future at stake.[42]

Such groups, by providing support for people studying the issues of war and peace, foster civic courage where students and teachers alike challenge popularly held views about war and modern defense systems. Questioning the dominant social order and challenging values about violence and militarism can be frightening and painful. Being in an affinity group where people trust each other allows contact with others who share concerns, so that together members can define a common reality and grope for alternatives. With this type of support people can actually become powerful as they practice peace in a group where others value their contributions. In a small group individuals can translate their personal doubts and fears into social issues, gaining political understanding and the collective strength to resist the oppression of the war apparatus.

Power for What?

The notion of empowerment suggests that people will become powerful. A key consideration for peace educators is: Do their students actually become empowered through taking peace education classes in such a way that they use their power to bring peace to the world? To answer this question, the author of this book conducted a follow-up study of students in peace education classes at the university level. The results of this research indicate that people can change their attitudes about war and peace issues as a result of a class, but most students don't become involved in political efforts to make the world more peaceful. They learn how they formed their attitudes and beliefs about violence. They also learn new information about war and peace issues. But few students take steps to transform their lives to become active working for peace. They continue their lives after the class in much the same way as they did before. Whether they become actively involved in the peace movement depends upon their peer group. Those graduates who had friends involved in peace activities tended to become more involved in working for peace than other students who didn't have regular contacts with people promoting peace.

Ervin Lazlo, a leading futurist who works with the United Nations, posits a three-stage transition towards a less violent world.[43] The steps are (1) build consensus, (2) change lifestyles and (3) participate.

Peace education obviously contributes to building a consensus about how to reduce violence in this world. Peace educators, by educating about the problems of violence, try to raise people's consciousness about problems that come from the use of force and to form notions of what can be done about those problems. Although educators themselves should not tell students what to think or imagine, they encourage students to develop their own images of a less violent and more wholesome future. Building such a consensus does not, by itself, make the world more peaceful. Education may liberate an individual's consciousness, but that education will not influence the nature of social reality until that individual starts to exercise his or her power either as a citizen or as a private individual. In order for peace education to contribute to making the world become less violent, graduates of peace education will have to either change their lifestyles or enter the political arena to change policies promoting the use of force.

Changing lifestyles, an important part of making the world less violent, is often overlooked in discussions about the effectiveness of peace education. People who incorporate peacemaking skills into their lives help reduce the level of violence in the world. They may not change public policies but they challenge the use of physical force whenever it occurs in their lives. In this sense peacemakers aren't necessarily using their power as citizens to change social policies, but rather using their power as human beings to influence the world around them by living more peacefully.

As a result of taking a peace course students participating in this study indicated that they think more seriously about violence in their lives. They try to reorient their lives towards compassion and caring, away from hatred and anger. They try to love themselves and use their capacity for love to improve their relationships with others. They are less likely to spank their children. They talk to their friends about the ways of peace. They become vegetarians. They are more aware of violence in the media and stop going to violent movies. They use conflict resolution skills to manage conflicts in their lives. They pay more attention to their own rhythms, trying to find peace within themselves. They continually challenge their own thoughts and beliefs about violence, as well as those of their friends and people around them. They read about these issues and try to stay informed about current events. These changes no doubt create small "pockets of peace" within a violent culture, but don't necessarily challenge political establishments that use violence to promote their ends.

Many believe that peace will come about by changing government policies promoting violence. Peace movements throughout history have attempted to do that by drawing to the public's attention the horrors of violence and by lobbying for less violent policies, the cessation of war, reductions in defense expenditures, cancellation of weapons contracts, etc. People involved in these efforts use their power as citizens, the rights and responsibilities they have within their countries, to influence official policies. Some run for office. Others work for candidates promoting peaceful causes. Some demonstrate and even practice nonviolent resistance to draw attention to violent policies. These kinds of activities allow people to use their political rights to create a more wholesome environment for all living creatures.

The author's research shows that students in peace education classes do change their attitudes and beliefs about violence and even change their lifestyles in more peaceful directions but they don't necessarily participate in political activities to challenge public policies. These observations indicate that the reconstructionist theorists were too optimistic about the ability of education to change the world. At best schools and community education programs may influence the way people think. Peace education classes do not directly influence the way the world is constructed. They may not even be able to change an individual's attitude about the world. People are influenced by peers, by social traditions, by family members, and by political trends. Many citizens who embrace peace education as a way to promote peace are optimistic about their efforts to make the world better, but the use of force is so deeply ingrained in human society that peace education efforts may only represent early fertilization of a peaceful culture. Peace education in many countries of the world grew at the end of the nineteenth century as a response to the extreme violence of modern warfare. It was championed as a way to avoid destruction wrought by mechanized armaments. In spite of almost one hundred years of peace education practice, the world has become more violent. Nuclear weapons have been developed. The use of handguns has become more widespread. And wars flourish in many parts of the world. Clearly, peace education is not a sufficient strategy for peace. The full maturation of such a peace culture will require changing attitudes, governments, cultural norms, economic institutions, and social values.

Peace studies classes may empower individuals to confront violence but they don't change society. It will take a long time to change the nature of political reality. Peaceful attitudes contribute to building a consensus that may one day become an important part of a political base that could change policies endorsing war. Empowerment education helps build this consensus by presenting alternative ideas about human behavior and the knowledge of what paths have to be followed for there to be peace. However, education forms a small part of an individual's total consciousness. Other factors influence an individual's lifestyle and political orientation. People do not become powerful just because they have taken a class. Peace education classes can provide important knowledge about the role of violence in the human community, but alone they do not propel people into taking the kind of risks that are necessary to challenge the political structures that promote violence. It is only with the strong support of peers that most individuals will attempt to use whatever power they have as citizens to change political realities.

3. Practice of Peace Education

*We should ask what our schools, colleges, and universities have been do-
ing to advance worldwide human survival and dignity. To what extent
and in what ways have they sought to prepare our students to meet the
twin challenge of peril and change that looms so large in front of each
and every one of us.*

Burns H. Weston

Peace education has been practiced in a variety of forms for hundreds
of years, originating in the Western world with those teachings of Christ
that promote pacificism, and the practice of those Christian churches—
such as the Mennonites, the Quakers, and the Brethren—that pursue nonviolence. In the East nonviolence has been preached by Buddhists, and in
India, followers of Gandhi have discovered dynamic ways to apply the
Hindu concept of *ahimsa* (nonviolence) to everyday life and political struggle. Many native peoples, such as the Hopis, have practiced peace throughout their history.

In the 1980s many people are waking up to the threats of violence in
this world and seeking educational solutions at the grass roots level. Peace
movements use educational means to promote their causes. Inhabitants of
war-torn areas such as Central America and the Middle East see a need for
alternatives to the violence that surrounds them, while millions of other
world citizens concerned about the nuclear threat are creating and joining
different peace organizations to express their concerns about violence.
Some of these people go door to door in an effort to educate people about
alternatives to violence. Some work through their churches. Others sponsor
and attend public forums. Housewives in Holland, teachers in Japan, pea-
sant leaders in Chile, businessmen in California, parishioners in Central
and South America, university professors in England, community
organizers in India, and mothers throughout the world—all are turning to
peace education to find solutions for violent behavior and bring peace to
the world.

This chapter will attempt to deal with some of the complexities of
peace education practice by first providing a brief history of peace education that will include a discussion of the relationship between it and
research. It will then discuss comparative notions of peace education as it

is carried out throughout the world with special emphasis placed on the role of the United Nations and peace education in churches. Finally it will conclude with a section about why "peace education" is an appropriate term to cover all the varied education activities attempting to alter patterns of violence.

Brief History of Peace Education

Much of the impetus for the modern attempts at peace education in Europe came from the two world wars in this century. Prior to World War I various peace societies had sponsored world peace conventions, the first of which was held in the Hague, Netherlands, in 1899 on May 18, a day thereafter commemorated as peace day. A further Hague world peace conference in 1907 tried to place limits on war by establishing the Hague Tribunal for the service of states willing to arbitrate their disputes by submitting them to an international court. After World War I peace activists and educators promoted, in many European countries, "education for international understanding," which focused on different cultures and political systems. The organized peace movement during this time supported the League of Nations and international agreements such as the Kellogg-Briand Pact, signed in 1928 by fifteen countries, that attempted to do away with war by agreement among nations. Later this pact was ratified by most nations of the world. The signers declared that they condemned war as a way of settling quarrels and agreed to try to solve their disagreements by peaceful means. The pact was hailed as a great achievement, but it proved useless in preventing war, as it provided neither means for enforcement nor ways for nations to work together.

World War II created new interest in "education for world citizenship." Educational efforts for peace in this period focused on politics practiced by the dominate world powers. With the advent of the Cold War, peace educators looked for an educational approach to international cooperation to build a lasting peace. Leading scientists at this time founded the Pugwash Movement, which holds scholarly conferences on the problems of modern warfare and issues position papers that have motivated scholars throughout the world wanting to address the serious threat of modern warfare.

The Swedish chemist Alfred Nobel left a large legacy to establish an annual peace prize, which, since 1900, has awarded prizes to individuals in the world who have done the most effective work in the interest of international peace. Sweden, Denmark, Norway and Finland have made "education for international understanding" a compulsory subject since the 1940s. Since the 1960s the Finnish government has sponsored disarmament education and established the Finnish Peace Research Institute, which held in 1983 the first international symposium on children and war. Another peace research institute in Finland, the Tampere Research Institute, publishes the journal *Current Research on Peace and Security*. Under the leadership of Johann Galtung, the Norwegian government established in 1960 an International Peace Research Institute (PRIO) to study problems related to structural violence and international conflict. This institute publishes *Journal of Peace Research* and *Bulletin of Peace Proposals,* two leading international journals of peace research. The Swedish government funds the Stockholm International Peace Research Institute (SIPRI) to monitor the world's arms race and trade in arms. This organization produces the most widely recognized and accepted reports on world arms traffic.

In 1964 at the Cleron conference sponsored by UNESCO that took place outside Geneva, the International Peace Research Association (IPRA) was founded. This organization encourages scholarship focused on problems of peace and security, has sponsored many international and regional conferences on war and global tensions, and publishes, on a quarterly basis, *International Peace Research Newsletter.* Every other year IPRA sponsors general conferences whose proceedings contain some of the most up-to-date research findings on the problems of war, peace, and global security. In 1971 IPRA established a Peace Education Commission, which published in 1974 a *Handbook on Peace Education.* These activities have helped define peace research as a legitimate area of scholarly endeavor.

Peace research in its modern form was born in the 1950s, largely in response to public concern about the threat of modern war. Many scientists who harbored misgivings about modern technological warfare suggested a more scientific approach to peace and initiated research projects to examine in a systematic way the problems of peace and war, violence and nonviolence, conflict and conflict resolution.

Peace research institutes throughout the world have produced a large volume of literature on the structures of violence in daily life, both at the personal, national and the international level. Resident scholars produce position papers on the nature of the arms race, the dynamics of world tensions and conflict, and problems of national and world security, which become part of a scholarly dialogue about the problems associated with militarization. They provide information about these problems and often suggest recommendations which, it is hoped, will become part of the public debate about national security and world conflict.

Peace education, to a large extent, owes its rebirth in modern times to the peace movements that have brought the problems of war and peace into the public limelight. There seems to be both an indirect and an inverse relationship between the growth of peace movements and the growth of peace education. Indirectly, heightened concern about the threats of war and the problems of violence has put pressure on educational institutions to respond to these problems. Inversely, peace education seems to grow when peace movements falter. Such a relationship was demonstrated in Northern Ireland where, when peace movements were seen to fail, leaders in various communities concerned about the level of violence in Northern Ireland suggested peace education as a means to teach new ways to deal with traditions of conflict that had grown up in that country. As the peace movement was floundering it turned its energies towards peace education. Likewise in the United States, the nuclear freeze movement with a great deal of enthusiasm promoted a nuclear freeze in the early part of the 1980s. When this campaign failed to change the policies of the United States government, its leader, Randall Forsburg, began to argue against a political strategy aimed at the nuclear policies of the United States government and for an educational strategy to change the attitude of the American public towards the use of nuclear weapons. The changes required to make the world more peaceful are far greater than the original adherents of the nuclear freeze imagined. Trying to convince the peoples of the world that nuclear weapons must be outlawed may take hundreds of years.

In attempting to address the problems of violence in the world, peace educators practice in a wide variety of settings. Many peace educators, as mentioned above, are scholars at universities or researchers at institutes where they teach and write about the problems of war and peace.

During the 1950s in the United States some scholars worked to promote research about war and peace. In 1952 a "Group for Research on War and Peace" was formed at the Eastern Psychological Association meeting. Academics at that meeting established a network to exchange articles and scholarly projects devoted to providing information about the problems of war and national security. This activity was coordinated by Arthur Gladstone at Swarthmore College, who edited the *Bulletin of the Research Exchange on the Prevention of War*.[1] Through this exchange a network of contacts was developed that stimulated seminars and sponsored peace scholarship. The locus of this work shifted to the University of Michigan in 1955, where, under the leadership of Kenneth Boulding and Anatol Rapoport, a decision was made to initiate a more scholarly journal, which appeared in 1957 and was named *Journal of Conflict Resolution*. This journal is currently one of the most important scholarly journals in the field, and the work of these early pioneers in the 1950s helped place peace studies permanently on the world's intellectual map.

As a response to the Vietnam War, colleges and universities in the United States started programs with an emphasis on peace studies.[2] Various associations and centers began to develop curricula that could be used in the schools to teach about nonviolent conflict resolution. These and many other groups have joined the Consortium for Peace Research, Education, and Development (COPRED) which was founded in 1970 to

promote the expansion and integration of peace research, peace education, and peace action in North America, and to act as a liaison with the
International Peace Research Association (IPRA), which promotes similar
functions in other parts of the world.[3]

COPRED sponsors a journal, *Peace and Change,* which provides an opportunity for peace researchers to publicize their findings about war and peace
issues.

In recent times concern about nuclear weapons has spawned in the
United States new interest in peace education. In 1980 a commission was
appointed by the United States Congress to study whether the United States
should establish a peace academy. In recommending that such an academy
be established, the commission reported, "Peace requires knowledge,
judgement, and skill no less complex than what is required for war."[4] In
1984 both houses of Congress passed legislation to create a national peace
institute in response to the efforts to create a peace academy, and this signed
legislation has created the United States Peace Institute, which sponsors
peace research projects.

At the elementary and secondary level peace education has been promoted from a variety of sources. National organizations have been
developing curricula and helping local school boards, teachers and school
personnel implement peace education programs. A national organization,
Educators for Social Responsibility, has created curricula for pupils in
elementary, middle, and senior high schools. In 1983 the National Education Association published a curriculum for high school students, *Choices:
A Unit on Conflict and Nuclear War,* that has been the object of much controversy, even receiving criticism from the Reagan administration. In April
1983 the National Catholic Association encouraged all Catholic schools to
infuse the concepts of peace and justice into the education of students in
order to enhance their mission. In some communities throughout the
United States, parents have pressured their local school boards to offer
courses that will provide an awareness of war and peace issues. By 1986 in
New York City; Cambridge, Massachusetts; Berkeley, California; and Milwaukee, Wisconsin, school boards had adopted resolutions supporting
peace studies. An example of such a resolution comes from the April 19,
1983, meeting of the Milwaukee Board of School Directors:

> Whereas there is a growing concern among educators regarding their
> responsibility toward students and the issue of nuclear weapons develop-
> ment and use;
>
> And whereas education's primary function is to prepare students for the
> future;
>
> And whereas there are strong indications that children are aware of the
> danger of these weapons and may be questioning what future exists for
> them;

And whereas the morale of students and their interest in school is directly affected by their perceptions of hope for their future;

Therefore, be it resolved that the Milwaukee Board of School Directors declare it appropriate to introduce into the school program, activities and curricula related to peace studies and the dilemma of the nuclear arms race.

Passing such a resolution represents an early stage in the process of getting a school district to take seriously the task of teaching peace. It legitimizes peace education by providing direction for teachers and administrators who want to pursue efforts in these areas.

In the United States some faculty on college campuses are developing courses that address peace issues or are integrating peace and war concerns into their existing courses. Still, a great many colleges and universities have been slow to respond to these issues:

In our universities, we have done virtually nothing to address the situation, to explore it as compassionate thinkers and scholars. This is an intellectual and moral scandal, and we should not forget that. A provost of a small college upstate who was awakening to this idea recently wrote to me on just that score. He said, in effect: "I have a minor nightmare that in the year 2050 there will be some hypothetical survivors looking in disbelief at our 1980 and 1981 catalogs. It's as if, living on the edge of a cliff, the Academy seemed not to care."[5]

The first peace studies program in the United States was started in a small Brethren school, Manchester College, in Indiana in 1948. Peace studies courses began to emerge in the late 1960s, and by the 1970s degree programs were set up at Colgate University and Manhattan College. In 1974 the World Policy Institute published a report that indicated that peace studies courses existed on about fifty campuses in the United States.[6] An updated survey conducted in 1983 indicated that thirty-eight colleges and universities in the United States had peace studies programs,[7] while other campuses had peace studies committees to plan courses and set directions for further peace studies activities. Another study released by the same organization in 1987 indicated that 235 campuses had peace studies programs. These programs take many different shapes. They vary from a Ph.D. in Peace Science to academic undergraduate minors. Some are multidisciplinary, while others have in an ambitious manner attempted to create their own academic departments within larger college and university structures. Many of those programs act as research centers, publishing position papers, sponsoring conferences, providing fellowships, and bringing in renowned scholars to discuss the problems of war and peace.

In the 1980s concern about the effects of a nuclear holocaust has motivated faculty at universities throughout the United States to develop new courses that deal with topics such as problems of war and peace, economic development and well-being, human rights, culture, community development, values and change, and alternative world order. Faculty throughout the United States are responding to the concern for peace by offering courses such as "Problems of War and Peace," "Planning Alternative World Futures," "Approaches to World Order," "Theory and Practice of Nonviolence," "The War Economy," "Global Environmental Politics," "An Introduction to Peace Studies," and "Peace, World Order and War."[8] These courses provide college students with an awareness of war and peace problems and a sense of what needs to be done in order to achieve peace.

Comparative Peace Education

The practice of peace education varies throughout the world. Current names for peace education, as it is being practiced throughout the world, include "education for world citizenship," "disarmament education," "nuclear age education," "A-bomb education," "development education," and "human rights education." What is presented in the name of peace education depends upon varying notions of security and peace, differing religious traditions, and cultural values. In each country peace educators initiate programs based on the political realities of their nations, and their curricula emphasize concepts valued by widely diverse cultures. In some academic settings peace education falls into the heading of world order studies, while in Catholic schools it tends to be called education for peace and justice.

Education for world citizenship originated in the interbellum period between the First and Second World Wars. At that time peace studies attempted to reduce the threat of war by preparing students for world citizenship, which would make them respectful of different cultures and values by providing a knowledge of different cultures, political arrangements, religions, and values—hoping to produce an aware citizenry that would eschew the use of violence to settle international differences.[9] A proponent of this approach, the British philosopher Bertrand Russell, said in the 1930s, "Education could easily, if man chose, produce a sense of solidarity of the human race, and of the importance of international cooperation."[10] Education for world citizenship or education for international understanding exists in many different countries. It teaches about cultural traditions and tries to promote cooperation among people.

In the 1970s many European nations promoted disarmament education,[11] which emphasizes the tremendous cost of the arms race and the disparity between the developed and the underdeveloped nations of the world. The following definition of disarmament education was provided in the Final Report and Document of the World Congress on Disarmament Education:

For the purpose of a disarmament education, disarmament may be understood as any form of action aimed at limiting, controlling and reducing arms, including unilateral disarmament initiatives and, ultimately, general and complete disarmament under effective international control.[12]

Based upon the principles of the United Nations Charter, disarmament education attempts to provide an awareness of the consequences of armaments upon human communities. It teaches about the cost of the arms race, educates about arms control efforts, and provides an awareness of the production and use of weapons.

Recently in the United States a debate has emerged regarding the most appropriate way to promote peace education activities. Some educators working with public school systems prefer to call it "nuclear age education." Most college and university teachers call their efforts peace education, as evidenced by the term "peace and conflict studies," a name used widely in the United States in many universities and colleges. "Peace education" is seen as being too controversial, because it suggests to some capitulation to the Soviets. The argument runs: If we teach young people peace education, they won't support the arms race, and the United States will fall behind the Soviet Union. If the United States falls behind the Soviet Union, it might be vulnerable to attack. Since the Soviet Union is an aggressive country bent on world domination, to promote peace education would result in the overthrow of the American system. With that argument dominating the popular mentality, peace education is the subject of a great deal of controversy. In England this line of reasoning conjures up images of Neville Chamberlain attempting peace advances to Hitler, and "peace education" is derisively called "appeasement education" by its detractors.[13]

In order to avoid some of the controversy associated with the name "peace education," Educators for Social Responsibility, an organization whose constituency consists of elementary, secondary, and university teachers in the United States, prefers to call its efforts "nuclear age education," as exemplified by the special edition of the *Harvard Educational Review* titled "Education and the Threat of Nuclear War." Nuclear age education provides an awareness of issues raised by the development of atomic weapons. As the editors of this special edition note,[14] the forty years since the development and use of these weapons have been filled with silence. Using the rubric of nuclear age education, teachers, civic leaders, and administrators are working at the local school level to provide an awareness of the consequences of living with nuclear weapons. Their educational programs address the sense of powerlessness and deep fear that young people in industrial nations have of a nuclear holocaust:

Many young people feel that the situation is now hopeless and that nuclear war will occur before they have a chance to complete their lives. Some adolescents say the nuclear danger dominates their lives and is their greatest concern.[15]

Responding to these fears, peace educators have found that they can argue successfully in schools and universities for education programs with the name "nuclear age education" to discuss many of the topics germane to peace education.

Since the 1960s teachers in Japan have been organizing to present what they call "A-bomb education" in the schools.[16] This approach emphasizes what Japanese citizens experienced as a result of the bombing of Hiroshima and Nagasaki and hopes to pass on an awareness of these tragic experiences so that the horrors are neither forgotten nor repeated.

Peace education efforts in Japan take a special form based on the experiences of Japan during the Second World War. Immediately after the Second World War the Allied Forces prohibited teaching about the A-bomb in school. In 1951 when a peace treaty was signed the press code was lifted and the teachers in Japan began seriously to address the legacy of the bombings of Hiroshima and Nagasaki.[17] During the 1950s children in Hiroshima were dying from the aftermath of the atomic explosions, and popular attention was focused on the survivors of the blasts. One important story was *Sadako and the Thousand Paper Cranes,*[18] which told the tale of a young girl dying of leukemia. In response to the horrible results of the two atomic bombs, a Peace Park was built in Hiroshima in 1958 with its central feature a statue of Sadako. School children in Japan visit the Hiroshima Peace Park to commemorate the beginning of the atomic era, to learn about the horrors of war, and to focus on different aspects of peace. Ten years later the Hiroshima Teacher's Union was shocked to see how little awareness children in Japan had about the nuclear war, and in 1969 formed an organization, the Hiroshima A-bomb Teachers Organization, with six hundred members. This organization has worked with the Nagasaki A-bomb Teachers Organization, formed in 1971, to promote peace education:

> Many teachers held themselves personally responsible for the war because of their having gone along with the popular emperor-worship that was central to Japanese prewar education. Since the war they have been determined to develop and maintain a peace-oriented curriculum. In postwar education, they have given greater attention to individual expression and the discussion of peace values than was ever the case in the past. Peace curricula have been established at all levels within the education system, from primary schools up to the level of the Japanese Peace Association, which is a university peace research organization.[19]

This group has helped establish in 1972 the Hiroshima Institute for Peace Education, which develops curriculum and peace education materials for schools throughout Japan. The institute's purpose is "to pass on the lessons of Hiroshima to the next generation for the benefit of all mankind."[20] It seeks to achieve this aim by "conducting scientific research on peace education and promoting peace education widely throughout the world."[21] Research results are published in the institute's annual report, *Peace Education Study*. This institute promotes peace education throughout Japan by sponsoring national symposia, and it serves as a clearinghouse for international exchanges on peace education.

Hiroshima University's department of education has since 1975 required a course on peace education as part of its curriculum. In 1975 this university created an Institute of Peace Science, which conducts research on peace problems. In addition, Nagasaki Institute of Technology founded in 1978 an Institute of Peace Culture. These efforts gradually spread throughout the rest of the nation and to the rest of the world through the work of scholars at these institutes, who have compiled the experiences of the survivors of the atomic blasts in widely translated materials that provide citizens throughout the world with an awareness of the horrors of nuclear weapons.

In many countries of the Third World, educators have little interest in nuclear age education with its focus on nuclear weapons. Rather, they are concerned about the problems of underdevelopment, starvation, poverty, illiteracy, and the lack of human rights. In speaking about the inadequacy of Western notions of peace education when applied to the Third World, an Indian peace educator has commented:

> There has been too much obsession with the threat of nuclear weapons and inter-state war. In the Third World, the problems of hunger, malnutrition, underdevelopment, social injustice and terror are much more important and they contribute more to the eruption of violence both at national and transnational levels.[22]

Peace education in the Third World is often referred to as "development education," and it addresses the problems created by imperialism, racism, and lack of human rights.[23] Development education provides awareness of political and economic conditions by encouraging people to participate in decisions that will transform their social realities. It has been linked to a call for a new economic order brought forth during the 1970s from Third World countries understanding that the existing economic order, marked by extreme inequalities between the North and the South, does not augur well for world peace and international cooperation. It seeks an international understanding of the crises that exist in the Third World and global solutions for the problems of underdevelopment.

Although Europeans have led the struggle to legitimize peace education, they have not been alone. India has developed its own form of peace education based largely on the work of Mahatma Gandhi, whose peace efforts were guided by a world view based on the spiritual unity of human beings. According to this view peace educators have to address not only the problems of violence but also the spiritual advancement of people everywhere. Gandhi's teaching renounces the exploitation of nature and human beings for the sake of material welfare and prosperity. Consequently peace education in India stresses self-reliance and a simple lifestyle:

> Therefore peace education as a lifestyle movement emphasizes the need for a critical awareness of this situation and stresses simplicity of life so that human survival can be guaranteed against the ills of over-industrialization and overconsumption.[24]

Indian society has for a long time emphasized *shanti,* or peace, and its traditions differ from those of the West. The Hindu concept *ahimsa,* or nonviolence, is deeply rooted within Hindu traditions. Hindu rituals begin and end with a call for peace, and for the Hindu spiritual peace leads human beings to perceive the truth. A Hindu respects all beings because each carries within the *Atman,* or spirit of truth and peace. Where Western societies emphasize the problems of war brought about by the nation-state, Indian tradition is more concerned with the individual being at peace.

From this perspective peace education in India works towards the creation of a nonviolent society that will eliminate inequities and build a new social order free from exploitation.

> A program for peace education in India must be able to deepen the understanding of the forces and factors creating imbalances in the society as well as ways and means to put it again on an even keel. Thus the major task which a peace education program must put before itself is to create a new consciousness among the people for building a new social order.[25]

As mentioned earlier in this chapter, peace education in India is considered a part of development education. Based on the traditions of *satyagraha,* the principles of passive resistance established by Gandhi as a means of gaining political and social reforms, peace education efforts have more closely resembled community development projects. "Satyagraha" means literally "holding fast to the truth,"[26] but for Gandhi it meant "soul force," which implied a commitment to nonviolence. *Satyagrahas* were campaigns based on nonviolent principles. These campaigns used moral and spiritual principles to educate about various forms of oppression which occured in Indian life. The participants in these campaigns were called *satyagrahis:*

> To Gandhi satyagraha was much more than a nonviolent technique: it was an educational process that would not only create among the satyagrahis an acute awareness of injustice and exploitation, but also restore their dignity and self respect.[27]

These satyagrahas had specific goals to accomplish, but they also strove for a spiritual transformation of their participants into active people with some control of their destinies. In this way, participants used nonviolent techniques to gain pride and dignity, as well as to free themselves from the social constraints imposed on them.

Many universities in India offer academic degrees in Gandhian thought. In addition, peace education in India is supported by various peace centers and foundations such as the Gandhi Peace Foundation in New Delhi, which supports research on the works of Gandhi, publishes scholarly treatises, and produces an international monthly journal, *Gandhi Marg*. The School for International Studies, Jawaharlal Nehru University in New Delhi offers seminars on Nehru, nonalignment, and world peace and publishes the international quarterly *The Nonaligned World*.

In Central and South America peace education has followed the direction taken in both India and Africa by focusing on issues of development and literacy. Working largely outside established government schools, peace educators have worked in conjunction with church leaders such as Don Camera and Clodivus Boff, leading adherents of liberation theology, to establish base communities which employ literacy programs based on the work of Brazilian educator Paulo Friere to teach people to read and write. These programs provide social literacy, which is both seen as a critical understanding of the structures of violence as well as the capacity to transform those structures. This type of education does not focus as much on arms and technical weapons as on the causes and effects of economic underdevelopment:

> Disarmament, as viewed from Latin America, would first of all involve eliminating the basic ills that lead to social violence and hence the use of arms. Arms are not a cause but an effect; they are not the problem but the symptom of a deep-seated ill which must be tackled at its roots.[28]

This type of peace education involves adults and nonformal adult educators. The educators rely on local leaders, called *animators,* to gather people into a base community. The educator discusses with participants their personal circumstances to generate from them a language that becomes the basis of a literacy program, leading to abstract concepts which include historical circumstances that cause oppression.

Peace research activities in Latin America are coordinated by the Latin American Council for Peace Research (CLAIP), whose headquarters are in Mexico.[29] This organization addresses the acute war problems in Central America and coordinates conferences with peace researchers from other Latin American countries such as Chile and Brazil, both of which have peace research centers. CLAIP focuses attention on the problems of refugees throughout Central America, promotes peace studies in Latin American universities, participates in the activities of the International Peace Research Association, and hopes to foster national associations of peace research in the countries of Latin America and the Caribbean.

Special mention should be made of the unique circumstances of Costa Rica. In 1949, under the leadership of Jose Figuers, the people of Costa Rica constitutionally abolished their army. This small Central American country has since that time had one of the strongest democracies in Latin America, and it has been recognized throughout the world as a neutral country. In response to the peaceful traditions of this country and also to an invitation from the President of Costa Rica, the United Nations established in 1983 in Escazu, Costa Rica, a University for Peace. This university does not yet formally matriculate students and offer degrees but rather serves as a forum for international dialogue and discussion about the problems of war and violence. It hosts international and regional conferences and provides opportunities for scholars in residence to pursue peace research.

A type of peace education closely related to development education is human rights education, sponsored by northern European countries, Japan, and UNESCO. Human rights education addresses injustices brought about by political repression, human suffering, misery, civil strife, and violence.[30]

International relations can also be a part of peace education, although there has been a distinction made in academic circles between international studies that focus on the existing world order, and those aspects of international studies that point out alternative ways to achieve peace. In many colleges and universities international relations prepares students for careers in various international settings. Rather than focusing on attaining peace, these courses highlight existing political realities and social systems. Whereas international relations programs include security studies to provide an understanding of defense systems and how various countries approach collective security, peace education programs tend to study alternatives to existing defense policies. International studies can provide important insights into how different cultures approach issues of security and international relations can help students develop a broader global consciousness.

The Role of the United Nations

During the First World War many peace activists directed their energies towards the creation of the League of Nations, an organization designed to arbitrate conflicts and avert war. Limited in scope to resolving conflicts between nations (many of which it was not able successfully to mediate), the League of Nations became a rallying point in many countries for peace education. In England a League of Nations Union promoted Education for International Understanding and Education for World Citizenship. These hopes for an international agency to resolve conflicts were transferred to the United Nations, which was created after World War II with a broader focus to provide a center for worldwide dialogue, awareness, and problem solving.

The founding of the United Nations provided an impetus for an international effort to teach about the problems associated with war, violence, injustice, illiteracy, poverty, and other sources of human conflict. In keeping with the principles of the United Nations Charter that promoted international cooperation and peace, the United Nations Educational, Social, and Cultural Organization (UNESCO) in 1953 sponsored an Associated School Project to study disarmament, the international economic order and human rights in schools throughout the world. The six main objectives of this project are:

> i) to improve the capacity of secondary school teachers to teach about world problems;
> ii) to increase young people's awareness of world problems;
> iii) to provide young people with skills which will eventually be useful in solving such problems;
> iv) to develop more effective teaching methods and materials to improve the teaching of three specific world problems (disarmament, the New International World Order, and human rights);
> v) to shed new light on how these three issues can effectively be studied in different countries; and
> vi) to understand better the complexity of world problems and facilitate finding solutions to them as a result of knowing other people's views and opinions regarding them.[31]

The Associated School Project has been carried out in many countries of the world, such as Australia, Finland, the Federal Republic of Germany, Greece, Italy, Japan, New England, Norway, Spain, Sweden, Switzerland, United Kingdom, United States, Bulgaria, the German Democratic Republic, Hungary, the Soviet Union, India, and Argentina. From this initiative national commissions in these countries were asked to develop special programs to increase knowledge of world problems, to promote international understanding through the study of different cultures, and to foster concern for human rights. These national commissions have helped endorse peace studies and education for international understanding, and they have legitimized similar educational activities throughout the world.

In 1974 UNESCO recommended a generic approach to the study of world problems, appropriately named "education for international understanding, co-operation and peace and education relating to human rights and fundamental freedoms."[32] UNESCO's endorsement of educational efforts designed to provide an understanding of world problems has promoted, at the national level, educational projects focused on such areas as multicultural education, human rights education, world studies, and development studies. This recommendation also emphasized the study of such issues as human environment, food supply, and an increasing world population so that citizens throughout the world can appreciate the magnitude of these global problems.

In 1978 the United Nations approved a Special Session on Disarmament, the World Congress on Disarmament Education, which was held in Paris in June, 1980. The final document reflects the United Nations' recognition of education for peace as basic to the achievement of disarmament:

> Education is considered as an essential instrument for two main reasons: Firstly, educational systems can offer effective teaching on world problems to young people everywhere, thus fostering ideas that will lead to a better society; secondly, the school itself provides a solid framework for concrete action, both curricular and extra-curricular, which may promote greater international cooperation.[33]

At this conference a United Nations World Disarmament Campaign was launched. The document produced by this special session focuses on disarmament education, saying, among other things:

> It aims at teaching how to think about disarmament rather than what to think about it. It should therefore be problem centered so as to develop the analytical and critical capacity to examine and evaluate practical steps toward the reduction of arms and the elimination of war as an acceptable international practice.
>
> Disarmament education should be based upon the values of international understanding, tolerance of ideological and cultural diversity, and commitment to social justice and human solidarity.[34]

As a result of these activities scholars throughout the world have researched alternative security systems that could provide the basis for the abolition of war; educators, politicians, and concerned citizens have been able to appeal to these statements as a rationale for introducing the various concepts covered by peace and world studies in school. The United Nations Department of Disarmament Affairs provides fact sheets on disarmament issues. It publishes *The Disarmament Yearbook* and the journal *Disarmament.* Other useful publications are the *Disarmament Campaign Newsletter* and the UNESCO *Courier,* both available from United Nations headquarters in New York.

Adult Education and the Role of Christian Churches

Peace education takes place in many more settings than formal schools. In communities throughout the world, organizations, church members, and elected officials have participated in forums designed to make adults more aware of war and peace issues. Members and leaders of these organizations use educational methods to influence public opinion about the threat of war. These organizations are led by peacemakers, who provide a stimulus for idealism in the terribly frightening modern world. As educators, in a different sense from formally trained teachers, these adult leaders hope to educate people throughout the world about the folly of using weapons and arms to settle disputes. "The colossal growth of the popular peace movement in recent years has been, in many respects, a very significant adult education movement."[35] In response to various demands supported by peace movements throughout the world, peace activists have been turning to education to promote their causes. The form and content of adult education for peace varies in different parts of the world.

In the Scandinavian countries, folk schools supported by the state and available to adults in those countries have been offering peace education classes. In the United States a movement called Beyond War has been organizing forums in people's houses to discuss the dangers of the current arms race and the need to change our way of thinking about conflict and our relationship to other people and the planet. In England the Campaign for Nuclear Disarmament has since the 1950s held forums, seminars, and adult discussion groups on problems associated with a commitment to militarism. These peace groups and others throughout the world often show films and hold day-long conferences to build broad support for their efforts and to provide community education programs for adults concerned about war and peace issues.

Christian churches have played an important leadership role in promoting peace education throughout the world. In 1983 the World Council of Churches issued a statement on peace and justice. That same year the Catholic Bishops in the United States issued a pastoral letter renouncing, among other things, the first use of nuclear weapons. That same year the Christian World Conference on Life and Peace issued a strong statement on "Peace, Justice and Common Security." Similar statements were also released that year by the Synod of the Federation of Protestant Churches in the German Democratic Republic, by the Bishops in the German Federal Republic and by the Church of England.[36] In 1986 Methodist bishops in the United States issued a strong statement denouncing nuclear war. These statements provide a moral force to the peace movement and a legitimacy to efforts to curtail the commitment to militarism. More importantly, they provide texts that become the basis of adult education programs. As church members examine these statements carefully, they challenge their own commitments to national security and develop a new awareness of the terrors of war and uses of violence.

Churches have generated many educational guides and resources that are available to community groups, parishes, peace organizations, and other groups that wish to educate their membership about the threat of war. (Appendix A contains a listing of church material related to war and peace.) One such publication, *Militarism and the World Military Order: A Study Guide for Churches,* has been published by the World Council of Churches and translated into many different languages and distributed throughout the world. In the United States the United Ministries in Education (UME), a covenant-based ministry created by eight national churches—American Baptist Churches, Christian Church (Disciples of Christ), Church of the Brethren, Episcopal Church, Moravian Church, Presbyterian Church of the United States, United Church of Christ, and the United Presbyterian Church in the United States—has published *Militarization, Security, and Peace Education: A Guide for Concerned Citizens,* by Betty Reardon. This book, designed for adult learning seminars, contains objectives for peace education, a discussion of the problems of militarization, and suggestions for action. In the Netherlands the Interchurch Peace Council has issued important policy-related statements concerning the threat of war. In East Germany the Protestant churches sponsor a ten-day "peace week" to focus of the dynamics of peace.

The role of religions in promoting peace education is not limited solely to adult education. In the Netherlands and in Australia, church-supported schools have taken the initiative to introduce peace education at the elementary and secondary level. Other church-sponsored schools throughout the world promote concepts of peace and justice not often found in traditional schools run by the state. In Latin America priests and bishops have played a key role in thousands of base communities, which are communities of prayer and gospel-sharing that provide mutual aid and often are geared towards changing society.

In industrialized countries various churches support peace and justice centers which provide tapes, books, films, discussion groups, and places for meetings, as well as other resources for education and action. The American Friends Service Committee, run by Quakers, has ten such regional centers in the United States. Within the Catholic church some of these centers provide a place for meditation and study. The style and emphasis in these centers vary from diocese to diocese in different parts of the world. Some of them provide meals for the homeless and a retreat space where educators can reflect upon their peace education activities. These centers allow people working for peace to meet with others and to recharge their batteries for the sustained struggle to bring justice to this world.

These peace efforts within churches and various adult communities challenge traditional educational practices. Whereas traditional education promotes peace through strength and a belief in the national security apparatus, peace activists and peace educators are questioning both the politics of the status quo and traditional educational goals and methods. Likewise, the traditional role of the church is being challenged by liberation ministries. Spurred by an awareness of the terror of nuclear weapons and political oppression, educators throughout the world are questioning traditional notions of security that come from being armed, and are creating a new type of education that empowers people by asking them what kind of society they want to inhabit. The practice of these new forms of education often originates in informal educational systems, in church parishes and adult education settings, but are starting to have an impact upon formal educational systems. As peace movements gather strength, educators in formal systems are placed in an existential dilemma: Do they want their efforts to continue to support the status quo, or are they willing to use their skills and professional status to help create a new social order that promotes a world based on peace and justice?

Why "Peace Education"?

Derek Heater has suggested that "world studies" is the generic umbrella for all these different disciplines, focusing on world problems and how to solve those problems.[37] Although these disciplines go by separate names, such as peace education, development education, human rights education, international studies, nuclear age education, A-bomb education, disarmament education, etc., Robin Richardson has stated that these different disciplines bear "a family resemblance."[38] They are not distinct, but rather share similar interests. Their adherents emphasize different educational approaches to peace and conflict, but they share the common goal of providing a better understanding about how to minimize conflict in the world.

The title *Peace Education* has been chosen for this book to represent these different approaches to studying about war, peace and conflict because it provides a paradigm for the consensual basis that guides intellectual inquiry. "Peace Education" is also preferred as a generic term because it includes the concepts implied in other educational approaches. All these different approaches complement each other and contribute to the rich diversity of the emerging academic discipline *irenology*, from the Greek word for peace, *irene*. From the Third World comes an emphasis on human rights and social justice. Japan contributes an understanding of the horrors of a nuclear war, and the Northern industrial societies add their understanding of the psychological effects of violence. Peace education covers the causes of war, the study of nuclear weapons, arms, the national security state, international relations, human rights, global cultures, and the quest for peace that has influenced human behavior throughout history.

Peace education is in some ways distinct from another academic field that has been labeled "security studies," which focuses on how nations defend themselves. However, because peace educators need to understand both defense and war systems, security studies belongs within the general heading of peace education.

Peace education, as an overall paradigm, contains within it many of the stimulating and motivating aspects of the concept "peace," which has provided inspiration for human beings throughout recorded history. Carl Jung refers to peace as an archetype that exists within the collective unconscious. According to him and others, all people desire peace and social justice. As a crucial part of all the world's major religions, concern for peace includes faith about the world becoming better and incorporates the spiritual aspects of human nature. Peace education supports some of the more noble aspects of the human condition, while the nomenclature "nuclear age education" underscores the worst aspect of human nature, its ability to destroy life on this planet. Peace education, then, becomes prescribed as a name for educational efforts to build a better world, including within it the skills and techniques of conflict management — skills that aren't traditionally taught in such fields as international studies or world order studies. The specific nature of peace education has unique historical roots within each country.

Peace eduction includes the Gandhian search for truth. It includes the depressing study of the threat of mass destruction from nuclear weapons, as well as the uplifting visions of peaceful coexistence, moral and social responsibility to children, teachers, schools, and society for human dignity and respect. It studies conflict between people and allows human beings to draw upon their urges for social justice to create a more humane order. Studying the existing world order can highlight tensions but also can emphasize successful attempts of people to solve their disputes nonviolently. Peace education allows teachers, students, and peace activists to inform others about the threats that dominate human existence as well as the possibilities for removing those threats.

4. Key Topics of Peace Education

We believe that a comprehensive and responsible plan for nuclear education is an imperative because our young people are growing up in a world of nuclear realities and perils. These are facts, and ignorance of them and of how to deal with them in itself is a danger to democracy. Indeed ignorance constitutes a peril to human survival. Youth, in the final analysis, need to be taught the realities of the nuclear age because they need to know about them. Our entire educational apparatus was avowedly brought into being precisely for the purpose of providing youth with indispensible knowledge about the world in which they must live. They, as we, have a right to know the facts. If the schools fail to implement this right, they fail to fulfill the central purpose for which they came into being. How can young people identify their interest, choose their alternatives, and instruct their government about what it ought to do for them if they are not provided with the necessary knowledge?

Willard Jacobsen, Betty Reardon, and Douglas Sloan,
Introduction to special issue of *Social Education*
dedicated to Nuclear Weapons

Preparing to teach about the dilemmas of war and peace presents a challenge to both teachers and community educators. Most people who want to teach about these topics were not formally trained in peace issues. For example, church attenders may have knowledge of those parts of scripture that discuss the search for peace and justice, but probably have never studied in depth many of the complex issues surrounding foreign policy.

Suppose that members of a church approach their minister about declaring their church a sanctuary for refugees from Central America. Part of their proposal might include a series of forums on the history of United States relations with Central American countries.This would provide important background information that would help parishioners determine whether or not they want to turn their church into a sanctuary. The forum organizers themselves have to spend considerable time learning about who are appropriate speakers, where they are located, and what issues should be covered. In this way their peace activities are preceded by learning about issues so they can make an informed assessment of the situation before proceeding with a plan of action. The first step in getting started with peace education activities requires learning the various topics that encompass the conceptual and academic terrains of peace studies.

Those who wish to initiate peace education activities face many problems in learning about the topics of peace education. The first is that the topics themselves are so broad. They include the history of different peace movements, foreign affairs, multi-cultural studies, the sociology and psychology of aggression, the economics of the arm race, religion, philosophy, social change theory, and conflict resolution. Learning about so many issues can appear overwhelming. The second problem is that it's hard to find out where to go to learn these topics. The activities of the peace movement are not covered in most traditional programs. Therefore the material that peace activists and educators want to learn is neither easily available nor taught in most existing curricula. If one wanted to learn about medicine, one could go to medical school, or a medical school library, or a nursing school. No similar academic institutions exist for peace studies. Since the 1950s some universities around the world have started to initiate peace studies programs where individuals can acquire background information that will help them make informed decisions about the issues of war and peace, but these fledgling programs do not have many graduates. The vast majority of peace educators, have never been formally trained to teach about peace issues.

Lacking such formal training, teachers from a wide variety of backgrounds approach peace studies with the expertise of their own academic disciplines, whether it be as activists in the peace movement, or as scholars of Eastern philosophy. Since there are no basic texts for peace studies courses, professors at different institutions, as well as concerned teachers and citizens, bring to peace studies content from a wide variety of disciplines. Because of this diversity, learning about peace issues is a complex task requiring investigation into fields as different as psychology and international law.

The main topics of peace education that will be discussed in this chapter are (1) existing security policies; (2) the quest for international order; (3) creative resolution of conflict; (4) understanding violent behavior; and (5) strategies for peace. These topics have been chosen because they represent the content taught in most peace studies programs. Since many books have been written on these topics, it is not possible in such a brief overview to offer a thorough analysis here. They will be presented in such a way as to provide the reader with an introduction to key ideas and concepts of a peace studies program. (At the end of this book is a bibliography, broken down by the sections listed below, that provides background reading on these topics.)

Existing Security Policies

Peace educators challenge students to think through what constitutes national security at the global, national, regional, local, and individual level. What is the best way to provide security for citizens throughout this planet? In peace studies classes students address questions about appropriate security systems: Would weapons in space increase or diminish our collective security? How can governments, both national, regional and local, best provide for the security needs of citizens? What can individuals do to protect themselves and create security for their neighbors, family members and loved ones? Have nuclear weapons, justified as a contribution to national security, made the world more secure?

A key part of the security arrangements provided citizens in modern states is the defense establishment. In order to be literate about defense policies, peace educators study all different aspects of defense—the history of the defense establishment, the cost of defense budgets, the type of weaponry advocated, and the implications of relying on particular defense postures. In 1959 in his final speech to the nation as President, Dwight Eisenhower warned about a growing military industrial complex:

> There is no way in which a country can satisfy the craving for absolute security—but it can easily bankrupt itself, morally and economically, in attempting to reach that illusionary goal through arms alone. The military establishment, not productive of itself, necessarily must feed on the energy, productivity, and brainpower of the country, and if it takes too much, our total strength declines.[1]

The total expenditures on defense are growing to the point where in 1985 the nations of the world spent over one trillion dollars on wars, weaponry, and defense planning. The publics of most countries, ignorant about these expenditures, know little about what their taxes buy, nor do they understand the economic ramifications of bloated defense budgets. Increasingly countries in the Socialist bloc, the Third World, and Western democracies are being stifled by what Helen Caldicott calls the "iron triangle"[2]—the network of private contractors, defense experts, and government officials, all of whom profit from the weaponry they promote. Poor countries in the Third World borrow money to buy modern weapons, and increasing amounts of their scant resources go to pay back loans rather than provide food and other basic necessities for their people. (At the same time that so much money is being spent on weaponry, 41,000 people a day, mostly children, are dying from starvation.)

In spite of the tremendous diversion of resources which this expenditure represents, most citizens are unaware of what their tax dollars are buying. Consequently, an important part of peace education is to provide information about both the weaponry and costs which constitute modern defense systems that are supposed to provide security. For example, in the U.S. President Reagan raised the defense budget from $140 billion in 1980 to $300 billion in 1983. For the first six years of his administration, 1980–1986, $1.6 trillion was spent on defense, a sum equivalent to all the money spent on defense between the years 1946 and 1980, which amounts to spending $91,000 an hour for every hour going back to Christ's birth. This enormous sum of money, as Seymour Melman has pointed out in *The Permanent War Economy,*[3] means that money is not invested in industry and social services in ways that could help sustain a healthy economy.

Traditionally, studies about defense matters have been labeled "security studies" and pursued within the field of political science. Students of peace education should take these courses and learn the basic vocabulary in order to acquire nuclear "literacy" so that as future citizens they can vote in an intelligent manner about these crucial issues. Without such an understanding citizens accede to recommendations from national leaders about the weakness of defense systems and accept the validity of threats posed by other countries, which are used to justify increased arms buildup. These arguments, by frightening people, create an atmosphere where taxpayers don't question the demands of defense leaders for new weapons and treat defense as a sacred cow that can't be challenged.

Within the heading "defense establishment" peace studies students learn about nuclear weapons — the physics and chemistry of how they work, their effects on the ecosystem, and the history of their production and first use. In order to understand the threats those weapons pose, students should investigate what could happen if their area were bombed with thermonuclear weapons. Recent studies have indicated that the repeated use of nuclear weapons would create a phenomenon referred to as *nuclear winter,* where so much damage would be done to the atmosphere and so much dust created that the whole ecosphere could be seriously altered; this, in turn, would drastically affect life on this planet.[4] If these research predictions are true (and they can't be tested short of a nuclear holocaust), the implications are that if one of the superpowers were to launch a "successful" thermonuclear first strike, totally wiping out the enemy to the point where no retaliation was possible, the ecological damage to the planet might be such that all people in the country that launched that strike could slowly die as the planet is surrounded with radioactive dust and the temperature on earth drops. Peace studies students should understand the implications of these policies by reading books such as *The Fate of the Earth,* which discusses in detail the philosophic and scientific arguments surrounding the use and production of nuclear weapons.

The study of national security systems also includes the history of arms control negotiations. Current arms policy rests on deterrence theory, which necessitates that either of the superpowers have sufficient capability to wipe out the other side should there ever be a first strike. Many world leaders, sensing the danger of new weapons systems and the cost of their production, have urged the countries possessing nuclear weapons to sign arms control agreements that would halt or even reverse the arms race. The desire to reduce these stockpiles is so great that in many European nations "peace education" is referred to as "disarmament education." Many educational leaders in these countries are convinced that the path to peace must include a disarmament process whereby the huge arsenals that now threaten human existence are reduced and ultimately eliminated. Learning about different disarmament strategies, as well as the history of arms control negotiations, will prepare citizens throughout the world to participate in an informed manner in the ongoing dialogue about disarmament.

As important as it is to learn about the defense establishments that dominate security debates, students in peace education classes should examine all different aspects of the need for human security. Peace studies classes should include discussions of local police and how their behavior contributes to security within that area. What role does a government have in promoting security for its citizens? What rights do citizens have to determine security policies at the local and national level? What can citizens do to make their world more secure? What contributes to insecurity and how does insecurity foster violence? What are the alternatives to existing security arrangements? These complex questions will both encourage students to understand current policies that often escape public scrutiny and challenge them to derive alternatives to improve their lives. They are so complex that they themselves range over a wide variety of traditional academic disciplines, including criminal justice, sociology, political science, and psychology. The search for security takes the inquiring learner deep into the realms of the human psyche as well as the labyrinths of foreign policy decisions.

The Quest for International Order

Social scientists have observed that the greatest cause of war is the current alignment of nation-states. Nationalism and differing economic investments have intensified struggles between countries and divided the world into armed camps bristling to protect and expand economic interests. Not only do nation-states extract important resources from each other, but nation-states also have particular ideologies and beliefs that cause hostilities. Because conflicts between nations can cause war, peace studies addresses national differences so that peace education students understand what contributes to the disagreements between nations, as well as methods to bridge those disagreements. Presenting information about the world's superpowers allows students to draw their own conclusions about superpower conflicts. Peace studies students should take courses in international relations to appreciate the diversity of perspectives that dominate the world's political systems.

World studies, often referred to as "education for international understanding," teaches about problems faced throughout the world and differing approaches to solving those problems. Included in these studies are attempts by countries in the so-called Third World to develop new information systems that tell their issues to a world dominated by media produced in advanced worlds, regional formations like the European Economic Community or the OPEC oil trading cartel, efforts to develop a new international economic order, and the challenges of grass-roots peace movements to traditional defense alliances. World order education promotes communication between different people in the hope that an awareness of problems in the world will enhance cooperation and discredit the use of force in international relations.

An important part of education about international order is developing a vision of the world in which human needs are met, respect for cultural differences flourishes, justice thrives, resources are distributed equally, and starvation does not exist.

> War, huge military expenditures, waste of resources, pollution, diseases, and national disasters are the enemies of the human race against which all people can direct aggressive tendencies.[5]

One strategy for dealing with the problems faced by planetary citizens is to promote through education a concept of world citizenry, where people take responsibility for their brothers and sisters around the world and work to create a world community. This strategy is widely promoted by the Baha'i, a religion that promotes the commonality of human beings throughout the world. As Teilhard de Chardin wrote, "we are now at the beginning of . . . the planetisation of Mankind."[6] Developing a sense of the world as a global community requires an interest in the problems of people throughout the planet, a concern for peace and justice, a knowledge of the war problem, a tolerance for racial and cultural differences, a reluctance to use violence, an unselfishness, and an attitude of globalism and humanitarianism rather than patriotism. In peace education classes students can question their different loyalties. What role does loyalty to a cause, or a country, or a neighborhood play in promoting or inhibiting cooperation in human communities? These loyalties inspire and motivate human behavior. One approach advocated by Global Education Associates promotes *Gaia consciousness,* an awareness of the intricacies of the planet Earth and a commitment to respect basic ecological requirements of the earth. If peace education can augment traditional chauvinistic loyalties with respect for the earth, for the worldwide human community, and for the sacredness of life, there will be less support for militarism and the use of force to settle disputes.

Because violence against human beings takes more forms than the threat of war, peace education should provide an awareness of all threats to human security. The planet is crowded and getting more so. Three-quarters of the world's population live in permanent misery. The ratio of the Gross National Product per individual in the northern industrial societies is ten times that of those who live in the Third World, and is increasing. Pressure on the ecosystem has reached the point where one species a week is becoming extinct, and it is predicted by the year 2000 that one species a minute will become extinct. Totalitarian governments are repressing political freedom. Human and natural resources are being wasted. These global problems cause structural violence and need to be addressed if the world is to move towards a more peaceful state where human beings can achieve their potential. In addition to eliminating war and decreasing funds spent to support the war system, the core values for such a world system are ecological balance, economic well-being, improved communication, human growth and development, and peaceful change.[8]

Another approach to solving problems which contribute to war and structural violence is the creation of world organizations and the reform of existing organizations, such as the United Nations. Other international attempts to resolve worldwide conflicts include the World Court, various treaties such as the Law of the Sea Treaty, international laws and a wide variety of international organizations as diversified as the International Red Cross and the World Council for Curriculum and Instruction. These nongovernment organizations help promote a more coherent world system, by allowing citizens from throughout the world to articulate concerns and develop strategies to address those concerns.

A thorough examination of the problems of war and peace requires students and teachers to analyze the causes of violence, provide information about the various aspects of violence and ultimately examine suggestions to transform violent behavior. In studying international order, such a framework would prompt peace educators to study how different nation-states have been formed, what the salient policies of states are, and how nationalistic behavior can be transformed into some system of regional or world government that lessens the possibilities for war on this planet. There are no easy answers as to how the existing system of political alliances and allegiances can be transformed, but peace educators should at least examine in their classes the various approaches that have been mentioned to promote a new world order.

> I think the lesson is slowly being learned, and that world order projects and studies, as a consequence, are increasingly aware that transformation of the world system presupposes a long ambiguous struggle dependent on the emergence of a robust global social movement. There is no "quick fix" in the offering, only the slim hope that there will be enough time for a global learning process among elites and masses to evolve in such a way as to be able to encourage a series of political adjustments in the world that gradually shift the weight of behavior in directions that are humane and ecologically sensitive.[9]

Learning about world order and attempts by nongovernment organizations to promote a new world order can involve peace education efforts in "track II" diplomacy, where ordinary citizens attempt to circumvent traditional governmental policies ("track I" diplomacy) to reach out to citizens in foreign countries. These citizen exchanges, sometimes facilitated by the development of high technology, allow people from different lands to explore areas of agreement and discuss ways to reduce tensions between countries. Although ordinary citizens do not set foreign policy, such exchanges can help reduce hostilities between different political alignments.

Creative Resolution of Conflict

If one of the goals of peace education is to bring peace to the world, students of peace education will have to learn how to resolve conflicts nonviolently. Conflict — a daily reality that comes from differing needs, values, goals, resources, scarcity, and competition — seems to be increasing in our modern world. It is international and inevitable. The ability to resolve conflict successfully is probably one of the most important skills an individual can possess, yet there are few formal opportunities to learn it. Some courses, often taught at the college level by faculty from communication departments, deal with intercultural communication and conflict resolution. Other departments, such as social welfare or psychology, that focus on human interaction may also offer courses dealing with conflict between individuals and within organizations. Various organizations such as the Society for Professionals in Dispute Resolution (SPIDR) or the International Society for Intercultural Education (SIETAR) publish journals and sponsor annual conferences where individuals can improve their skills in conflict management. Because of high levels of civil suits and domestic violence, there has recently been a proliferation of conflict resolution centers which help mediate local conflicts. (In the United States there were 15 such centers in 1975 and 350 in 1987.)

Like other human skills, conflict resolution can be taught because it consists of a set of skills often referred to as conflict "resolution strategies," which may be classified into three categories — avoidance, defusion, and confrontation.[10] Avoiding conflict can aggravate a particular problem as resentments build up and emotions intensify. *Defusion* is essentially a delaying action that attempts to cool off a situation, or to keep issues so unclear that confrontation is avoided. Because conflict frightens individuals they often tend to seek ways to defuse it, trying to understate its significance in the hope that it will go away. Conflict is a necessary and creative dynamic in most relationships that should be confronted to help two people or a group of people make good decisions and grow closer.

Defusing or avoiding conflicts can become destructive if people are afraid to express disagreement or feel put down for their opinions and feelings.

In order to be dealt with constructively conflict has to be confronted. Expressing hostile feelings is a good way to avoid withdrawal, but in order to express these feelings constructively people have to be committed to a win-win situation where participants' feelings are expressed and all parties are willing to compromise. Peace education seeks to avoid power confrontations where people try to impose their wills upon others and depends upon compromise and negotiation to resolve conflicts. Some people prefer to use the term "conflict management" rather than "conflict resolution," because even though disputants are able to settle their disagreements, bad feelings may linger; hence a particular conflict is not resolved in the sense that it disappears, but rather has been managed in such a way that the disputing parties have been able to reach an agreement.

One way of discussing conflict is to think of it in terms of a continuum going from cooperation to competition to warfare. Cooperation involves people working together to resolve their disagreements. Competition implies that there will be winners and losers. Some forms of competition are mild and friendly, while others are intense and destructive. Conflicts can be managed nonviolently by talking them through, by using votes, compromise, and consensus strategies, by creating alternatives, by agreeing to disagree, by seeking mediation or arbitration, and by practicing nonviolence. Warfare represents the most violent way to resolve conflict.

Conflict resolution involves problem-solving between individuals, groups, organizations, and nations. The Martin Luther King Center for Nonviolent Social Change in Atlanta, Georgia, recommends six steps for resolving conflicts between parties. The first step is to gather information that accurately represents both sides of the dispute. The second step is to educate people about the problem, and to provide information that accurately represents both sides of the dispute. The third step is to build commitment among parties to participate in a process that will resolve their conflicts. The fourth step is to negotiate a compromise that all parties can agree to. The fifth step is to put that compromise into place and act on it. The final stage is to attempt to further reconcile differences between parties and evaluate the agreed-upon compromise. The success of this process depends upon the disagreeing members achieving an understanding of both the position and frame of reference of their opponents.[11]

Two Harvard law professors, Roger Fisher and William Ury, recommend that rather than bargaining over positions, conflict resolution focus on the interests of people involved in a conflict:

> To sum up, in contrast to positional bargaining, the principled negotiation method focusing on basic interests, mutually satisfying options, and fair standards typically results in a wise agreement. The

method permits you to reach a gradual consensus on a joint decision
efficiently without all the transactional costs of digging into positions
only to have to dig yourself out of them.[12]

This approach generates options that allow both parties to come away with
a sense that they have gained from the interaction. Digging into positions
and holding onto them keeps parties locked into a competitive win-lose
situation whereas the search for alternatives allows both parties to seek a
solution that satisfies their needs.

Conflict resolution gives peace education students skills they can use
in their daily lives to express their frustrations in ways that don't abuse
others. In order for these skills to be successful, all parties must be willing
to change their behavior. On an individual level an angry lover may strike
the object of his or her love before seeking therapy to resolve differences.
At a social level, lawsuits are most often initiated before aggrieved parties
turn to negotiation. On an international level the success of conflict resolution and nonviolent strategies depends upon nations being committed to
not using force or military means to settle their disagreements.

Unfortunately, the general pattern of violent behavior is that, faced
with a crisis of some kind, one or more parties decide to use violent means
to get their way. Usually the aggressive party chooses violent means believing it can win. That party is not interested in compromise or negotiation
until the use of force breaks down or is stalemated. Quarrels are picked.
They don't just happen. Solving a dispute in a way that is acceptable to both
sides is not a goal of countries going to war, individuals fighting, and con-
testants suing each other. At best it is a secondhand solution. Conflict
management works only when both parties agree to submit to a problem-
solving procedure.

Understanding Violent Behavior

Violent behavior causes tremendous problems in human communities.
Students of peace education need to understand the causes of violence and
why people use force to impose their will on others. As human beings have
progressed they continue to exhibit violent behavior. Dictators torture their
opponents. Religious fanatics wage holy wars. Prurient interests promote
violent pornography. And movies celebrate gruesome behavior. A sad
irony of the development of civilization is the accompanying sadism and
destruction. Studying the many different causes of violence draws the peace
educator into complex debates about human behavior. In order for
violence to be eliminated these causes must be understood and corrected.

Aggression has been defined as "behavior whose goal is the injury of
some person or object."[13] People commit aggression in order to get
something they want. Three different types of theories have been advanced

to account for aggressive human behavior. The first says that aggression is unavoidable because it is deeply rooted in human nature. Others, often associated with Konrad Lorenz,[14] state that human beings have a predisposition to aggressive behavior programmed in the human genetic code. Others say that violence is deeply rooted in the human psyche.

Those theories based on biological determinism—i.e., aggression being programmed into the genetic code—often refer to the *territorial imperative,* where humans, like wild beasts, stake out territory and then use violent means to protect it. Because such behavior is instinctual, it is seen as belonging to the human species. Some scientists have even argued that men, because they have Y-chromosomes, are by nature violent, that violence is inherent to the male species, stemming from high levels of testosterone in the male.[15]

At the psychological level, Sigmund Freud emphasized how violence is deeply rooted in human nature, being an expression of the unconscious barbarity of man.[16] Under this theory, violent behavior expresses urges that exist deep within the human psyche. The way to deal with these aggressive drives is to channel them constructively and learn nonviolent ways of expressing them. Activities such as the Olympics allow a release for aggressive impulses in ways that don't harm.

The second set of theories about violence views individual human aggression as the result of hostility brought about by frustration. According to this approach human beings are goal-oriented. As long as they make progress towards achieving their goals they do not become frustrated and consequently violent. This explanation of human behavior states that frustration builds up to a point where it gets released in aggressive behavior. In cases of acute frustration human beings have bloodthirsty fantasies. War represents a state of crisis where problems can't be solved within the limits of discourse and negotiation. Each of us is capable of committing violent acts because in times of acute frustration we want to sadistically destroy our enemies. The strategy for dealing with this type of aggression is to get rid of frustration by doing away with poverty, misery, starvation and various barriers that keep human beings from reaching their full potential.

On a deeper level an Italian psychologist, Franco Fornari, argues that war and violent behavior come from deep-seated frustrations.[17] Under this line of reasoning, violent human behavior expresses an individual's deep-hidden sadistic impulses, as he or she tries to destroy an enemy that is projected out from dark parts of the self. Each person has "a terribler" that provokes nightmares and other frightening images about the world. Violent behavior provides the possibility of destroying anxiety-provoking images that have been projected onto the enemy. The way to eliminate war and violence, according to this theory, is to raise children in ways that reduce internal tensions by eradicating the element of domination from the parent-child relationship (and the teacher-student relationship!). Allowing children the opportunity to express themselves freely, teaching them to articulate their needs, and responding to those needs reduces the production of angry dark sides within an individual which become the driving force for aggressive, violent behavior.

The third set of theories concerning individual aggression and violence emphasizes the role of social conditioning in aggressive behavior.[18] According to this approach, human beings acquire violent behaviors by observing friends, family members, images in the culture, and significant others. Since human beings learn violent ways to express their aggressive tendencies, they will practice violence if they get rewarded for it. The way to extinguish violent behavior is, in the first place, not to practice violence, and in the second, not to reward it. Positive reinforcement of nonviolent behaviors is the best way to change aggression. According to this theory, peace educators should model nonviolent behavior, set up cooperative classrooms and deemphasize competition and opportunities for students to lord over others.

Societies reinforce violent behavior in individuals when the collective power of a group, state or nation is used to wage war. People identify with these collective bodies and want to defend their group interests when they are threatened. It has been demonstrated that war can be influenced by the aggressive actions of individual leaders—such as Alexander the Great, Genghis Khan, Napoleon Bonaparte, and Adolf Hitler.[19] These individuals, although not the sole cause of wars, played an important role in building public sentiment to support warlike actions. Another reason that social units support war is through a phenomenon known as *displaced aggression,* where a frustrated person may not be able to express his or her frustrations at the cause of ill feelings, so he/she places them on some other source, such as the "commies," or other groups which are said to cause evil in the world.[20] Societies also build upon individual tendencies for aggression by promoting militarism. Social values stating that one group is better than another and emphasizing values "higher than" life prepare people to fight. People are desensitized to violence when they are constantly exposed to violent images. In modern industrial societies children and adults are constantly exposed to violent images. Environment plays a large role in promoting aggression. Learning how to compete, and that every situation is a confrontation which translates into a win-lose situation, teaches people to devalue cooperation. Societies also prepare their members for war by making citizens obedient to authority.

Within certain countries (e.g., Afghanistan, El Salvador), individuals wage wars of national liberation because they feel they have a right to overthrow tyranny, and a right to self-determination. Much violence takes place throughout the world when people take up arms to overthrow one type of government and replace it with another. Increasingly in many countries resistance movements are practicing nonviolence to resist oppressive dictators. Such was the case in 1954 in Guatemala, in 1986 in the Philippines, and currently in countries throughout the world, such as Chile, where resistance movements are pledging themselves to discredit the violent practices of the ruling government. National wars of liberation can be studied to understand how physical force is relied on to overcome oppression and can be contrasted with nonviolent attempts to reach similar goals.

Wars between nations are caused by differing economic systems, religious and ethnic differences, political ideologies, and the desire to assert authority. Wars are glamorized in ways that cause people to think they are wonderful. An article in *Esquire* magazine stated that for many men fighting in a war was their greatest time: "War is, for men, at some level the closest thing to what childbirth is for women: The initiation into the power of life and death."[21] As long as war is seen to be an enduring part of the human species and is glorified as a noble enterprise, human beings will allow their governments to practice it.

Strategies for Peace

Peace education includes a sense of what can be done to achieve a more peaceful world. The topics covered in the study of war and violence are so depressing that peace education students could become extremely cynical about human institutions and group behavior. Intellectual awareness and arguments are not enough, though. Students must also be taught what can be done about this situation, by learning different strategies for becoming more involved in shaping the destiny of their culture. In this sense peace education requires people to become more active participants in the societies they inhabit. Peace education should not only lead to inquiry into these problems; it should also help formulate solutions to these problems.

Three basic types of strategies address issues of war and peace. The first deals with transforming an individual's personal life so that it is less violent. The second concerns joining some type of group to provide information and support for those attempting to bring peace to their lives. The third involves working on a political level to change official policies concerning violence and peace.

If we want a less violent world, we must reorient our values and our lifestyles. Many individuals desiring peace do not think it is possible to change the defense policies of their governments, but do think they can change their own lifestyles. We will not make the world peaceful if we cannot make ourselves more peaceful by adopting nonviolence as a way of living and conducting our affairs. We must learn a morality of caring where we use love to channel aggressive impulses into behaviors that respect the dignity and sacredness of life. Peace is not simply the absence of violence, and the opposite of violence is not passivity. Nonviolence implies taking an active stance in the world to manage conflicts constructively and to work for peace and justice:

> Non-violence cannot then be understood as passivity or indifference to the dynamic of life (i.e. communication between men). It is not the posture or removing oneself from conflict that marks the true non-violent man, but quite on the contrary, it is placing oneself in the heart of the dynamic. Non-violence means an active opposition to those acts and attitudes that demean and brutalize another, and it means an active support of those values and expressions that foster human solidarity. Non-violence, in essence, means taking a stand in favor of life and refusing to delegate individual moral responsibility to another person or group; it means taking control of one's life and aiding others in doing likewise. Non-violence is an attempt to find truth and love even in the midst of hatred, destruction and pride.[22]

For many concerned about the threats of violence, embracing nonviolence means adopting a way of living based upon love of fellow human beings, creatures, and plants. Peacemaking implies a commitment to engage conflict situations actively and to use nonviolent techniques to resolve disputes. The world's history has been strongly affected by the practices and beliefs of such important peacemakers as Jesus Christ, Mahatma Gandhi, Danilo Dolci, Henry David Thoreau, Kenneth Kuanda, Dorothy Day, and Martin Luther King, Jr. Peace education students, by studying nonviolent leaders, can learn how to adapt their own lives to the principles of nonviolence. Nonviolence is demanding. Mahatma Gandhi, one of the world's greatest practitioners of nonviolence, admitted that the more he learned about nonviolence—or *ahimsa,* as it is called in Hindi—the more he realized that he was imperfect in practicing it. "Nobody can practice perfect nonviolence. We may not be perfect in our use of it, but we definitely discard the use of violence and grow from failure to success."[23] Individuals practicing nonviolence search deep within their souls to discover the sources of hatred and learn how to control their aggressive urges with love. Nonviolence practice does not just involve using civil disobedience against oppressors but demands a rigorous discipline where an individual orients his or her life towards working harmoniously with others.

In addition to practicing nonviolence, individuals can join organizations dedicated to peace. Currently in the United States there are approximately 3000 such local groups, which vary from church organizations concerned about nuclear policies to feminist groups addressing domestic violence. (For a complete listing of these organizations write *American Peace Directory,* Ballinger Publications, 54 Church St., Cambridge MA 02138.) One state, Pennsylvania, has over 100 local peace groups. These organizations together constitute a modern peace movement that is worldwide in its scope, with different branches, chapters, and activities taking place in countries as diverse as the European nations, Japan, Israel, the Philippines, and Argentina. Peace organizations allow people to join with others to reverse the tide of militarism that currently floods human endeavor. Studying the history of peace movements will help students discover which strategies were successful and why others failed. The thousands of organizations that constitute the modern peace movement allow volunteers and paid staff to use their political talents by directing their efforts to influence policies that will help create a peaceful world. Involvement with these organizations amplifies an individual's political power, provides an opportunity to share concerns about violence, supports concerns about the role of violence in people's lives, and encourages the creation of options to build a more peaceful future.

Citizens who live in democratic countries can vote and use creative political energies to influence public policy to bring a halt to militarism:

> Facing the peril of nuclear annihilation, it is now imperative that we all grow up, become adults, and learn to use this magnificent democracy which we are all anxious to preserve. We are not children, and the "experts" are not our benevolent parents who have our best interests at heart.[24]

Debates in peace education classes about various measures proposed by world leaders to reduce the threat of war will help generate goals that provide a focus for organizing and further education. The World Disarmament Campaign, based in the United Kingdom, has produced a set of proposals, many of which have already been adopted by the General Assembly of the United Nations. These proposals are listed below in order to stimulate thinking about what steps can be taken on a global level to reduce the threat of war:

For the Prevention of Nuclear War

1.1 A joint declaration by the nuclear powers of an immediate, verifiable freeze of all nuclear weapons and their delivery systems (ballistic and cruise missiles and longe range bombers) covering development, testing, production and deployment.

Freezing should be accompanied by concrete measures for reducing and destroying nuclear weapons, with the USA and the USSR taking the lead in cutting their nuclear weapons by a wide margin.

1.2 A permanent comprehensive nuclear weapons test ban on the lines already discussed by the USA and the USSR and called for by the United Nations.

1.3 A permanent agreement on the demilitarisation of outerspace.

1.4 The establishment of nuclear free zones.

1.5 An agreement between the USA and the USSR and all other governments concerned on the reduction and destruction of strategic and
other nuclear weapons.

1.6 The conclusion of agreements between the USA and the USSR and
all other governments involved regarding the reduction and destruction of all existing nuclear weapons in Europe and the prohibition of
the deployment of new nuclear weapons in Europe.

1.7 A declaration by all nuclear weapons powers that they will not be the
first to use nuclear weapons, nor to use them or threaten their use
against any country not having nuclear weapons on its territory.

1.8 The adoption by all states of a declaration proclaiming any use of
nuclear weapons to be a crime against humanity.

1.9 An urgent international study of the possible "nuclear winter" effect,
with steps to ensure that all governments and peoples are made fully
conversant with its findings.

For the Improvement of East-West Relations

2.1 The active pursuit of detente, particularly by strict adherence to the
provisions of the Helsinki Final Act.

2.2 The conclusion of non-aggression pacts between all NATO and WAR-
SAW TREATY member states in which they reiterate their promises not
to initiate the use of force, conventional or nuclear.

2.3 The conclusion of an agreement on the mutual reduction of all armaments (nuclear and conventional) throughout Europe, starting in
central Europe.

2.4 The acceptance by the USA and the USSR of the good offices of nonaligned states in facilitating arms reduction negotiations, such as the
approach of the "Four Continents Peace Initiative."

2.5 The extension of the mutual monitoring of military maneuvers and
military activities throughout the world, in order to create an atmosphere of confidence.

2.6 The eventual dissolution of the NATO and WTO military alliances and
their replacement by an all European security system, sponsored by
the United Nations, to which all European states—East, West, and
neutral—can belong.

2.7 Agreements to curtail total military expenditure by all governments,
on the lines about to be explored by the United Nations.

For Resolving World Problems and
Strengthening the United Nations

3.1 Reaffimation by all governments of their adherence to the obligations, taken by them under the Charter, to the United Nations, as the
highest world authority, and recognition by them of the need to

strengthen and use its peace-making machinery to the full in resolving international disputes, to develop a rule of international law and to create conditions in which states feel it is safe to disarm.

3.2 The full implementation of the Non-Proliferation Treaty and the strengthening of the international non-proliferation regime through the implementation by the nuclear powers of the clause requiring a reduction of their nuclear armaments.

3.3 The immediate conclusion of an international convention banning the production, stockpiling and use of chemical weapons.

3.4 The adoption of measures to reduce the international arms-trade.

3.5 The development of appropriate provisions for the verification of all arms control and disarmament measures.

3.6 Cooperation with and financial contribution to the United Nations World Disarmament Campaign for the distribution of information and educational material on disarmament matters, by governments and non-governmental organizations.

3.7 Recognition of the right of conscientious objection to military service.

3.8 Acceptance of the integrity, free from foreign intervention, of nation states within frontiers recognized by the United Nations.[23]

Suggestions such as these will help students understand the full ramifications of current national security policies and the difficulties in disarmament strategies. What can citizens do to make sure that suggestions such as these are included in national debates on security? If the world is to move beyond war, there must be wide-scale agreement upon a set of policies such as those listed above. Such policy statements provide positions peace educators can introduce into the public arena to provide alternatives to existing war system.

Conclusion

Peace education presents many challenges. Before teaching the topics mentioned in this chapter, peace educators will have to study in a great variety of academic disciplines in order to become well versed in these areas before attempting to teach these topics to others. This often requires research into peace efforts that are neither covered well by standard media nor written up in traditional histories. To master the broad range of subjects covered in peace studies requires a creative, truth-seeking mind.

Learning and assimilating so much material presents difficult tasks because peace studies is such a new field. Most people teaching about war and peace probably have not received in-depth training in all the areas mentioned in this chapter. Consequently, they have to seek out ways to learn this material and engage in a variety of continuing education, taking workshops and reading on their own in these different fields to become conversant with the various topics of peace education. This suggests a need for inservice training, seminars, workshops, and institutes where professional educators, church leaders, and concerned citizens can become conversant with issues as diverse as the arms race and the ecological balance necessary to preserve life on this planet. Some people form study groups to investigate the patterns of violence in their own lives, where they learn to challenge each other about their commitment to nonviolence.

Both in studying the various topics that comprise peace studies and in teaching those topics, peace educators should remember the three-part format mentioned in Chapter 2 of this book — where people learn about how certain attitudes are formed, learn information about violent and peaceful behavior, and explore ways of transforming patterns of violence into nonviolent behavior. Most specifically, for some of the topics mentioned in this chapter, this format would encourage both teachers and pupils to find out the root causes of nationalism, learn about differing political beliefs surrounding the promotion of patriotism, and explore ways by which the commitment to nation-states can be transformed into a quest for global order. Similarly, pupils and teachers can examine the causes of violence within themselves. What are their own patterns of violence? How did they learn violent behavior? They can also learn about violence in their societies and use that information to discuss ways to promote peacemaking.

In order to face these challenges educators have to learn the various topics of peace education and teach that knowledge in ways that help people consider what kind of world they want to live in. What will the future be like, and how can they contribute to it? Learning these topics, however, is not enough. Peace educators also need to know how to initiate educational programs that will promote dialogue about these issues in their classes, so that their students can conceive of peace and not become embittered and cynical citizens in a violent, nuclear world.

5. Getting Started

Education is the fundamental method of social progress and reform.

John Dewey

Initially, an individual may wake up one day feeling a concern about the threats of violence and a desire to do something. Responding to these issues requires courage, skill, and a great deal of knowledge, not only about the topics of war, peace, and conflict, but also about how to initiate new courses, workshops, programs, and research centers that can demonstrate how to eliminate violence from human existence. What a person does depends to a large extent upon where that person is located. That person may discuss his or her concerns about conflict and security with fellow workers, or initiate discussions about violence in various other settings — veterans organizations, neighborhood groups, fraternal orders, churches, or social clubs — choosing to conduct adult education programs in those settings. If that individual does not belong to such a group, or does belong and feels that those organizations are not receptive to these ideas, he or she may choose to gather together a few friends into an affinity group to learn more about how violence affects their lives and to formulate actions to express their concerns. Community educators may plan public educational events on war and peace topics. Church members may organize forums on peace and social justice issues for other members of that congregation. Teachers can incorporate peace and conflict studies concepts in classroom activities and start sharing with other professionals and students concerns about violence, while teacher trainers may introduce peace and justice concepts into teacher education classes. In discussing how people can get started with peace education activities this chapter is divided into two sections, one dealing with nonformal education settings and the other with formal school settings — elementary and secondary schools, universities and colleges. This latter section discusses the relative merits of infusing peace and justice concepts within existing courses versus starting new concepts or programs. This chapter concludes with what the author considers to be the best way to permeate schools with peace education: establishing peace education activities in all aspects of professional teacher training.

75

Peace Education in the Larger Society

People alone feel isolated and powerless in relation to their concerns about conflict in their lives. They can break out of this isolation by joining a peace group. Currently the peace movement is large enough that most areas will have a peace and justice organization.[1] Many of these organizations conduct community education activities, publish newsletters to inform the broader public about war and peace issues, and sponsor public events — such as talks, forums, and speaker series — that provide information about security issues. In one of these organizations an individual could contribute to ongoing educational activities or even suggest new ways to reach the public.

Community education about the problems of war, peace and conflict in nonformal settings involves much more than teaching. Adult educators have to be successful organizers if they are to reach wide audiences. They need to listen carefully to the people they are trying to educate and understand the cultural traditions of the community in which they are working, so the peace education programs respond to people's interests, as opposed to responding to a predetermined agenda irrelevant to that community. Getting peace education events started involves at least seven different stages — coming together, needs assessment, setting goals, planning events, developing publicity, implementing events, and evaluating peace education activities.[2]

During the initial moments of a group, the "coming together" stage, members get to know each other and develop a sense of trust that provides the basis for commitment to the group. Before dividing up tasks and planning an event, group members should identify the different abilities and interests of those in the group. They should also decide on a facilitator who will have responsibility to make sure the group meets it goals and stays on task. (This responsibility can be rotated.) Early in its history a group can develop a sense of cohesion by becoming a planning group.

The second stage involves a needs assessment to determine the educational background and needs of the people they hope to educate:

> First, determine whether the needs, assumptions, assertions, and values which you have clarified and articulated in the statement of purpose are shared by others in your community.[2]

This assessment of need for peace education can be done with a sample conducted over the telephone or through a mailed questionnaire. Because the return rate from mailed questionnaires is so low, it might be best to personally interview people at public places to gather data that can help determine the content and form of a peace education program.

In the third stage the group sets goals for itself and decides what it hopes to accomplish. These goals should reflect the findings of the needs assessment and include a goal statement about what can be learned as a result of a particular program.

During the fourth stage the group should determine how to implement its program. This stage of the planning process involves deciding how the program will be conducted. Peace education programs can vary from a single event with a speaker or a film, to a day-long conference, to a whole week of activities focused on peace and national security issues. At this stage a flow chart with a timetable should clearly delineate what has to be done, by what time it has to be accomplished, and who has responsibility for different aspects of the program. A budget should be developed with a fundraising schedule to raise money to pay for travel costs of guest speakers, honoraria, rental of films and slide shows, publicity costs, and other costs associated with educational events.

The fifth stage centers around publicity. In modern times most people receive their news through the media; therefore a successful peace education planning group should devise a strategy to gain coverage from the media. Minimally such a strategy would deliver press releases to all major media, print and electronic, that would provide a brief summary of the event — who is going to be featured, where and when it will be held, and the name of a contact. Maximally, the media coverage will extend to the event itself, with coverage on prime-time television and articles in leading newspapers. Any effective peace education group will, over time, develop a list of media contacts — people who can be relied upon to provide coverage of peace education activities — and reach out to other groups with constituencies that may be interested in peace issues. Such groups include political organizations, labor unions, professional networks, church groups, minority and ethnic organizations, and women's organizations.

The sixth stage is the implementation of the event itself. Care should be taken to make sure that people will be comfortable, that there will be time for audience participation, and that the event keeps to its stated time. Individuals should be designated as press contacts. The group should provide a sign-up sheet and announce how those in attendance can join or become more active in future events. Peace education in these kinds of settings involves organizing — trying to get people involved in an issue so they will want to pursue it further. With a successful event the group will meet its expenses, have more members, and create more public interest in peace issues.

The final stage is an evaluation of both the program and the process used to deliver the program. The various actions that members of a planning group performed constitute a significant occasion for learning. Participants can gain an understanding of their own behavior in groups by seeking answers to the following questions: How did different people carry out their assignments? What went well? What failed and why? How could this event be done more effectively? Evaluation allows participants to learn from what they have done and to understand their strengths and weaknesses. This evaluation process allows the group to set new goals for itself and to support its members for both the risks they have taken and the care they have given to peace events. As a learning group, members should examine carefully what has been done and discuss in greater depth the content of the educational activities. Was the audience interested? How could they reach more people? Was the presentation appropriate?

Community education for peace is an important part of all peace organizations. Individuals concerned about violence on this planet want to communicate their concerns to others and need to keep abreast of the latest developments in conflict areas that vary from domestic abuse to tensions in the Middle East. Using the techniques described above can provide information about crucial peace and justice topics, help generate support, and broadcast concerns to a wider audience. This type of community education is demanding and requires a lot of time to make contacts. Sometimes the best way to communicate with a broader audience is to publish a newsletter, which requires further funds for printing and mailing. An important challenge of community education for peace is reaching new people. Many peace organizations that use community education tactics make the mistake of "speaking to the converted." Peace educators, in their attempt to address the concerns of a wide variety of citizens, need to plan creatively how to reach new audiences.

• **Peace Education Within Churches or Synagogues.**Churches provide valuable forums for peace education activities.[4] Throughout the world churches have social missions that support peace and social justice concerns. Churches and synagogues have at least three levels at which educational activities can be planned. At the most superficial level they can be used to house peace education events. In order to do this a peace education group should approach the local minister or rabbi to get his or her support. If that person expresses reluctance, peace educators can identify parishioners who can approach the head of the church. The best strategy would be to get attenders of that church involved in the peace education activities, so that as concerned churchgoers they become advocates for particular programs. It is harder for a priest, rabbi, or minister to say "no" to a member of his or her own parish than to refuse someone from the outside.

In developing peace education programs through a church or synagogue, the educator should understand its structure. Many parishes have directors of religious education whose tasks include developing educational programs and in-services for people involved in church activities. Most churches or synagogues have "Sunday schools" for children which are appropriate places to introduce peace and social justice concerns. This can be done by running workshops for the Sunday school teachers, acquainting them with key topics as well as teaching methods for introducing peace and justice topics into their classes. Another approach to raising churchgoers' consciousness about war and peace and social conflict issues would be a study group for church members. An international organization called Pax Christi does exactly that within Catholic churches. Other religions have similar groups that can provide study guides, films, and speakers that will enhance parish educational programs.

Further peace education activities within the structure of organized religions can take place in church-run schools. In some countries of the world (e.g., Ireland and the Netherlands), the majority of children attend church-run schools. To initiate peace programs in parish schools, peace educators should contact principals and superintendents to see what they are already doing about peace and social concerns. In-service workshops for teachers can help them figure out how to incorporate issues of conflict and national security into their classrooms. In planning workshops peace educators should consult teachers to focus workshops in ways that will be most useful.

Adults and concerned citizens who practice this type of peace education in nonformal settings do much more than a traditional teacher. Skilled in the methods of group dynamics, peace educators in nonschool settings have to work through the conflict that invariably comes with the introduction of new activities. Establishing learning communities can provide personal support and motivation for those trying to challenge traditional notions about violence in our world. These types of educational activities are time-consuming and demand much of the peace educator, who may have been trained to believe that education only involves delivering a lecture.

Getting Started in Formal School Settings

Teachers all over the world are waking up to the threats that war and violence pose to contemporary life. Once concerned about the ominous nature of violent behavior, teachers in formal school settings grow to understand that they can use their professional skills to address the problems of security in contemporary life by creating curricula to address these threats. (Appendix B contains a list of some of these curricula produced in the United States.) Teachers at all levels—from those working with young children in day care centers to university professors graduating Ph.D. candidates in peace studies—are finding ways to incorporate peace and conflict studies concepts into their classes. Some teachers are writing their own curricula, while others are emphasizing in their ongoing courses the problems that come from a commitment to militarism. At universities and colleges professors are establishing peace studies programs and research centers.

In formal schooling institutions there will be a wide variety of responses to peace education. Some teachers will not care at all about these issues. Others will be hostile to alternative approaches to world peace. Many, critical of alternatives suggested by the peace movement, will actively attempt to block efforts to introduce peace studies in school settings. Some teachers, aware of the threats of violence, may even be concerned, but not want to revise courses or teaching styles to incorporate peace and justice concepts. Their daily routines and class lesson plans are already so full they don't see how they could possibly introduce anything new. Many teachers feel they have developed a successful routine and can't be bothered with changing their pedagogical activities. They don't want to take on something as controversial as peace studies that would "rock the boat." In spite of the routine of tradition, however, many creative teachers are introducing peace studies in their classes.

Schools have often been criticized because traditional curricula have no relevance for student's lives. John Dewey noted that one of the weightiest problems of education is the isolation of the curriculum from life experiences.[5] Alfred North Whitehead also called upon educators "to eradicate the fatal disconnection of subjects which kills the vitality of our modern curriculum," and advocated the study of "life in all its manifestations."[6] Because students face the problems of violence in their lives (i.e. they are afraid of being beaten up, they worry about being sexually harassed, they have to decide whether to join the military, or they fear for the future because of the threat of nuclear weapons), the introduction of peace materials can provide relevance to a student's learning experiences. The world is a violent place. Why should teachers turn their back on this turmoil and teach as if it didn't exist, ignoring students' real concerns over the way violence and militarism impact upon their lives?

• **Becoming Informed.** Teachers can become better informed about war, peace, and conflict by studying the vast amount of material available. The fields of history, sociology, psychology, political science, and anthropology all address the causes of violence and the tension of international relations. Literature and the arts contain references to war and the problems that violence cause on the human condition. (Appendix C contains a list of literary works on these topics arranged according to different levels of reading interest.) Teachers can form study groups to discuss some of the current literature and research on the problems of violence in social structures.

Teachers desiring to learn more about peace studies have access to excellent resources. In practically every country that has a peace movement, there exist professional teachers' organizations promoting peace education. A prototype for such an organization is England's Council for Education in World Citizenship. Formed in 1939 as an outgrowth education committee of the League of Nations Union, this organization has promoted the study of foreign languages and cultures in schools, has initiated pen-friends exchanges among pupils in different countries, has sponsored exchanges of pupils between countries, has provided information for teachers through newsletters, has held conferences, lectures, and debates on topics of world order, and has prepared a variety of audio-visual and printed materials for classroom use.[7] In Japan, teachers helped found the Hiroshima Institute for Peace Education in the 1970s; that institute sponsors national symposia on A-bomb education and has published a variety of teaching materials for classroom teachers. Internationally, UNESCO has published classroom materials that promote international understanding. More recently in the United States, Educators for Social Responsibility has been designing and delivering in-services for teachers on nuclear education and has numerous publications available for classroom teachers. (Appendix D contains a listing of peace education organizations in the United States with their addresses and purpose statements.) Many of these organizations circulate newsletters providing teachers with up-to-date material on peace studies. Others publish journals which contain in-depth analyses of the problems of war and peace. Through these organizations teachers can learn about other educational attempts to attain a less violent world.

Although the above-mentioned organizations may be most useful because they have a specific focus on peace education, traditional teachers' organizations can also play a role in promoting peace education. Two organizations, the World Council for Curriculum Instruction and the Association for Supervision and Curriculum Development, have already published peace education and global education resources for teachers. In the United States the two largest professional teacher unions, the National Educational Association (NEA) and the American Federation of Teachers (AFT), have actively promoted education for world citizenship in the interbellum period, and the NEA has most recently produced a curriculum for nuclear age education called *Choices*. Concerned teachers can promote peace education in these organizations by making sure that annual conferences sponsor workshops and forums on peace and justice topics. Members within these organizations can assert the right of teachers to teach about political and social issues and can help sensitize professional educators to the urgency of the task of educating for peace.

• **Building a Network.** The key to getting started in peace education is to develop a network of like-minded people who share concerns about the ominous threats of violence in our world. Many teachers who feel isolated with their concerns for peace welcome the opportunity to talk with others about how to incorporate peace and justice in their classrooms. A good way to start such a network is through a social activity such as a potluck or a luncheon meeting. Informal word-of-mouth can be used to identify other school personnel who may be interested in peace studies.

Start with a small group to brainstorm names of others who might be interested in focusing attention on the problems created by violence in this world. Within these networks faculty can receive support for the peace education efforts by sharing classroom activities and creating curricula.

One such network in Madison, Wisconsin, Teaching Toward Peace, consists of teachers at all levels of the public schools. This group has a mailing list of 150 teachers and administrators, 20 of whom attend monthly meetings, promotes educational activities in conjunction with television specials such as *The Day After* (a made-for-tv movie about what happened to a town in Kansas after a nuclear attack), schedules in-service workshops for teachers on peace education, sponsors a peace week every April that is coordinated in every school in the district, and has written an elementary school curriculum used throughout the district. As a support group, Teaching Toward Peace helps individual members overcome isolation and provides an effective vehicle for promoting curricular changes.

In addition to networking within individual schools and school districts, peace educators have been forming regional and even statewide networks to promote peace education. One such example is the five-college consortium in Massachusetts—Amherst, Smith, the University of Massachusetts, Mount Holyoke, and Hampshire College—which has hired an expert on global security issues to sponsor programs and activities available to faculty and students at each of the member institutions. In Chicago, over 700 faculty at 40 different institutions of higher education have come together to create Chicago Area Faculty for a Freeze, a group that provides opportunities to share ideas and present scholarly papers on war and peace themes.

Peace educators in the United States have also been forming statewide networks. The State of California through its legislature has created the Institute on Global Conflict and Cooperation (IGCC) at the University of California at San Diego, which serves all the campuses in the state system. This institute has funding from the proceeds of research at the atomic laboratories run by the state university system. It provides professors and students in the University of California system a variety of supports, including grants for graduate students, a media library, a clipping service, lectures by experts in the field, a summer teaching seminar, and an annual conference on Global Conflict and Cooperation. In Ohio, a similar network—Ohio Peace Education Network (OPEN), pulled together by Governor Celeste—promotes peace education on the various state university campuses within Ohio and within public schools. In Wisconsin, educators from both public and private colleges and universities have formed a statewide institute, the Wisconsin Institute for the Study of War, Peace and Global Cooperation, to provide support for peace education.

Infusing Peace Concepts into Existing Courses

Educators wishing to teach about the social structures and behaviors that lead human beings to violate each other have to answer the following question: Should peace education be something that permeates existing courses, or should it be introduced as a subject in its own right?

Through an infusion approach teachers introduce concepts dealing with war, peace, and violence into existing courses and school life. (The infusion method was funded in the United States by the federal government during the 1970s for the study of environmental topics. As with peace studies, environmental studies was seen as an inchoate field, not a separate discipline, and environmental topics were taught in traditional sciences, such as biology, geology, chemistry and physics.) Infusion is the preferred method for teachers to get started with peace education at the elementary and secondary level, where teachers already have prescribed curricula, and there is little or no room for extra courses. Infusion does not require teachers to develop new courses and hence may not be as time-consuming. Infusion also does not require getting permission from department heads or school administrators. Teachers have relative autonomy in their classrooms to decide what and how they want to teach. To be sure they may have to teach preset curricula, but they can often alter those curricula to introduce new topics or develop new approaches, or even to initiate new programs.

At the college and university level it may be appropriate to design special courses dealing with nuclear issues, environmental destruction, or nonviolence; however, infusion also works well in higher education. There is no one discipline that determines the academic content of peace studies. Faculty from many different fields can find ways to investigate the problems of violence in their courses.

The range of topics presented by the study of violence is so great that instructors in practically every discipline could provide examples related to peace and conflict topics. Every teacher can infuse peace and justice concepts by using his or her own imagination to tailor the content to a particular group of students. The material selected must be appropriate for the age of students. The list below presents a brief guide for teachers on different peace and justice concepts that can be infused into their classes.

Mathematics	World problems involving cost of defense budgets and local impact. How many people would be killed by a 10-megaton bomb dropped in this area? How many by a 20-kiloton bomb?
Typing Classes	Instead of typing abstract paragraphs, type articles related to peace. Send letters to

elected representatives expressing concerns
about violence in community.

Art

Create school displays on war and peace
themes — posters and murals. Do specific
projects to highlight the necessity of peace
to the human community.

Drama

Act and produce plays that have war or
peace themes. Make films about violence in
student's lives. Critique war films.

Home Economics
(Clothing and Food)

Prepare and discuss foods from different
countries. Compare clothing from various
countries. Prepare a meal that would represent unequal distribution of world's
resources.

Music

Analyze contemporary music and videos:
How do they present violence and peace?
Study the works of numerous musicians
who have written songs with peace themes.[8]

Biology

Study the earth as a spaceship, the effects of
radiation upon ecosystems, the interrelatedness of living things, and ecology.

Chemistry

Study atomic particles, fission and fusion.
How is the biochemistry of organisms
affected by radiation?

Physics

Emphasize relativity and the physics of
nuclear weapons, the generation of power
and electricity, alternative energy sources,
and pollution.

English

Study violence on television and in commer-
cials. Read essays and novels on war and
peace. Write on topics centered around the
role of violence in daily life.

History

Study the role of peacemakers and peace
movements, places in the past and present
where nonviolence has occurred. What
have ordinary people done to bring about
social change?

Politics and Economics

Analyze the impact of the defense budget
on different communities, resource
distribution throughout the world, international organizations, and the activities of
peace groups on politics.

Athletics

Practice new games and cooperative exercises that deemphasize competition.

The above list is not meant to be exhaustive, but rather to convey how
broad the concepts of peace and justice are and to illustrate how teachers

from all curricular areas can use their creative powers to infuse these topics into existing courses.

On the college and university level, peace and justice concepts can become components of courses taught in fields as diverse as atmospheric science (the effects of radiation upon the stratosphere) and law (the study of international law and its ability to ease world tensions).[9] The concepts associated with peace and justice practically define the core of a liberal arts curricula, used to develop an appreciation of liberty, justice, and the pursuit of peace:

> Perhaps more than any other single subject, the study of war and peace in the nuclear age provides a vehicle through which we can accomplish virtually all the espoused purposes of liberal education.[10]

Liberal education hopes to give students an understanding of their traditions and teach them how to exercise their responsibilities as citizens. The study of war and peace allows students to examine basic assumptions of political policy and to develop their own conclusions about contemporary issues. Student concern about the threat of nuclear war was deemed so crucial by one educator, the president of Ohio Wesleyan College, that nuclear war became the focus of the entire interdisciplinary program required of all freshmen.

Once an educator has examined his or her existing courses to see where peace and justice topics can be infused and has determined exactly what to introduce, he or she needs to develop an instructional strategy to organize that content into specific lessons. Such a strategy will attempt to adjust the content to the abilities, needs and interests of students. Many peace educators have asked students to help plan peace events for the classroom. Working with the teacher to plan curricula gives students a sense of ownership and enables them to take steps to create a more peaceful world. Peace educators have many resources to draw from in organizing learning experiences — small group exercises, readings, essay topics, student projects, films, guest lectures, etc. People from the community can provide important resources for teachers who may feel inadequate to addressing the complexity of some of these issues.

The final stage in infusing peace and justice concepts into the classroom involves figuring out how to evaluate student learning. Evaluation helps the teacher figure out what students have learned and whether the curriculum design was effective. With data from these assessments peace educators can work to further redesign their curricula. As an expert in the field of curriculum development has put it:

> What is implied in all of this is that curriculum planning is a continuous process and that as materials and procedures are developed, they

are tried out, their results are appraised, their inadequacies identified, suggested improvements indicated; there is replanning, redevelopment and then reappraisal and in this kind of continuing cycle, it is possible for the curriculum and instructional program to be continually improved over the years. In this way we may hope to have an increasingly more effective educational program rather than depending so much upon hit and miss judgement as a basis for curriculum development.[11]

Teaching about war and peace requires a constant examination of thought patterns and behaviors, as well as an analysis of current events and reexamination of curriculum. Conflict and peace issues impact people in many complex and subtle ways. Teachers should always be examining their classroom activities to help students understand the effects of these issues upon their lives.

In addition to specific classroom activities, peace and justice issues can be infused into school and church life in a variety of creative ways. Libraries can feature these topics in special displays. Bulletin boards in individual classrooms and corridors can highlight war and peace themes. Assembly programs can present information about war and foreign policy. Special holidays such as United Nations Day or Martin Luther King's birthday can be celebrated with guest speakers. Certain schools and churches have declared peace weeks to focus attention on peace issues.

Infusing peace and justice concepts into traditional school activities allows students to think about the important war and peace dilemmas that face our civilization. As many faculty as possible should be involved in the effort to infuse peace topics into school activities. Such involvement underscores the importance of the topic and allows students to receive a comprehensive approach with many different points of view and challenges them to reflect more deeply upon these topics than if a single teacher or classroom pursues these issues. Students won't be able to solve these complex problems just because they have been introduced to them, but they can in school acquire skills and understandings that can become the basis for responding to these issues as informed adults. Essentially, infusion helps sensitize students to the different issues included under the heading "peace and conflict studies." The more frequently they have these topics brought to their attention, the greater their understanding.

Developing Separate Courses and Programs

As convenient as an infusion technique may be for teaching about war and peace, it has one main disadvantage. Infusion of peace and justice topics may present an overly simplistic view of extremely complex topics. Unless an instructor is willing to explain in great detail the complex aspects of international relations and human behavior that lead to violence, students may come away from classes where these topics have been introduced with shallow notions of how they can be solved. A more thorough approach to these topics would be to introduce whole courses and programs dealing with the topics of war and peace, where students and instructors can examine in depth the nature of the violent behavior. This approach is most applicable in formal school settings at the university and college level, although some high schools might choose to offer courses on international relations that would highlight how the behavior of nations contributes to the threat of war.

In proposing new courses, programs, or even departments, peace educators find themselves involved in educational change.

> The central point for those who want to initiate curriculum improvement is that changing attitudes towards acceptance of proposals is not merely a rational process. To be sure, sound rational argument can help a great deal, but it is a political process, too.[12]

The introduction of new courses shifts teachers away from classroom considerations into a political realm where they have to be prepared to present material, argue for its acceptance, and lobby for its approval. Implementation of new changes requires a process of learning and resocialization over a period of time. A well-developed curriculum, if not supported by powerful political actors, will not reach many learners. Literature on bringing about change in social organizations involves *action planning,*[13] a process whereby a change agent identifies changes he or she would like to see and then describes both the forces in that institution that will bring about these changes and those forces that will be barriers to the changes. Successful change strategies require negating the barriers and increasing the supportive forces so that change proposals win acceptance within social organizations.

Peace educators, if they attempt to bring about new programs, courses or curricula within existing school settings, will have to become acquainted with "the lay of the land." Who are the important people that have final say over curriculum revision, and how can those people be influenced? In order to work through the complex labyrinths of educational institutions, peace educators need to form a leadership group to identify what barriers exist in a given organization, to help with the difficult tasks of preparing proposals, and to get approval for those proposals.

A comparison of two case studies will help illustrate how teachers can go about introducing peace studies in a school system. One comes from Milwaukee, Wisconsin, the sixteenth largest city in the United States (population 600,000), the other from Madison, Wisconsin, a city of about 300,000 people.

In 1982 a group of citizens put pressure on the Milwaukee school board to start addressing issues of war and peace in the Milwaukee schools. As a result of this pressure the school board passed a resolution endorsing peace studies at the elementary school level, at the middle school level, and at the high school level. This task force met for a year and developed a set of guidelines which were approved by the school board early in 1984. The school board then passed these recommendations on to administrative personnel and had curriculum development specialists write peace curricula for the schools. The curricula were finished within a year, and were distributed to teachers in the system in the fall of 1985. By 1987 few teachers in the Milwaukee system were teaching peace studies. Each teacher had been given the curricula developed by the school administration, but most felt they already had too many things to teach, so they did not make a place in their classes for peace topics; nor did the school administration make any special efforts to prepare teachers for this activity by providing in-services on peace education. The curriculum itself is impressive, but has had little or no effect because the teachers don't feel they own it. They had no say in preparing it. The curriculum was handed to them by administrators. This "top-down" process of curriculum change resembles a similar process used in Berkeley, California, and Cambridge, Massachusetts. These attempts, although well meant, have not had a lasting effect in changing the daily activities of teachers or in introducing peace studies in schools.

The story of peace education in Madison, Wisconsin, represents a grass-roots, "from-the-bottom" model of educational change. There a group of twenty teachers got together at approximately the same time (1983) to discuss how they could focus attention on the problems of war and peace in the Madison school district. They recruited teachers from every building in the Madison system and broke up into action grups. One group produced a curriculum for elementary students, *Becoming Peacemakers,* and the other group worked on outreach. This latter committee contacted people throughout the district, trying to get them involved in their efforts. They planned workshops and produced a newsletter that was distributed to every teacher in the district. One member of this group worked in the department of staff development, another in the area of human relations. These two were able to order, duplicate and distribute materials through their respective departments. The outreach committee was able to create in Madison a climate supportive of peace studies. As a result of the dedicated efforts of a core group of about twenty educators, the curriculum developed by this group has received broad support within the Madison schools and is being widely used.

The lesson to be learned from these two histories is that there is no substitute for the intelligent participation of teachers in curriculum improvement. Teachers need to feel a sense of ownership of new curricula, and they are, in fact, the best people to develop new materials in their classrooms, because they can answer whether or not a particular implementation will benefit students and figure out what are costs in terms of time, energy, and anxiety in changing their routines to adopt peace and justice concepts. Curriculum improvement is most successful through a cooperative approach. Those who wish to change existing school practices to incorporate peace studies need to involve as many teachers as possible in the process of change. Involving teachers assumes they are intelligent professionals who can revamp their classes to reflect the dilemmas of war and peace.

> If decisions are to have meaning for the individual teacher and to provide direction for his work, he must be personally involved in making them.[14]

Teachers working together in a cooperative effort to revise school curricula will have important experiences in the process of peacemaking, which requires people to work together to achieve mutually agreed-upon ends.

Research from the field of curriculum development shows other factors that facilitate teacher innovation.[15] Foremost among these is the use of an outside consultant to provide new ideas and help teachers develop new skills. Because the field of peace education is so new that not many consultants are available for working with teachers at the elementary and secondary school level, teachers often have to become consultants themselves by reading and experimenting with different approaches to peace education. "Learning the new educational practice, therefore, is not a simple matter of absorbing the written transmission of information."[16] Teachers who experiment with peaceful approaches to their lessons need support to encourage them and give them helpful feedback about new suggestions for peace lessons. Supervisors wishing to encourage this type of change can provide substitutes so teachers can visit each other's classes and attend workshops and seminars where peace education strategies are presented.

- **Curriculum Implementation in Higher Education.** At the college and university level, professors have already begun to initiate courses dealing with war, peace, and global conflict. A sample of such courses with their syllabi can be obtained from the World Policy Institute in New York.[17] Some colleges, such as Gustavus Adolphus in St. Peter, Minnesota, and Alverno College in Milwaukee, Wisconsin, have attempted to infuse peace and justice throughout the entire campus life, including a strong focus on violence and peace in required introductory courses. Other campuses have created separate peace studies programs, while still others have even established research centers.

The first step in establishing peace studies on college campuses is the formation of a support group or task force of faculty willing to work to make sure peace studies becomes a permanent part of campus offerings.

Every campus will contain students and faculty interested in these issues. The question is, how to identify those people and get them working together to create a peace studies program? Once identified, they should establish a communications network throughout the campus to inform other faculty of their efforts and to provide a presence for peace studies on campus. Numbers are not as important as an active group of dedicated faculty who come from a wide diversity of disciplines, so that peace studies will have broad support across campus.

A planning group has to decide where a peace and conflict studies program would fit within the administrative structure of the college or university. Most peace studies programs are currently interdisciplinary and offer either a major, minor, or a certificate. An academic program has the advantage of being more flexible and cheaper to operate. A program might have a half-time faculty administrator and an administrative assistant to handle paperwork and answer phones. The program approach, because it relies on faculty from a wide variety of academic departments, has the further advantage of providing peace studies a wider base of ownership on campus.

A peace studies department requires full-time salary for faculty and secretarial help. It has the advantage of providing peace studies with academic respectability (because it is on the same institutional footing as other departments within a college) and stability. An academic department of peace studies allows professors within that department to focus all their energies on peace studies. This means that they can devote their advising time to peace studies majors and research activities towards developing peace paradigms. Faculty in interdisciplinary programs have to divide their attention between their home departments and peace education.

An important stage in the development of a peace studies program is the provision of funds to provide for a full-time director. These programs have been created by dedicated faculty who volunteer their time above and beyond their normal duties to create a climate where questions of war and peace can be seriously investigated on their campuses. Some foundations may support these activities, but the host institutions themselves should provide space, release time and support so that faculty can concentrate on advising students and addressing serious academic issues raised under the heading of peace studies. Institutional support should cover the day-to-day maintenance tasks — publishing flyers, bringing in speakers, promoting the program, raising funds, circulating newsletters, etc. — that give a peace studies program both an identity and a vitality on campus. Without institutional support these programs rely too much on the goodwill and dedication of a few select faculty members who can easily become "burned out" as they try to juggle peace studies with their existing commitments.

Other decisions have to be made about what courses to offer. United Ministries in Education provides a guide for self-assessment and planning that discusses how a peace studies leadership team could assess other faculty members to see what their interests are in peace studies and what courses they currently teach that have a peace studies emphasis.[18] Key components in a peace studies curriculum are political science, international relations, psychology, communications, education, literature, and sociology. Faculty should be recruited from these areas to offer courses that will provide depth to the academic program. An important step in developing an academic program will be to establish an introductory course that provides students with an overview of the problems of war and peace.[19] Most peace studies programs offer an internship, where students can acquire a sense of what a career in peacemaking might look like. Joseph Fahey, the director of one of the oldest peace studies programs in the United States at Manhattan College in New York City, has said the following concerning the role of internships in peace studies programs:

> The importance of the internship cannot be stressed too much. In almost every case it has helped students understand the relevance of their academic preparation to "real life" issues, and has inspired them to take their courses very seriously upon their return to the college. In addition, many have actually pursued careers in the area of their chosen internship.[20]

Internships developed through peace organizations and international relations institutes will provide practical experiences that will enable students to apply what they are learning in the classroom and will give them an understanding of what it means to work for peace.

After a planning group has set goals for itself and decided what it wants to implement, it needs to develop strategies about how to build a program. In many cases it is best to start with courses in established departments rather than to begin with a full-fledged program. Starting with existing courses helps identify students and faculty supportive of peace studies, and it slowly generates support for peace studies. An effective peace studies program will need a promotional strategy. Literature describing courses must be prepared for students, and a newsletter can keep supporters updated with how the program is progressing. Many peace studies programs also have an outreach committee that provides public events which include bringing in well-known speakers, holding forums, showing films, and providing information on controversial issues such as the Strategic Defense Initiative (SDI or "Star Wars"). These events promote a greater awareness of the threats of war and peace while providing a public presence for peace studies both on the campus and in the surrounding community.

Once an academic program has been established, a group of faculty may consider a research center, such as the Center for Peace and Conflict Studies at Wayne State University. Founded in 1965, this center houses a specialized library containing over 2300 books, over 200 periodicals, and filed materials on topics devoted to domestic and international conflict. This center provides a link between the university and the Detroit metropolitan area through the public schools and the Detroit Council for World Affairs, and publishes an annual *Peace Almanac* distributed throughout the world. Other centers publish newsletters and provide research moneys for faculty and students. These centers help legitimize peace research and peace education within academic institutions.

Teacher Training

In a world truly concerned about the well-being of its citizens, all teachers would be trained peacemakers. Their teacher preparation courses would provide them with knowledge of the war and peace dilemmas that face humanity, skills to deal with violence and violent issues in the classroom, and an awareness of how to structure classes in ways that would prepare young people to become peacemakers. In the current world, however, very few teacher education programs are preparing teachers with the requisite skills and knowledge to teach peace education.[21] Because peace education is such a new field of scholarly endeavor, few teachers currently see themselves as experts in the complex domain of peace education. Most approach this topic as students. Although investigating peace and war topics in an open classroom environment where students and teachers are learning together presents an important cooperative model, there exists a risk that many teachers are poorly prepared to discuss the complex nature of these problems and may be treating these topics in a glib or superficial manner.

Educators receive professional preparation in three different ways. Their preservice education, normally called undergraduate teacher education, consists of three areas: general education, professional courses, and student teaching. Once they have become teachers, school districts provide in-service education, which attempts to keep professional staff abreast of current developments. In addition, most teachers earn graduate credits and advanced degrees. A successful strategy to prepare peace educators would address all three of these areas of teacher training.

In a teacher training program that had the goal of preparing peace educators, prospective teachers would be introduced to peace education in all aspects of their undergraduate education. In the general education component, where teachers acquire knowledge of subject matter, they would study the history of war and peace; learn about the psychology and sociology of violence; takes courses in conflict resolution and human communications; and be introduced to the study of international relations. Such a comprehensive approach in the general education part of their training would provide them the knowledge they need to discuss in depth the complex topics of peace education in their classes. In the professional education component of their teacher training program prospective teachers should learn how to set up peaceful classes that promote problem solving and critical thinking skills. In their student teaching experiences supervisors and cooperating teachers can instruct apprentices on how to establish a peaceful classroom based on nonviolent principles. Teachers themselves, as part of their preservice training, need to learn how to resolve conflicts so that they can model peaceful behavior in their classrooms. Such a comprehensive approach would prepare teachers to teach about the role of violence in the social order and provide them with nonviolent techniques to establish peaceful classrooms.

In-service education consists of workshops and expert consultation. Most school districts require their personnel to attend in-services designed to make them aware of key current topics. Groups like Educators for Social Responsibility have been conducting workshops in the United States for teachers on nuclear education. In some states they are working through the state departments of education to inform different school districts about the availability of experts to run workshops on nuclear age education, while in other states teachers are organizing workshops within their school districts to have in-services that will provide awareness about peace education topics.

Robin Richardson from the World Studies Project in London has sugested a model for workshops and seminars in peace education which involves a cooperative process among workshop attenders and the leader.[22] The first stage builds a trusting climate by establishing the knowledge and opinions of the participants, by getting to know others in the group, and by being challenged and stimulated by "one's own ignorance." The second stage involves inquiry into the subject matter. The final stage is a synthesis stage, where participants embark on collaborative planning, generalize from their own experiences, and develop action proposals to implement in classes. Such a workshop allows participants to reflect upon their concerns and to build plans they can use in their teaching endeavors.

A different model of in-service education for teachers is a summer workshop. Harvard and MIT have been running workshops in the dynamics of the arms race that bring in faculty from throughout the world to focus on the dynamics of superpower tensions. The University of California at Berkeley offers a similar workshop for university professors who want to gain a greater understanding of the causes of international tensions and the arms race. These workshops usually last for one week and expose participants to a wide variety of expert opinions. The United Ministries in Higher Education Program and the Teachers College Peace Education Program at Columbia University regularly offer summer institutes for teachers that take place in different parts of the United States and Canada.

These workshops allow participants to examine practical ways to approach peace-related topics in classroom settings.

Another model for in-service teacher education comes from Sheffield, England, where the local authorities have appointed an advisory teacher for peace education who has the responsibility of stimulating and encouraging peace education activities in that school district. Her task will be to survey schools to see what they are doing, to create a forum for interested teachers to share classroom activities, and to develop peace education teaching materials appropriate for specific classrooms. She also has established a peace education center in the Sheffield school district that provides peace education resources.

At the graduate school level, schools of education can allow teachers to refine their awareness of peace education skills and knowledge. Currently some graduate schools of education offer courses in global perspectives which provide the following goals:

> (1) valuing diversity while acknowledging commonalities in all human beings, (2) making decisions and understanding the consequences of individual and collective behavior, (3) effecting value judgements among alternative solutions to world problems and (4) exercising influence competently through participation.[23]

Such courses help students develop an awareness of different cultures and an understanding of the interrelatedness of all people.

Graduate courses in nuclear education provide a forum for teachers to discuss the effects of living in a nuclear age and how fear of nuclear annihilation influences their students. In addition to providing information about the arms race, these courses prepare teachers for dealing with controversial material. They also promote teaching skills such as critical thinking and communication skills required for negotiation and mediation. Basic to these courses is the skill of questioning assumptions underlying foreign policy decisions. Teachers who take these classes learn how to help students understand their own assumptions about the threat of war.

Graduate courses in peace education should allow teachers to discuss their experiences of individual, social, and international peace, and the way to maintain and preserve peace in their classes. These courses help teachers identify the key topics of peace education, understand the key issues involved in educating for peace, and confront the various obstacles to peace that make their work so difficult. Teachers can acquire in graduate classes important skills by asking the questions, "What do we know about peace?" and "How do our teaching activities convey a method of nonviolent resolution of conflict?" To answer these questions teachers should share with each other ideas that work and problems they have introducing peace topics. Teachers answering questions such as these will generate practical suggestions to make their classrooms more peaceful.

Working Outside or Inside "The System"

Many teachers find themselves paralyzed by the institutions for which they work. They feel that their particular schools have no interest in peace topics, that they are overworked, or that hostility to alternative approaches is so great that they might as well give up attempts to promote peaceful change within that institution. Such individuals often teach their own classes in peaceful ways, infusing peace and justice concepts, but can be thwarted by hostile administrators. Those educators frustrated by working within large social institutions have a variety of different avenues to follow.

Many teachers join traditional peace organizations, where they enjoy the company of others who share their beliefs and work to promote the goals of those organizations. They can help produce community education activities which provide the general public with information about current topics related to peace. They can write for newsletters, or even become so knowledgeable about certain issues that they themselves are sought out as experts.

Teachers who are frustrated by a lack of support within a given institution can seek out support from parents who are concerned about violence and from active members of the peace community. Throughout the world, such teachers have taken upon themselves the task of writing peace curricula. A fine example of such curriculum is "The Friendly Classroom for a Small Planet," produced by members of the Fellowship of Reconciliation in Nyack, New York. This curriculum has been produced by an alternative press and widely distributed throughout the United States. One of its developers, Priscilla Prutzman, has become a full-time peace educator, working outside formal school systems to promote peace education. She runs workshops for teachers within New York City, and conducts in-services for school systems throughout the country.

In the Netherlands a group of educators sponsored by the church have developed a variety of special workbooks on peace topics that they are trying to promote within the schools. Educators for Social Responsibility in the United States also represents an organization of teachers promoting peace education. Members of this organization have developed many different peace curricula, speak at a wide variety of conferences, run in-services for school districts, hold institutes for teachers, and promote national speaking tours for experts who travel to different parts of the country. In Wisconsin the local chapter of Educators for Social Responsibility holds a summer institute at which it trains teachers to conduct in-services and work with their colleagues within school systems to promote peace education.

These types of activities greatly expand traditional notions of what teachers do. Most people think of an academic career as a fairly humdrum existence, where an individual spends his or her professional life teaching one particular subject. Peace education challenges traditional teachers in many ways. First of all, peace educators have to keep abreast of all the complex dynamics of war, peace, and conflict. That alone requires study and interaction with other human beings. Secondly, most peace educators also become change agents, where they have to figure out how to introduce peace education concepts within the schools. This demands new behaviors and challenges teachers to develop whole new areas of competence. Thirdly, peace education allows teachers to work for the betterment of the human condition and hence adds a degree of nobility to their calling. These challenges enable peace educators to make new friends, to derive satisfaction from working for social justice, and to receive praise from people appreciative of their courage to embark upon educational reform. All these activities involve teachers in groups and provide a purpose for their lives. Rather than being isolated teaching the same material year in and year out, they are expanding their horizons and drawing upon inner resources they may not have known they had. Similarly, peace education can provide rewards for individuals within church settings. Within major denominations that have produced letters and statements supporting peace, peace education allows church leaders to address concerns that are deeply felt within the church community. Since all religions express a desire for peace, getting started with peace education activities allows ministers, priests, and rabbis to become active and take leadership in promoting social justice concerns. Peace education also provides parishioners with opportunities to put their faith into practice.

Peace education efforts offer similar challenges to movement activists, allowing them to use community education techniques to promote their causes. Working outside the system, these activists are challenged to produce educational events and forums that will educate broad sections of the public. Such educational techniques include sophisticated public relations campaigns and effective use of the media to provide public exposure for individuals who care deeply about the fate of the planet.

As exciting as peace education can be, it must also be remembered that it can be painful. Most citizens prefer to stay home and watch violent shows on television, rather than leave the safety of their homes to attend peace education events. Peace educators often feel overwhelmed in the face of what seems to be tremendous apathy about problems of social justice. Getting started while facing such indifference takes courage and persistence because there are so many obstacles to overcome. Many people oppressed by violence in this world do not have the professional skills or resources that are available to teachers. Lacking support and financial resources, they can feel that their endeavors are useless. Cultural barriers and norms will challenge their endeavors. Colleagues will scorn their idealism. Students raised within militaristic traditions will resist learning peace. Public figures will attack their efforts, and, in many countries, government agencies will oppose their activities. While many desire peace, the peace educator has to tiptoe through hostile reactions, trying to explain the ways of love and caring to individuals raised in violent traditions who feel threatened by alternative approaches to peace. In the next chapter, we will look at ways to overcome some of these obstacles.

6. Overcoming Obstacles

School is both a child and mother of warfare ideology.

Jaime Diaz

Many peace educators feel a sense of urgency. They fear that nuclear war threatens the existence of life on this planet, or that levels of crime are destroying their communities, or that regional strife has to be curtailed. As important as it may seem to rush into educational programs that inform people about these threats, peace educators need to pause to consider what obstacles they face in challenging the ways of violence.

Violence has always been a part of the human condition and will not disappear. To be sure, human beings desire peace, but there exists considerable controversy about how to achieve it. Some who believe in peace-through-strength strategies promoted by governments have opposed peace education, which, by offering alternatives, threatens the hegemony of national leaders to continue military policies. Peace educators need to stand firm in their conviction that the public in a democratic society has a right to hear all different sides of controversial issues. They must be prepared to meet attacks head on with arguments that spell out the advantages to be gained by studying alternatives to violence. Some do this by soft-pedaling the topics taught in peace education classes, focusing on the role of violence in personal life and avoiding political policies, hoping that their approach to peace edcuation is noncontroversial. Others research the effects of violence and draw compelling arguments about why educators have a moral obligation to challenge conventional wisdom by teaching the topics of peace education.

Preparing a defense against opposition is an important part of getting started in peace education. Peace educators are fighting for the souls of their students. Are citizens only to be exposed to the violent images they see on television and the armed policies of their countries, or are they also to be exposed to nonviolent ways of conducting human affairs? This Faustian struggle concerns the dialogue that takes place within each individual between destructive and compassionate forces. Are the destructive human urges to overwhelm the capacity of human beings to love? Peace educators who take a stand for life against the destructive behaviors that dominate human existence need to be aware that their efforts will be threatening to many.

This chapter will discuss cultural obstacles to peace education and provide suggestions for how to overcome some of those obstacles. Because of wide-scale support for the use of force in human affairs, these barriers to peace education permeate all levels of society. Any threat to peace can become a threat to peace educators who need to identify the obstacles to the development of peace, devise ways to remove those barriers, and share with others attempts to overcome them. The obstacles include "macho" norms for behavior, reliance on technology, exaggerated enemy images, military traditions, economic policies, and the use of language. Because these cultural norms permeate educational institutions, peace educators need to be prepared to face resistance wherever they attempt to educate about peace.

Cultural Barriers

Individuals are influenced by cultures that impose values, attitudes and behaviors which, because they implicitly and explicitly support the use of force in human affairs, create many barriers for peace educators. Foremost of these cultural norms is violence. Teachers and students live in societies where they are constantly barraged by violent images. Armed force is promoted to solve social and political problems. People fear neighbors or strangers they meet during their daily routines. Young people are taught never to speak to strangers. Women distrust men because they fear physical assault. Patterns of domestic violence are carried out through generations. Children learn violent ways of dealing with others to control their behavior. Many homes contain guns. Television shields viewers from the painful effects of violent behavior. Political violence carried out by modern states promotes the notion that brute force and strength settle disputes. Movies glorify war, and military values influence many social institutions, including the schools.

The constant presence of violence supports a "macho" culture that promotes a strong country with an aggressive posture. Respect is thought to be gained by superiority and control. In a hierarchical world divided into winners and losers, "being number one" becomes an important cultural consideration. In a world dependent on military systems, being number one is not defined in terms of social justice or equity, but rather in terms of military might, so that powerful nations with vast armaments terrorize the weaker, less developed countries. This attitude, condoning willful exploitation of weaker countries, permeates the social fabric:

> Although personal advancement and the enjoyment of the fruit of one's labor is a great and humanizing virtue, advancement at the cost of others and the enjoyment of the fruits of the labor of the exploited other is a dehumanizing and destructive vice. To the degree that this attitude of egocentric individualism becomes ingrained in the culture of a people, authentic personal relationships and cooperation between people becomes impossible. Each one is out for his or her own self! May the best one win![1]

Might makes right. Compromise and negotiation are seen as signs of weakness. Competition permeates the natural order of things. Winning is everything, and it is difficult to come up with new ways of thinking to challenge this win-lose mentality. Who wants to be weak? A reduction in arms is seen as a sign of capitulation whereas flexing muscles, threatening, and pushing others around are applauded as signs of strength.

Social systems based on competition emphasize winning at any cost, so that foreign policy becomes a team sport or gambling game, where the tough get going and the quitters don't win. These cultural values promote a masculine dominance that makes alternative approaches unacceptable in the popular imagination. Doesn't everybody want to play on the winning team? Well, if you do, you'd better love a strong defense and be prepared to annihilate those people described as the enemy. "The idea of masculine superiority is perennial, institutional and rooted at the deepest level of our historical experience."[2] Men make wars, play popular professional sports, and establish the parameters for foreign relations and defense policy. Under the masculine paradigm, being gentle and promoting alternatives for conducting affairs of state seem unrealistic:

> Realism is a big word, particularly when it makes claims to "scientific" evidence. It is used widely to discredit those who find something wrong with the present international system. The kind of realism we are propagating today may result in widespread famine, growing inequalities, and World War III. If we accept the arms race, poverty, racism, and other charming attributes of the present system, we are being "realistic." There is something weird about a human mind capable of producing the contemptuous assertion that those who denounce these phenomena are idealists, idealogues, or dreamers.[3]

In the world of realpolitik, men in charge discredit alternative proposals as being utopian. However, these men with their armies and their technological weapons are contemplating the destruction of life on this planet. What is more realistic: to play ball for the armed forces or to argue for alternatives that guarantee a healthy planet for future generations?

In macho cultures, young boys are expected to be tough. Modern societies express sex role expectations that train men to kill, or at least be prepared to kill. Many men at age eighteen actually join the armed forces, while others are prepared for that by living in a culture that praises military behavior and values. The importance of a "macho" perspective on foreign policy has been well documented.[4] In policy debates about national security, values such as caring, nurturing, understanding, flexibility, and compassion are not seen as relevant. On the basis of these kinds of labels entire cultures endorse policies that rely on military might to promote national self-interest.

Fear of being an underdog keeps people from criticizing militaristic policies. At the end of the Second World War the United States stood in a position of military superiority in the world. Victorious against the Fascist powers and possessing the awesome power of nuclear weapons, it was seen as the leading and most powerful country in the world. Because United States citizens enjoy many economic benefits from their country's ability to dominate world affairs, those in power argue for huge military budgets to protect their privileged status, even though those budgets impoverish large numbers of United States citizens who are either unemployed or underemployed in nonmilitary sectors of the economy. Citizens in countries throughout the world are convinced that a strong military will increase the stature of their country. After the Cuban Missile Crisis, the Soviet Union pulled out all the stops to build a defense capability comparable to the United States. Soviet people made tremendous sacrifices in order to reach parity with the United States armament industry. Such military buildups divert badly needed funds from the domestic sphere but are tolerated because of the status they give a country. Within these violent cultures peacekeeping strategies that don't rely on military might, such as diplomatic negotiation, are seen as signs of weakness. Armaments become a symbol of national strength in a world where states are graded according to their military capacity in international relations. In a macho world, peace has a bad image.

The modern arms race is basically a technological race. Rather than building peace through compromise and treaties, countries are committed to "winning" the arms race through technological advances. The great nations of the world compete in research and development, where one new weapon system spawns another. People are reluctant to challenge such technologies because they are closely bound up in cultural notions of progress. Modern weapons built on the most sophisticated scientific principles and discoveries belong to the long list of technological accomplishments that characterize the advanced nature of modern societies. This way of thinking began with Descartes and Newton, who used the rational science of mathematics to describe the universe in ways that could be manipulated and controlled. Over half the scientists in the world currently work on defense-related research, and many leaders in the scientific and intellectual community lobby for defense contracts. The general public accepts modern weapons systems because they represent the latest stage in this transformation of nature into a domain dominated by human endeavor. An irony of the development of these new weapons is that they threaten such terrible destruction that many people in advanced countries are starting to question the wisdom of relying upon technological advances to achieve national security:

> Each of the Western nations is unique, yet all are easily moved by images of war, and all are united in worshipping technology as the solution to human problems. Undoubtedly, the U.S., the leader in the arms race, leads in this respect, too, just as it leads in the democratic culture of violence, and, by a huge margin, in the homicide rate, a fact that can be ascribed in equal measure to the mythology of the lawless frontier and to the promiscuous prevalence of handguns among the population. It is not reassuring to have a culture of this kind fermenting beneath 30,000 nuclear warheads and presided over by a President who is the creature of corporate capital and loves the good old Wild West. Nor is it any comfort to behold the grip that technology has over the average mind, despite all the evidence of the menace it presents.[5]

Many who feel inadequate to question such strong cultural norms as the positive value of technology balk at suggestions that sophisticated defense programs such as the Strategic Defense Initiative ("Star Wars") are the wrong road to peace. They accept the authority of government leaders proposing military projects backed by the latest scientific research to create a safe world and are reluctant to challenge the destructivenes of these technologies.

Perhaps the dominant cultural value that makes the work of peace educators so difficult is the fear of the enemy. The cold war between the superpowers plays an important part in the minds of people throughout the world. Depending upon the ideological commitments of the countries practicing peace education, discussions of the Russians or Americans will be fraught with highly charged emotions because of the emphasis given to creating an enemy image which justifies huge arms expenditures. These enemy images scare citizens into thinking that they are threatened by a treacherous, evil, and warlike people. Media coverage constantly highlights the negative aspects of life in countries that are perceived as being part of the enemy camp. In the United States fear of a Communist takeover even leads some to say that they would be "better dead than red."[6] Likewise, in Communist countries the Western nations are seen as imperialist agents bent on world domination.

This mass hysteria about perceived enemies has a profound effect upon educators who are often attacked because, by challenging dominant notions of peace through strength, they are accused of supporting a takeover by the enemy. Trying to get students in Western countries to see the Soviet people as human beings flies directly in the face of a long tradition of seeing them as enemies who can't be trusted. Such dehumanization of people into "enemy" forces creates an adversarial world divided into simplistic notions of good and evil:

> Once we have reduced our adversaries to subhumans and projected many of our evils onto them, it is easy to see ourselves as good, peace-loving and self-defense-oriented, and portray our enemies as evil, aggressive and warlike.[7]

Dividing the world up into "good guys" and "bad guys" allows one country to promote its culture, e.g., one that is fighting for Democracy, while at the same time, provides a justification for increased military might to protect those good qualities. Fear of Communism (or of imperialism) promotes an ethnocentrism that makes it hard for peace educators to create a climate conducive to understanding the complexity of international relations. If one country and its allies are always painted as "good," while other countries are "evil," students are reluctant to accept suggestions that there may be some value in reducing cold war hostilities and limiting arms buildups. Even worse, teachers who suggest in their classes ways to move beyond the cold war are seen by some as being traitors. The promotion of peace in such a hostile world does not become the creation of a better world order, but rather can be mocked as an attempt to undermine the dominant strength of a militaristic society.

Demonizing another country keeps people from addressing their own problems. In Western societies the Soviet Union becomes a scapegoat upon which the cost for expensive weapons systems can be justified. Public opinion becomes influenced by fear of other countries, rather than being formed by an analysis of what may be best for all. Enemy images keep people from examining their own national defense goals and using common sense to set national priorities. Such hysteria has the effect of making any presentation on peace issues suspect in the minds of people saturated with fears of being dominated by evil political systems.

Political Barriers

Governments and political parties perpetuate many of the cultural myths mentioned in the previous section. Because military men and military values dominate the councils of state, citizens are constantly being told that the world will be safer with more arms. As John Mack has pointed out, the United States government has been guilty of promoting a variety of types of thinking about nuclear threat which he calls make-believe.[8] These include optimistic projections in the 1950s about how the citizens of the United States would benefit from atomic power without highlighting the corresponding bad effects of the whole nuclear cycle, from the mining of uranium, to the production and potential use of weapons, to the disposal of nuclear wastes. The United States government has also issued decrees describing various scenarios of "limited" nuclear war, or even winning a nuclear war, that do not conform to existing knowledge about the tremendous destructive capacity of nuclear weapons. Using their ability to generate news, governments limit discourse about armaments or present such items in glowing ways that understate their true effect upon a populace both in terms of their use and their cost. Governments also keep information secret from their citizens, such as the United States government having suppressed information about the effects of the atomic bomb upon the civilian populations in Hiroshima and Nagasaki. Withholding such information makes it hard for citizens to draw accurate conclusions about national security policies.

One of the greatest obstacles to peace education is the structure of the world, divided into fiercely competitive nation-states. The desire for power and dominance seems so intricately related to national structures, that, as Machiavelli pointed out, political life is itself a sort of war, with competing individuals at each other's throats to get the most gain. The glorification of war and promulgation of patriotic values create a climate that makes it difficult for peace educators to introduce new ways of thinking about the uses and abuses of political structures. Power, jobs, and careers are all wrapped up in national security systems, which promote the idea that countries must expend their precious resources on armaments. In this way military leaders in positions of power control budgets and dominate official state ideology.

States use internal security forces to protect their dominance. The arms race has spawned a technology capable of keeping track of "deviant" citizens who press for alternatives to militarism. Surveillance has become increasingly sophisticated, with computers able to store huge amounts of data about groups that engage in "subversive" activities such as promoting disarmament. Technologies threaten the democratic rights of citizens to question defense policies. Elites in power use advanced technologies to suppress dissent and criticism of military expenditures.

Related to politics are the economics of the arms race. In the developing world, military hardware costs run up huge deficits and postpone the important work that must be done to increase the standard of living of the poorest of the world's citizens. In Western societies the defense budgets have become a sort of industrial policy, a Keynesian flywheel that keeps private investment and public dollars going into unproductive uses. Throughout the Western world, millions of people are making their livelihood by producing instruments of mass destruction. (In the United States it is estimated that one out of every ten people works for the Pentagon or for a firm that supplies the Pentagon.) In the Soviet Union the military industries are given top priority in the economic plan that sets goals for the Soviet economy. Workers in military industries receive special privileges not available to many citizens in that country. A push for disarmament severely threatens the economic well-being of millions of people who depend for their living upon this type of state spending. To dismantle or cut back defense appropriations threatens their livelihood. As Seymour Melman has pointed out, money spent on the military could much more productively be spent on other sectors of the economy, but powerful forces resist this trend towards economic conversion to peaceful production.[9] Men build their careers creating large weapons systems through wasteful military contracts, and peace education is seen as a threat to those people because it would require a reduction in the amount of money going towards war preparation.

The impact of the war economies upon peace education is powerful. In many countries young people can anticipate building lucrative careers in armaments industries. As engineers or scientists they can work on the "very frontiers of human knowledge" by participating in defense-related research. Peace studies and a concern for the problems of the world are seen as peripheral to the pursuit of a career in business, engineering, or science; therefore a large number of young people motivated by a desire to succeed in today's world have no interest in pursuing peace studies. As one professor teaching a course on nuclear war has put it:

> A lot of students don't want to take it. They said that they didn't want to think about a nuclear holocaust, that they had to get on with their careers.[10]

Careers available to people majoring in peace studies do not pay well. Peace activists work in penury.

National economic policy affects peace in other ways. Because of the huge expense of the national security system, many people are driven into poverty. As social service programs are cut to meet defense requirements, more and more people throughout the world are forced into substandard conditions in miserable circumstances. Some become active in resistance movements that try to set new national goals not so reliant on armaments. As opposition movements grow within a given country, national leaders argue for more guns and a tighter security apparatus to repress dissent. With more arms the struggle of liberation movements often themselves become violent, contributing to a sense of despair that the world will ever be peaceful. The cycle of violence deepens as arms expenditures receive top priority in budget debates, with the result that the weapons in turn become instruments for repressing citizens desiring social change. In order to convince citizens of the correctness of these positions, those in power develop distorted images. For example, President Reagan calls the Contras in Nicaragua, who commit acts of terrorism, "Freedom Fighters."

Language

This use of language to promote militarism presents many thorny problems for peace educators. Language, a conceptual tool, helps structure reality by delimiting the world with symbols, words, and concepts. Human beings use language to communicate their understanding of what they see, hear, and perceive about that world. As Benjamin Whorf pointed out, language is both a shaper of ideas and a programmer for mental activity.[11] Through the language they use while teaching, educators communicate certain norms and expectations about the world. In a violent world, peace educators must be careful about language used in the classrooms. Does their terminology contribute to the existing violent way of resolving disputes, or does it challenge the culture of violence by pointing to new peaceful ways of communicating, thinking, and learning in the classroom?

> In a global setting the school, which is asserted to be neutral in society, occupies a privileged position as a communicator of values transmitted to adapt students to the system in force, and as such it tends to be a sopor of conscience.[12]

Many so-called "normal" patterns of language used in schools condone and support violence. Expressions such as "I will kill you if you lose my book," or "Stick to your guns," casually reinforce violent human behavior. Peace educators should, therefore, help unravel the linguistic means by which a culture of violence is being created in modern states.

In a famous article published more than forty years ago, Harold Lasswell[13] warned that advanced industrial societies are headed towards becoming garrison states whose political leaders are increasingly dominated by specialists in violence. These leaders are not typical warriors but rather modern public relations experts who use management and technical operations to maintain their privileged positions. A garrison state depends upon symbols and images to create such a frightful world that citizens will support military policies. In the garrison state a frightened citizenry does not question expenditures on military means to eliminate threats from supposed enemies. Modern political leaders use language and symbols to create a system of political beliefs that is beyond challenge. Given the dangerous nature of the world, with criminal elements, "evil empires," and terrorists, the national security state seems entirely justified. These leaders depict their actions as fair and just while using the mass media to paint vivid pictures of threats, describing the world in such a way that huge outlays in military might and police force are seen as necessary to preserve law and order:

> Men who approve of violence and the military have constructed a violent language and world which provides a language trap which supports their world view.[14]

Thomas Merton described this use of language as the "logic of power,"[15] where those in control are convinced that whatever they say makes sense, and words become meaningless when applied to actions which contradict them.

Words contain evocative power which can be used to justify violent acts by glossing over their horror. During the Vietnam War, United States troops created "Free Zones," which meant that a previously viable area was so decimated that no one could move freely within it. Likewise, a "pacification plan" meant the total destruction of whole villages so that no living thing could occupy them. Another example is the incredible idea of "destroying a town in order to save it." These types of linguistic construcction mask the true horror of violent actions by promoting images acceptable to citizens asked to fund military enterprises.

> All who belong to the world of the warriors share a common language and a common style. Their style is deliberately cool, attempting to exclude overt emotion and rhetoric from their discussions, emphasizing technical accuracy and objectivity, reduced to quantitative calculation. They applaud dry humor and abhor sentimentality. The style of warriors is congenial to professional scientists and historians, who also base their work on factual analysis rather than on moralistic judgment. The philosophic standpoint of the warriors is basically conservative, even when they consider themselves liberal or revolutionary. They accept the world with all its imperfections as given; their mission is to preserve it and to ameliorate its imperfections in detail, not to rebuild it from the foundations.[16]

In 1947 the name of the United States War Department was changed to the Defense Department to convey the notion of passivity and minimize the perception of aggressive acts carried out by the United States military. Glenn D. Hook[17] and others have written extensively about how linguistic metaphors and convoluted statements have been constructed and promoted to advance nuclear weaponry. A prime example of this was how in the 1950s the use of atomic power was promoted through a program adeptly named "Atoms for Peace," which tried to convince the American public about the benefits of nuclear power, distracting them from the terror of nuclear weapons. In general the makers and supporters of these weapons have promoted a professional language that tries to underplay the horror of modern technological approaches to war to make the use of these weapons seem more palatable. Thus, policy makers discuss a "surgical" strike that would wipe out an enemy fortress and kill "only" thousands of people, as if that many deaths of innocent civilians were acceptable; the strike, being "surgical," uses a medical metaphor to connote something good, the elimination of a disease or a cancer. Language used in this way suppresses emotionalism in favor of supposedly more "objective" discussion of these weapons:

> Metaphors and euphemisms of those with power to shape the nuclear discourse have obscured the inhumanity, immorality, and the irrationality of weapons and their impact on society.[18]

One expression that illustrates how language clouds the real meaning of weaponry and war is "Nuclear war is winnable." Yet in a nuclear war everyone loses. A full-scale nuclear war could mean annihilation of life on this planet. Even to call such an event a war is an anachronism dating back to earlier days when wars supposedly had winners and losers.

As Robert Jay Lifton has pointed out, nuclear weapons make their possessors either mass murderers or self-deceivers,[19] but they are argued for as a crucial means for defending freedom, justice, and liberty. The publics of the nuclear countries are told that increasing nuclear weapons adds to their security, while official communiques fail to underscore the tremendous dangers brought about by relying on such weaponry. In this way language used in the public debate about these weapons creates a false sense of security: If we have more weapons we will be safer, and we all resemble the tortoise Ajax, as described in the following fable:

> Dr. Nicholas Humphrey, professor of animal behavior at Cambridge University, once told the following story, which we might call "The Parable of the Happy Tortoise": It seems that when he was a child, Professor Humphrey had a pet tortoise named Ajax. One autumn day, Ajax was looking for a place to spend the winter, and in his wanderings he happened upon a pile of brush and wood. As it turned out, that pile was being prepared for Guy Fawkes Day, celebrated in England every November 5 with bonfires. We can imagine the growing contentment of Ajax, as tinder was heaped up around him, offering more and more protection from rain and cold. On the appointed day, Ajax may well have felt differently about the arrangement, but not for long.
>   Dr. Humphrey asks: "Are there some of us who still believe that the piling up of weapon upon weapon adds to our security—that the dangers are nothing, compared to the assurance they provide?" The answer is yes. Moreover, those people are in control.[20]

With adroit use of language, public opinion is deliberately manipulated to facilitate the integration of nuclear weapons into pre-existing thought patterns and the acceptance of their existence and possible use. A missile as devastating as the MX is sold to the Congress and the citizens of the United States with the innocuous-sounding claim that it is a "bargaining chip," a necessary strategem in arms talks with the Soviets. In the public dialogue about the development of this weapon the negative consequences of its use are not discussed. Rather, it is extolled for its ability to bring peace and security; it is even called "the peacekeeper." Such euphemisms used by politicians and the military industrial complex have become known as Nukespeak.[21]

Language used to promote violence is not limited to linguistic symbols. French intellectuals have discussed the notion of *total language,* which includes the electronic media, the newspapers, printed materials, symbols and images that appear in the culture:

> In the root of total language is the notion of the totality of human expression as language (conscious or not) and therefore as communication. Today, total language is gaining importance and acquiring new dimensions with the advent of the electronic age and the attendant multiple messages of different types which are addressed increasingly to our impulses as opposed to our reason.[22]

The mass media play an important role in promoting violence by their willing portrayal of violent scenes as well as their biased reporting of national events. Many members of the mass media contribute to the propaganda war surrounding the use of force to maintain the national security state by participating in a cult of silence that surrounds violence and the use of brute power. One such example is a holocaust that occurred in East Timor in the 1970s, where the Indonesian state massacred over a million people. Because the Indonesians were seen as a client state and friendly to United States interests, little attention was given to these atrocities.[23] At the same time the Khmer Rouge were commiting genocide in Cambodia. These activities were extensively covered because aggression in Cambodia was being carried out by Communists, who were accordingly labeled as terrorists. Other acts of violence routinely commited in Guatemala, El Salvador, South Korea, Chile, and countries supportive of United States economic interests go routinely unreported, while the slighest violation of human rights in a "hostile" country like Nicaragua gets extensive media coverage. In this way the mass media support the national power structure, reflecting its biases and mobilizing popular support for its interests.

The mass media also condone violence through constant use of violent images to develop drama. So much violence and slaughter are daily exhibited on television and through movies that citizens throughout the world are becoming inured to violence, guns, and militaristic ways of solving problems, and children are desensitized to violence by their cultures. Men are taught, by watching the behavior of other men, to pull out a gun and blow away those people close to them when they are faced with frustrations. Police torture and force are seen as solutions to crime. Such a constant diet of killing, fighting, and violent drama broadcast into people's homes (and consciousness) through television wears down the natural resistance that humans have to blood, gore, and physical violence.

In order to restore the peace-loving instincts that also belong to the human species, peace educators should help students reevaluate the total language of human culture that embraces violence and the language claims of such concepts as security, power, dominance, and peace which support existing military structures:

> Peace education as "conscientization" then, is not a factory of dreams, but a school of realism. It is neither sectarian nor prophetic. Neither an ideology nor a religious offering of miracles.[24]

Peace educators take a realistic look at the world as it is constructed by modern language systems and recognize how those linguistic systems support different forms of violence that dominate human thought and action.

Peace educators can construct a new grammar for developing a nonviolent world and challenge current language patterns that support the culture of violence.

> As educators, we are powerful custodians of our culture's consciousness, and we have a vital role to play in challenging the hegemony of pernicious and outmoded realities. Merely to recite our species' long record of past mistakes is not, however, enough. We must put ourselves and our students in touch with their individual and social potentials as citizens of the world systems only now being born.[25]

They need to develop new conceptual and linguistic categories that will name a world based on caring and mutual respect rather than dominance and superiority.

As Dale Spender has pointed out, language is both a trap and a source of liberation.[29] Language traps us into existing patterns of thought, but also has the potential to liberate our thinking by providing new directions and new concepts. Language, when used carefully and creatively, can help people challenge commonly held assumptions and point to new ways of structuring reality. Peace educators can contribute to the creation of peaceful futures by carefully examining language usage and talking with students about ways to create a new grammar, vocabulary, and conceptual framework for a less violent world.

Conquering Barriers

The militaristic political and economic practices of nation-states present many obstacles for peace educators to overcome. In many cases research requests for grants to support the study of nonviolence or alternative international relations are denied by funding sources only interested in supporting the status quo through security studies or international relations. Peace educators can work to overcome these obstacles by teaching students that their governments should have different priorities, most specifically, that they should work to realize the goals set forth in the original charter of the United Nations:

> It is absolutely essential, as is noted in the 1974 UNESCO recommendation, that member states formulate policies for the improvement of international understanding and for overcoming the misconceptions and cultural ignorance which often permit the toleration of injustice as well as the nurturing of fear of the enemy, which in turn nurtures the arms race. If, according to the guiding principles of the recommendation, education is presented from a global perspective, students will come to understand that the human species has a common planetary destiny, that we have more in common than differences, and that respect for other people, their cultures, civilizations, values, and ways of life is absolutely essential to the preservation of the species, its cultural diversity and its physical survival.[27]

One way to counteract the nationalistic, and hence militaristic, goals of nation-states is to develop a planetary consciousness. Peace educators can teach that the human race depends for its own survival on cooperation between people and not competition between armies from different countries.

The most fundamental human right, the right to life, is guaranteed under the Declaration of Human Rights. This right cannot be obtained without peace:

> War, the indiscriminate consumer of human lives, is in direct contradiction to the principles of human rights. Disarmament education should illuminate this contradiction and stress the inadmissability of war.[28]

Governments assume they have a right to kill and repress dissent in order to protect their sovereignty. In challenging this behavior by appealing to human rights, peace educators are risking controversy, but these risks will be essential to the struggle to create a less violent world. Addressing the threats posed by modern commitments to defense and security requires that teachers confront dominant political values. As one student who had taken a peace education course noted:

> The saddest part to me is that the leaders of a country that is supposed to be concerned with human rights should be so obsessed with the production of weapons whose objective is mass violation of the major human right, the right to live.[29]

Education acculturates people to the prevalent beliefs in a society in a way that passes on the traditions and values of that society. Because peace education explores those issues, peace educators have been accused of indoctrinating their students. An editorial opinion column in the *New York Times* about a peace studies minor at New York University stated:

> The driving interest of "peace" scholars ... is in student activism. Mobilizing student support for the scholars' peace agenda is the unstated but seeming goal in this and other such programs.[30]

Peace educators are often attacked because they challenge mainstream views of security and defense. Opponents claim that rather than participating in "objective" presentations about the problems of violence that confront humanity, peace educators engage in rhetoric, present only one side, and try to convince students of the correctness of that position. Peace studies has been labeled as being value-laden, not the proper material for intellectual inquiry, by Baroness Cox, a sociologist, and Dr. Roger Scruton, a reader in philosophy at Birbeck College, London:

> Peace studies should not be taught in schools and universities because it lacks the intellectual rigour to qualify as a serious academic discipline, encourages prejudice and conceals a concerted attempt to manipulate the political thinking of young people.[31]

In contrast to what the above authors state, peace studies itself is seldom a separate discipline, but rather it is interdisciplinary, based on traditional subject matter—political science, history, communications, philosophy, sociology, etc. Because its programs typically consist of courses from these academic disciplines, peace studies is not a separate field and is no more subject to lack of intellectual rigor than its components.

Cox and Scruton further state that peace studies encourages prejudice and attempts to manipulate the political thinking of young people. This point can be countered on two levels:

(1) On one hand, encouraging of prejudice usually means presenting only one side of an issue, so that students in peace studies would not get a balanced point of view about war and peace. Peace educators wishing to avoid charges of biasing their material must insist that their courses present a balanced point of view, with as many sides as possible, so that students can make up their own minds about defense and security. Because problems of war and peace are extraordinarily complex and don't allow simple solutions, discerning students are likely to discredit teachers who provide only one point of view.

In some peace education classes teachers present a perspective that opposes traditional points of view which support peace through strength. By presenting different points of view, peace educators aren't prejudicing their students, but rather are increasing their ability to understand complex phenomena:

> Our task as educators is to open minds, not to close them: We wish our students to acquire not only a viewpoint, but a self-critical perspective on that viewpont.[32]

Peace education can contribute enormously to students' rational thinking capacities by encouraging them to think critically about existing national security policies and evaluate these policies. The key to peace studies and the best rejoinder to those opponents who argue that peace studies prejudices students is to teach peace studies in a manner that encourages students to become more competent in analyzing, comparing, and verifying competing claims of fact by presenting different points of view about the problems of defense and violence in social systems.

(2) The argument that peace studies is somehow value-laden while traditional studies of history and other academic disciplines are not is a polemical argument constructed to discredit a point of view that threatens people in power. Education is neither neutral nor objective in the sense that excludes the teaching of values:

> By what we teach or fail to teach, and by how we teach it, education has far reaching consequences. Education is never politically neutral. By the very nature of the activity education cannot be a private or "objective" enterprise that is "value free." It is a public and social activity that is always value laden. Education can pretend to be nonpolitical by attempting to take an "objective" stance toward the present social realities within which it takes place. But then it has the inevitable consequence of fitting people into those social realities as they presently exist.[33]

Exploration of war and peace issues, as advocated by peace educators, is controversial because it challenges traditions valued by those who control societies.

Peace education, like all curricula presented in schools, contains certain values; in this case, the values of nonviolence and social justice. It is not, however, uniquely value-laden while other subjects are value-free, and as such does not prejudice students any more than any other subject. The claim laid against peace education that it is value-laden and hence not "objective" rests on the assumption that correct knowledge taught in the school is "objective," but this, too, is a straw-dog argument. Werner Heisenberg, a physicist, established in 1920 the *uncertainty principle*,[34] which states that objectivity cannot be provided in scientific investigations because as soon as you start setting up an experiment you are meddling with matter and hence altering its configuration. Thus, scientists and educators present neither facts nor knowledge claims that are truly objective. As educators, their role is to present as many different points of view as possible so their students receive a comprehensive understanding of the complex role of violence in human affairs. They can provide many different points of view about a subject, but this principle would be more accurately described as a principle of fairness or comprehensivity rather than a principle of objectivity. Peace educators themselves reflect different points of view about the best way to achieve peace. Some may be hawks, desiring to increase weapons; others may be doves, wishing unilaterally to reduce stockpiles; still others may be owls, hoping to reach wise conclusions about the complex and perilous problems that confront humanity because of the arms race.

Claims of objectivity on the part of the detractors of peace education hide the value-laden assumptions of people supporting the status quo:

> Especially in the field of scientific knowledge an ideological or value base for the knowledge proposition is denied and under the guise of value neutrality, "facts" and "theses" are propagated as objective and universal truths.[35]

A claim of objectivity is a claim that an assertion is not prejudiced from a particular value position. However, as Heisenberg demonstrated, all claims have a value perspective. All courses contain hidden within them the value perspectives of their instructors. The way material is presented, the knowledge that is considered relevant, and the conclusions that are drawn present some value perspective or another. But a course or discipline can be balanced or fair when it provides many different points of view, not just one:

> Peace studies has no quarrel with the ideal of "objectivity," in the sense of striving to overcome the limitations of one's social perspective and to present opposing arguments as fairly as possible. Such objectivity is indeed part of our agenda. But we cannot avoid opposition to those ideologists who, by claiming that their own social perspective is "scientific," seek to impose their own ideology of pseudo-scientific neutrality as a requirement on the rest of the university.[36]

The criticism of indoctrination leveled against peace studies boils down to an attempt to discredit peace studies for not reinforcing the existing set of militaristic values that govern most societies. These values condone violence as a means to entrench existing power structures and powerful economic interests. Peace educators, because they call into question the culture of war, are accused of manipulating the political thinking of young people.

Such claims of prejudice leveled against peace studies fly directly in the face of commonly held assumptions about education, such as the openness of intellectual inquiry. In a democratic society ideas are supposed to compete for approval. Hence a commonly held value in universities, colleges, and high schools is that students should be exposed to a broad set of viewpoints and allowed to draw their own conclusions:

> The purpose of schooling is to broaden and enrich the minds and hearts of students so that they can shape their own values and arrive at their own judgements.[37]

Peace educators who establish an open climate in their classes where students have the freedom to express their own ideas and can draw their own conclusions about violence in the world can avoid indoctrinating their students by carefully following the difference between description, analysis, and prescription. In teaching about war and violence which beset citizens in this world they should then present different aspects of these problems and help students analyze these different perspectives, so that students can draw their own conclusions. Peace educators should avoid prescribing "correct" viewpoints or telling their students what to do about these problems. They can lay out various options for students, without prescribing how students should respond to these problems.

> It should be stated that however much our educational aim is to encourage a positive expression of opinion towards equality, justice, disarmament — in other words peace — this does not mean that we deny students the possibility of arriving at other opinions. The freedom to come to one's own decision must always be possible for students.[38]

Helping students analyze the problems of war and peace will increase their analytical skills and help clarify their own values.

The public debate over peace education, by trying to rule out the peace perspective presented by pacifists and others opposed to escalating the arms race, is itself guilty of indoctrination. A good example of this involves the Reserve Officer Training Corps (ROTC), a college- and university-based program in the United States that trains future military officers. Members of the armed forces can go into any secondary school in the United States to recruit for ROTC. However, when conscientious objectors attempt to speak to high school students, they are often excluded by administrators who don't want students exposed to that point of view. Such exclusion was challenged in 1984 in Chicago by Clergy and Laity Concerned, an organization that trained people to make presentations in public high schools about alternatives to military service. When representatives from Clergy and Laity Concerned were denied the opportunity to provide high school students with information about conscientious objector status, they sued and won in the federal courts, so that schools now have to provide access to both points of view to young people considering their future status with the military.

Attempts to block courses in peace education deny students exposure to a wide variety of viewpoints about national security. People who oppose peace studies because it prejudices the minds of students can themselves be accused of narrow-minded "either-or" behavior: Either you support the status quo or you are a traitor (or you are indoctrinating students, or you are teaching value-laden subject matter, etc.). Problems of national security and peace are so complex that many different people have advanced solutions to these problems, reflecting a wide variety of viewpoints. Attempts to stifle dialogue about alternative viewpoints commit intellectual prejudice by not allowing students to hear all different sides of these controversial issues.

Obstacles Within Educational Institutions

Raising such issues in a classroom can present real threats to a teacher. He or she may be criticized by other colleagues, attacked by angry parents, or censured by patriotic administrators. An educator's ability to raise questions about political reality depends to some extent upon the institutional setting in which he or she works. Tenure and other conditions supporting academic freedom allow individuals to be outspoken in their pursuit of truth. However, for many peace educators, challenging the existing political arrangements may threaten their jobs. Consequently, it is crucial for teachers about to embark on peace courses to understand the nature of the institutions for which they work. Violence in the world permeates individual schools, colleges, churches, and settings for adult education. Working successfully within these structures will be a key ingredient in establishing peace education classes. Different educational settings contain different obstacles to peace education.

When the author of this book first taught a course in peace education, leaders of the business community in Milwaukee sent a letter to the Chancellor of the University of Wisconsin-Milwaukee attacking the course, saying:

> It is clearly evident from the outline and from the text used that it's [the course of peace education] not a scholarly objective presentation of academic subject matter. It is rather a "how to" course designed to produce anti-defense activists and protestors on the streets of Milwaukee.

In response, the head of the Academic Program and Curriculum Committee mentioned that this course had been approved by the appropriate faculty review bodies and that major universities offered a variety of courses "from Greek Philosophy to Military Science and from Bio-Chemistry to Peace Education." Because of long-held traditions of academic freedom, this course was supported by administrators and faculty throughout the university who protected the right of professors to teach courses they deem important.

Similarly, when a teacher from a middle school in Waukesha who is active in Wisconsin Educators for Social Responsibility (WESR) wrote an article for the local newspaper praising peace education, another business leader in Milwaukee ridiculed these efforts in an opinion column titled "Activists Posing as Teachers Seek to Give the Peace Away." He preferred the acronym WENI to the acronym WESR. "WENI," he said, "stands for Wisconsin Educators for National Irresponsibility." He went on to attack peace education for promoting pacifism and disarmament, which would abandon the United States to the rapacious forces of the Soviet Union.

In England in 1984 the director of Teachers for Peace in London received a phone call from a reporter from the *Daily Mail* asking about the activities of her organization. The next day the newspaper featured a center section entitled "Communist Teachers Spreading Peace in British Schools." The article contained her address, and she subsequently received bomb threats. In Australia there have been strong attacks from the new right on peace studies programs, and in the United States the October 1986 edition of *Commentary* directly attacked the peace studies program at Tufts University. The independent peace movement is severely repressed in the Communist countries of Eastern Europe. Student organizations and liberation groups that challenge official military policy are repressed throughout the world.

As frightening as these attacks may seem, they have not destroyed peace studies. In many cases they bring increased attention to the peace studies program in question, and this attention has stimulated various supporters to come out of the woodwork. In some cases, peace educators face risks to their jobs. In other cases, hostile attacks have elicited support for peace studies programs. But it must be remembered that peace education will be controversial. Such great peacemakers as Martin Luther King, Mahatma Gandhi, Oscar Romero, and Jesus Christ have all died violent deaths.

Elementary teachers may run into controversy when peace concepts clash with parental values. Throughout the world various organizations are trying to notify school administrators that teaching peace or nuclear age education is not appropriate for schools. Some parents may belong to such organizations, or, because of the controversy surrounding peace education, may challenge a teacher's inclusion of such material in the elementary curriculum. With this potential challenge in mind elementary teachers should

be up-front about their peace education activities, discussing them with
school principals and providing justification for them to other teachers and
school authorities, so that, should a challenge or a question arise, those
people who often have initial contact with the public are prepared to defend
the teaching of war and peace issues. Elementary teachers should also be
prepared to explain to parents what is being taught about peace in the
classroom and to defend those activities.

At the secondary level peace educators use textbooks that emphasize
exclusively the accomplishments of military heroes and national leaders.

> Prejudice and ethnocentrism seem more strongly reflected in history
> and social education texts than in others. Further, history at the secon-
> dary level emphasizes wars, and only rarely the story of avoided wars or
> of events in which there has been peaceful resolution of conflict. Such
> history reinforces the attitude that war is inevitable, and that there are
> few if any alternatives to war for playing out international competition
> in the pursuit of national goals.[39]

Most history textbooks present in great detail the accomplishments of the
war machine, yet they contain little or no information about the peace
efforts that have always existed throughout history. Emphasis falls on the
dropping of the atomic bomb, rather than on the negotiations that were
taking place between members of the Japanese government and representatives of the United States to end the Second World War. Interesting
discussions could take place about why those negotiations failed and
nuclear weapons were used. Early histories of the United States underscore
the warlike nature of Native Americans and neglect the deep peace traditions of certain Indian tribes. Historians can study in detail the work of the
United Nations in keeping peace and the role of its peacekeeping forces in
trouble spots throughout the world. There are many topics that could be
presented in history classes that would provide understanding of the role
of peacemakers in history, but few teachers are prepared to teach such
material. The never learned it in school, and it would take a special effort
on their part to research nonviolence.

During their teenage years young men are susceptible to conscription.
Many secondary schools support the Reserve Officer Training Corps (ROTC)
and other programs that promote military service. An acute problem in
many high schools centers around career choices for young people. Peace
educators should become aware of alternative careers for young people in
helping professions and human services so that students understand they
don't have to enlist upon graduation and can apply for conscientious objector status. Since the armed forces recruit strongly at the secondary level,
providing students with knowledge about their various options presents a
more balanced approach to help young people select careers.

At the university level there seems to be callous indifference to the threats posed by living in the atomic age. Many university professors are aware of the threats implied by living in a nuclear area, but why don't more of them direct serious scholarly attention to issues of the arms race? Explanations for this seeming lack of concern for addressing the violent nature of the world in college clasrooms comes from examining the nature of traditional disciplines. Professors, deeply embedded in the academic traditions of their respective fields, have their research and teaching agendas set by the established limits of those disciplines. Academics are often reluctant to delve into new disciplines like peace and conflict studies that don't conform to accepted values. Peace education studies the prospects for a refigured world to reduce conflict in novel ways. Speculative research in these areas may not receive recognition in traditional academic journals and departments upon which professors depend for their livelihood.

Henry Nash makes the point that peace and conflict studies require looking into the future and seeing there disastrous consequences as a result of current policies.[40] Academics are uncomfortable gazing into a crystal ball and predicting the future because they can't be sure of the outcome. Consequently, they focus their efforts on the past and study causes and events that might provide a deeper understanding of current states of affairs. Academics are also uncomfortable with the topics of war and peace, because studying these issues raises concerns that often imply action:

> There is also the conclusion toward which any such course on nuclear war must inevitably move: The probability of world disaster is drastic if changes in national policy are not made.[41]

College professors are committed to the notion of value-free inquiry, and are concerned that teaching about issues of war and peace may lead "to emotionalism, over-simplification, and even indoctrination."[42] If the study of nuclear age education or peace education reduces to a conflict between education and indoctrination, academics might tend to back away from controversial topics to pursue their commitment to what they consider value-free inquiry.

Professors at institutions of higher education have to face many obstacles in getting new courses approved on topics of war and peace. They are busy people with classes to teach, administrative duties, students to advise, and research agendas. Many of these professionals find it hard to drop their existing commitments to develop new courses or sit on committees to promote peace studies. Because there are few research funds in these areas, they are likely to pursue research projects in more traditional areas that have a greater probability of being funded. The irony of these traditions is that by ignoring the threat of modern war, they may be avoiding preparing their students to take responsible positions in the modern world. Many people at all levels of education, teachers and students, would prefer

Many people at all levels of education, teachers and students, would prefer not to spend time dwelling on topics as depressing as nuclear winter. However, if the citizens of modern countries aren't made aware of such issues as they attend school, they may be exposed only to the official practices of their governments as expounded by political leaders and supported by mass media. Within this climate there is a strong ethical argument for educators at all levels to teach about the threats of violence and the alternatives of peace so the human race can become more aware of the disaster facing it. Taking the risks to raise such intellectual questions within the confines of educational institutions helps guarantee the future of academic inquiry. Without such a commitment teaching can become a hollow charade that deceives the young about the nature of the world they will inhabit.

At the adult level in churches and community settings the main obstacle is in overcoming what many people perceive as apathy or disinterest in the topics of peace and global awareness. Various schools of community organizing teach that there is no such thing as citizen apathy. If the citizens are not concerned about an issue, those who have knowledge and awareness of that issue have been negligent in their presentation of the issue to the public. This shifts the blame for lack of concern from the general public, which may be uninformed or misled about security issues, to educators, who understand these issues and have the responsibility to organize educational programs that will provide public awareness in compelling packages. The arms race threatens all people in the world, not only because of the destruction it portends, but also because it robs valuable resources from society. Peace educators create educational programs that provide the general public with a greater awareness of these problems and discuss with adults the threats of violence in their daily lives. By gearing peace education classes to a practical level, where adult students can gain a better understanding of issues that directly affect them, they have a chance of motivating adult learners. In this way peace education can become "reeducation" of adults into the crucial threats of violence that make their worlds insecure. Lifelong learning should be geared towards helping citizens in all societies reflect constructively on the crucial role of violence in their lives.

Many adult educators don't see themselves as radicals and want to avoid controversy. Peace education requires bravery. They must risk censure and attack in order to provide awareness of these issues to the citizens of the world. Keeping silent on these issues helps legitimize existing militaristic policies of nation-states. Peace educators, creatively constructing programs that crash through the conspiracy of silence surrounding these issues, will help the human race to move beyond war and realize its potential to live peacefully on this planet.

7. The Peaceful Classroom

Education for peace assumes peace in education.

Magnus Haavelsrud

So far this book has discussed peace education from the point of view of content: what sorts of things are taught in peace education classes; how they are introduced into the school curriculum; and what obstacles educators should be aware of while teaching this content. If the foregoing represents the "what" of peace studies, this chapter will present the "how." How should peace educators teach about war and peace, and what is the optimal pedagogy for peace education?

Teaching various aspects of war and peace provides students with an awareness of the problems brought about by a commitment to militarism, an understanding of the causes of violence and an appreciation of different steps that could be taken to reduce violence in human communities. In addition to providing such information about peace issues, peace education tries to transform individuals so they develop a particular type of personality, most specifically, a personality that desires to promote peace at all levels — personal, societal, and global. Although awareness is an important part of creating this type of personality, peaceful individuals have to acquire skills and dispositions to act in nonviolent ways towards each other. Such skills and dispositions do not come from information provided in the classroom; rather they are habits, values, and proclivities that arise in an individual as a result of a complex series of life experiences.

In discussing characteristics that help develop peacemakers, Elise Boulding says there are six different aspects to an individual's development. They are psychological, emotional, cognitive, spiritual, the development of role-taking skills, and the development of knowledge.[1] The way an individual develops is determined to a large extent by behaviors of people in that person's environment — family members, friends, neighbors, people in school, peers, fellow workers, figures from the media, and significant others. The aspect that teachers most readily influence, a person's knowledge stock, comes from many different places — the media, the family, the culture, the neighborhood, etc. However, teachers, educators,

121

parents, ministers, and concerned adults do much more than teach facts, and skills. They also influence psychological, emotional, and spiritual growth, creating environments where individuals learn by observing the behavior of others, by trying out new behaviors, and by receiving feedback about their own behaviors. Values and morals can't easily be taught.[2] They are acquired through experience with other human beings. Thus the environment in which a student learns becomes extremely important. Teachers have a key role to play in creating a learning environment conducive to developing the seeds of compassion and nonviolence.

In 1937 Maria Montessori said, "Our hope for peace in the future lies not in the formal knowledge the adult can pass on to the child, but in the normal development of the new man."[3] She believed that educators should establish environments that allow the natural peace-loving instincts of young people to flourish. These instincts might be characterized as concern for other human beings, aversion to violence, desire for freedom, and harmony with others. In a Montessori classroom teachers step aside and allow the child to grow. Such a teaching style promotes free choice and initiative on the part of the learner, who is not passively receiving instruction from authoritarian teachers but rather learns in the classroom settings to engage his or her conscience with other human beings. Dr. Montessori believed that each child is a messiah capable of saving the human race:

> If at some time the Child were to receive proper consideration and his immense possibilities were to be developed, then a Man might arise for whom there would be no need of encouragement to disarmament and resistance to war because his nature would be such that he could not endure the state of degradation and of extreme moral corruption which makes possible any participation in war.[4]

A Montessori classroom is a carefully structured environment where children learn by pursuing their own interests, where they learn to cooperate with other children by working on mutually agreed-upon tasks, and where the children develop at their own rates. Because, as Dr. Montessori believed, all children have tendencies of compassion and care for others, such free environments allow those capacities to develop so that as adults they have dispositions that abhor violence and express concern for the well-being of others.

An irony of peace education is that an educator need not necessarily teach the topics of peace education in order to conduct a peaceable classroom.[5] Likewise, a parent fairly ignorant of the principles and practices of the peace movement could establish a home environment conducive of peace. In order to act peacefully, students need not necessarily be taught information about war, peace and violence. They do, however, need to learn the ways of peace.

> A peaceful and warless world cannot be created by providing information and developing intellectual virtues alone, but, first and foremost, by fostering moral self-discipline and by making an aesthetic approach to education, in all its aspects and stages, for the development of men and women to their full humanity, and their capacity to live in creative peace and cooperation with one another and all existence.[6]

This learning can occur in a variety of places, but like other learnings that take place in education settings, it should be intentional. Children will be pulled in a variety of directions. Their friends will play war games. The media will expose them to killing and violence. Adults concerned about the effects of violence on children can create environments that will draw out children's natural instincts towards peace.

What are the characteristics of such an environment? A good way to answer this question is to describe the type of person that environment should produce. Elise Boulding, one of the leading thinkers in peace education and peace research, provides such a model:

> The child who becomes an altruist, an activist, and a nonviolent shaper of the future is then one who feels autonomous, competent, confident about her own future and the future of the society, able to cope with stress, relates warmly to others and feels responsibility for them even when they are not directly dependent on her. She has had many opportunities to solve problems and play out different social roles in the past and her successes have been recognized and rewarded; she has been exposed to a wide variety of events, accumulated a fair amount of knowledge, and has a cognitively complex view of the world. She has been inspired by adult role models, but also nurtured and helped by her own peers. In terms of our model she has had optimal opportunities to develop each of her capacities, cognitive, emotional and intuitive, during her maturing years; her predispositions for bonding, for altruism, for play, for creating alternatives have more than counter-balanced her predispositions for aggression. Her social spaces have been filled with challenges she could meet, role models which have provided rich sources of complex learnings about possible social behavior, and positive reinforcement for her attempts to make constructive changes around her.[7]

A person who has a peaceful disposition would know how to control destructive aggressive tendencies. He or she would be saturated with the idea that human beings are born into a world that requires all creatures to live in harmony. Plato and Aristotle discussed raising the citizens of Athens with a moral judgment, a sense of right and wrong that meant the learning of something like good manners or good form—a dynamic concept of nobility, of virtue, of wisdom and courage. In order for there to be peace in this world, human beings have to live with each other in communities based on sharing and mutual self-help. The deep-seated urges that propel human behavior have to be directed away from violence and directed towards the peaceful resolution of conflict. Men and women have to be free and courageous enough to choose the path of love and unity with all human beings, instead of the path of hatred and fragmentation of human society. People need to learn how to give vent to their frustrations and anger in ways that don't harm others.

As Paulo Friere has pointed out, education can either domesticate or liberate. In order for peace studies to contribute to the creation of a democratic society, it must abandon hierarchical procedures and establish democratic classrooms that promote equality, mutual respect, participation, and cooperation. People can learn in democratic classes how to live democratically. If the student is to be empowered to bring peace to this world, she or he cannot be a passive recipient of information, but must be an active creator of knowledge. If, as John Dewey said, "We learn the things we do," then students who learn to sit quietly as passive receivers of "truth" from an authority figure will have learned to function well in an authoritarian society. Some methods of teaching are clearly more empowering than others, and peace education has to rely on those methods that provide examples of how individuals can peacefully coexist on this planet. The goal of creating people with a disposition towards peace leads to a peace pedagogy, or a theory of how peace education ought to be conducted. Peace education points to new ways of educating as indicated by Table 2 on page 125.

Teachers who are authorities use their expertise to teach others. However, many teachers go beyond being authorities to using authoritative behaviors to control children in their classssrooms. Using competitive rewards to pit individuals against each other, authoritarian classrooms are divided into winners and losers, where students who are accustomed to a routine of losing acquire a sense of worthlessness, helplessness, and incompetence. In authoritarian classrooms the teacher always knows best, and pupils do not to participate in the development of classroom limits and boundaries for classroom behavior. Children expect the teacher to determine rules and express little interest in classroom management. Children are governed by a teacher's sense of right or wrong, and the ethics of adults are seen as superior to the ethics of children; teachers punish nonattentive pupils, and students become rivals for marks rather than equal participants in a learning process. The majority of students learn to fail, which in turn leads to apathy and a negative self-attitude.

A peaceful classroom, on the other hand, is an open environment where each student has an equal chance to learn, and the welfare of each

Table 2. A Typology of Educational Goals Based on War and Peace Goals

MEANS	GOALS	
	WAR	PEACE
Politics and Power	direct violence physical strength paternalism wars competition oppression win/lose	safety spiritual-soul strength participation negotiations cooperation justice win/win
Education	selfish behavior authoritarian methods traditional teaching moralistic explana- tions of behavior coercion structural violence	responsibility open classroom innovation causative or social- science explanations of behavior self-motivation freedom to pursue interests

individual is given attention. Students and teachers learn to interact with each other in constructive ways. Everybody contributes his or her perspectives on reality, and students and teachers set limits for behavior. In order for peace education to be a moral craft resting on the recognition that students and teachers share something of value, with a profound respect for all those engaged in the learning process, peace educators have to establish trusting environments where "people might test their capacity to face truth and enhance their ability to change their minds."[8] This type of teaching differs sharply from indoctrination, in which the instructor determines the agenda, and from advocacy, in which the leader rallies others to a cause. Peace educators don't consider themselves the possessors of truth. As advanced learners who may have examined the problems of war and peace in some detail, they engage their students in a cooperative learning adventure to determine what can be done about such profound human problems. Teachers in peace studies classes exhibit humility within a truth-finding process.

Two brothers — David and Roger Johnson, from the University of Minnesota — who have done considerable research into different classroom climates have discovered that there are three main goal structures for the classroom, where a goal structure specifies the type of interdependence that exists among students. The three ways that students will relate to each other and the teacher in accomplishing instructional goals are cooperative, competitive and individualistic.[9] A cooperative goal structure exists when students realize they can obtain their learning objectives "if and only if, the other students with whom they are linked can obtain their goals." [10] A competitive goal structure exists when students realize they can obtain their learning objectives "if and only if, the other students with whom they are linked fail to obtain their goal."[11] And an individualistic goal exists when the achievement of a goal by one student is unrelated to the achievement of the goal by other students. In this latter type of classroom, whether or not a student achieves a particular goal has no bearing upon whether other students achieve their goals. In a competitive classroom there are a limited number of rewards; therefore a large proportion of students experience failure, and the environment discourages students from taking on challenges because they fear failure. Those students who are successful in competitive classrooms may learn that winning is the sole goal in life, and that people who don't win have no value. Bertrand Russell noted that a competitive philosophy of life, which views life as a contest in which the winner gains respect, breeds a vicious cycle where intelligence is ignored for strength.[12] Competitive people do not learn for intrinsic reasons. Learning becomes a means towards the goal of winning. Learning should be rewarding for its own sake; it should not have as its goal getting the better of another person.

In a cooperative classroom, students rely on each other. They learn together, and the success of learning activities depends upon the cooperative contributions of all. Everyone in the classroom has different capabilities, but they learn from each other in order to complete tasks. In a cooperative classroom, students learn social skills and democratic values beneficial to society as well as to each individual. Cooperative goal structures, as described by the brothers Johnson, create a democratic classroom where students have the freedom to participate in and influence the decision-making structures that determine their learning environments. Democratic classrooms do not imply that individuals are free to do whatever they want. Students either determine how the class is to be structured or, using a Montessori model, they rely on the structured environment created by the teacher where they choose learning projects.

Competition is not entirely eliminated in a cooperative classroom. Pupils will still strive for excellence. They will compete to complete tasks within prescribed time limits and to achieve standards agreed upon by the group. However, these classrooms should have no room for the "zero sum" aspect of competition where when one person wins, another loses.

Peace education builds upon the traditions of cooperative education to build democratic classrooms and rests on the following five principles of peace pedagogy. Research supports the conclusion that democratic experiences in schools can contribute to the knowledge, skills, and attitudes essential for democratic citizenship.[13] Peace education (1) builds a democratic community; (2) teaches cooperation; (3) develops moral sensitivity; (4) promotes critical thinking; and (5) enhances self-esteem. Peace educators have numerous opportunities to use these principles to provide democratic learning experiences that allow students to learn behaviors conducive to creating peaceful human societies. These principles, although they are meant to guide a teacher's facilitation of learning experiences and the mode of classroom interaction, can be used in home, in school, or in community learning settings. They are not mutually exclusive. Some build upon and reinforce others. Together they provide guidelines for how to establish a peaceful classroom.

- **Building a democratic community.** In order for there to be peace in the world, individuals will have to learn to live with each other without resorting to destructive violence. Education which fosters disunity cannot foster a sense of hope. Where there is no sense of community and no sense of belonging, people will not develop a sense of responsibility for others. In a global community, human beings depend on each other. Citizens need raw materials and food produced in other countries. Companies need markets for their products, and we all depend on the planet Earth for food, water and shelter. Human beings rely on each other for collective security and gather together into interdependent communities to satisfy their needs. Millions of people throughout the world are forming intentional base communities to deal with the perverse effects of direct and structural violence. Peace education can contribute to student understanding of sharing and mutual help by building classroom communities, as model laboratories for learning democratic behavior.

To do this, teachers should shape learning programs with the help and participation of students. This means, on the one hand, building programs based on students' interests and experiences, and on the other, working with students to determine classroom limits and agreeing upon accepted behaviors.[14] Peace educators should encourage students to share their experiences with violence so members of the class can learn that their own frightening experiences aren't unique. They can also learn from each other strategies for coping with fears and anxieties that come from living in a violent world. Students with different perspectives will actively (and emotionally) disagree with each other, but hearing (and respecting) each other's views while figuring out how to respond to violence becomes an important part of building a democratic learning environment.

In this democratic process of examining the causes and sources of violence in our lives, the teacher serves as a facilitator who keeps the class moving. He or she asks questions or provides new resources which shed insight into problems. Often opinions need to be clarified and summarized.

The teacher does this in a way that helps relate discussions to the goal of that particular lesson. The teacher also checks periodically to see if a discussion is moving in a way agreeable to the group. Another important function of the teacher in peace education classes is to make sure everyone's point of view is listened to in such a way that looking at different perspectives becomes a positive learning experience rather than contending to prove who is right. The peace educator shows a warm concern and interest in the participants, affirming them for their contributions. Thus, the teacher in a democratic classroom becomes a mediator, one who maintains the cohesiveness of the learning group.

A democratic classroom calls for a dialogue between all individuals who should feel comfortable and believe they have something to contribute. The teacher encourages those who are reticent to speak and endeavors in supportive ways to discourage too much talking by those who monopolize time. An open dialogue between learners and educators requires respect and trust, which are in turn the key ingredients of community. A learning community can be enhanced by having participants share experiences from their lives. The instructor can share his or her feelings and experiences and offer opinions as hypotheses subject to collective examination. Such interactive pedagogy allows students to get to know teachers in new and exciting ways that enrich the notion of a learning community of intelligent beings exploring complex problems.

There are many techniques that teachers can use to set up democratic classrooms. One of the most important is to get students to know each other through a variety of introductory exercises. Students can also help determine a constitution for a class or at least agree upon mutually acceptable guidelines for appropriate behavior. At the end of each class period, students and teachers can spend about ten minutes discussing what went on during the class itself.

The purpose of such a processing session is not to rehash the ideas brought up in the classroom discussion but rather to explore how people feel about their participation and the participation of others. Such process sessions can help provide a sense of ownership for the class: We are all in this together. How can we make it better? What went wrong? What worked? How can it be improved next time? Processing a session can also provide participants with significant feedback about their own roles in the class interaction.

Becoming a democratic citizen requires more than an abstract understanding of democratic principles. Behaving democratically is a way of life. Peace educators can prepare their students for this way of life by building classroom communities where individuals pursue their own personal goals while remaining respectful of the goals of others and tempering their actions through considering the consequences of those actions upon other members of the community. By participating in the establishment of learning communities, teachers and students can acquire an appreciation for the techniques of democratic decision-making.

• **Teaching cooperation.** Part of existing within a democratic learning community is learning how to cooperate. In cooperative learning situations, teachers structure small groups to work on projects. Hence, peace studies pupils need to acquire group skills. The Johnson brothers label the collaborative skills essential for learning cooperatively as being *forming, functioning, formulating,* and *fermenting.*[15] Teachers in peace education classes can teach students to become proficient in group processes by determining what skills students need, helping students get a clear understanding of specific group techniques, setting up practice situations, providing feedback and support, and making sure the techniques are used often enough so they become part of a student's behavior.

Forming skills are those skills that help organize a group: staying with a group, communicating clearly to others, and encouraging all members to participate. These skills make sure that group members are present and working with each other.

Functioning skills involve managing the group's efforts to complete tasks and maintain effective working relationships among members. They include getting a learning group started and stating the agenda for a particular session in such a way that all participants understand what is expected. Group members should understand and respect established time limits and should agree upon a set of operating procedures. They should be able to ask for help or be able to explain or clarify what is going on to others within the group. Members should be able to paraphrase others' contributions, energize the group with new ideas, and describe their own feelings when appropriate. Functioning skills assist the group in operating smoothly.

Formulation within a learning group structure builds deeper understanding of the material being studied by summarizing what has been discussed, checking other people's contributions for accuracy, seeking elaboration from others, and making explicit the reasoning processes used to support certain conclusions. Sometimes at this stage a group may have to present its findings to others—in which case the group would have to decide how best to communicate its conclusions. Such reformulation of the material can have important effects on the quality of reasoning and retention.

Fermenting implies a higher level analysis of what the group has accomplished. At this stage, group members challenge other points of view. Academic controversies arise which cause members to reexamine the material, to assemble rationales for their conclusions, or to argue for alternative positions. This involves the ability to criticize ideas and not people, to integrate a variety of different points of view into a single position, to expand upon other findings by group members, to probe for deeper understandings, to generate further answers to difficult questions, and to test reality by checking out the group's conclusions. These skills allow a group to reach high-level conclusions that demand considerable intellectual rigor and debate.

Learning these collaborative skills is a lifelong task. Although people may be familiar with one or the other of them, a person's ability to perform these skills can always be improved in new situations. A key component of being able to work cooperatively with others is the ability to manage conflicts. To achieve a more creative resolution of conflict, people have to improve their communication skills within group settings. Classrooms provide an ideal environment for testing out new techniques in conflict resolution. Peace educators can help students learn conflict resolution skills by setting up simulations and psychodramas, and role-playing different conflict situations. Structured role-playing allows participants to experience conflict directly and learn from others who evaluate their performance. These skills can be used with families, churches, community groups, and at work. Ashley Montague has extolled the value of cooperation to human communities:

> It must never be forgotten that society is fundamentally, essentially, and in all ways a cooperative enterprise, an enterprise designed to keep men in touch with one another. Without the cooperation of its members, society cannot survive, and the society of man has survived because the cooperativeness of its members made survival possible — it was not an advantageous individual here and there who did so, but the group.[16]

Cooperative learning provides tremendous advantages for peace education students. Research shows that cooperative learning environments promote higher achievement levels among students and provide important levels of peer support unavailable in either individualistic or competitive learning environments.[17] Students also can acquire important emotive gains from cooperative classrooms. They tend to know their peers better, and the liking for each other they generate from working together increases their motivation to learn. In small group settings, students encourage each other to achieve. Cooperative learning situations, based on positive interdependence among group members, teach individuals to care for other group members and provide important survival skills that help foster good working relationships throughout their lives.

• **Developing moral sensitivity.** The basis of morality is sensitivity and care for other human beings. Democratic classrooms provide good training for developing a moral disposition, because students get to know each other and they rely on each other to correctly complete their tasks. In a cooperative learning situation, it's hard for one pupil to ignore another because they depend on each other to successfully complete group assignments. Heterogenous groups give students experience with diversity and help them learn to acknowledge viewpoints different from theirs. Cooperative goal structures promote appreciation of ethnic and cultural differences, because heterogeneity provides different perspectives which improve the functioning of a problem-solving group. Through the shared responsibility that takes place in group learning situations, every member's contributions are realized and valued in helping the group reach its goals. When peace educators involve students in group projects, students can learn to make choices with a view of what is good for both themselves and the group. Developing feelings of responsibility for others in learning can become the basis of moral thinking. Similarly, in real life, good citizenship involves working with others to incorporate their wishes and interests in setting policy and making decisions.

By confronting the real-life situations which cause and perpetuate violence in human communities, peace education allows in-depth study of social problems and the values that relate to those problems. Peace educators should pose problems of war and peace as moral dilemmas, allowing students to research the complex positions that support such decisions as the dropping of the first atomic bomb, the bombing of Dresden, the escalation of the arms race, etc. Examination of such dilemmas promotes moral reasoning precisely because the nature of these issues is so complex that they don't provide easy or pat solutions. To understand their complexity fully requires delving deeply into human nature and the type of social organizations that support militarism.

Carol Gilligan, in her book *In a Different Voice,* has noted three stages of individual moral development.[18] The first stage is oriented toward individual survival. At this stage, morality is seen in terms of self-centered responses to sanctions imposed by society. People grow out of this stage as they move from selfishness to responsibility with an increased attachment to others. The second stage involves increased social participation, which develops a morality based more on shared norms and expectations, manifested as an increased capacity for caring. The highest stage in Gilligan's schema is the morality of nonviolence, where care becomes a universal obligation. Nonviolence, the injunction against all hurting, is elevated to a position governing all moral judgment and action. Peace educators are perhaps best prepared to foster this kind of moral development in their classrooms because of their understanding of nonviolence. They can promote nonviolent behaviors by setting up classrooms that are respectful of all members' interests, concerns and needs. They can use affective group techniques that allow learners to practice nonviolence and help students become more moral by confronting their own commitment to violence. It goes without saying that by running a nonviolent classroom, teachers will be modeling important moral behaviors for their students.

Peace education has at its core deeply moral considerations. Peace studies serves the cause of life at both physical and spiritual levels, promotes the preservation of life, and advocates the sacredness of all forms of life against violence and injustice. Students in peace studies classes think systematically about controversial social issues and rethink their positions on important social, ethical, and legal questions by identifying key aspects of violent behavior, taking positions on those issues, exploring different stances and patterns of argumentation, refining and qualifying their position, and testing factual assumptions. Peace educators, in a rigorous intellectual climate where all points of view are respected and issues are thoroughly explored, can use a dialectical style to question students' assumptions. Such an approach to the classroom does not teach that all in the world is wonderful; nor does it gloss over the misfortunes of others. It does not teach selfish individualism where the goal of life is to get ahead, but rather poses a world beset by serious problems that require the cooperative efforts of people working together to find solutions.

Paul Goodman complained about the moral indifference of American people:

> It is appalling how few people regard themselves as citizens, as society-makers, in this existential sense. Rather, people seem to take society as a pre-established machinery of institutions and authorities, and they take themselves as I don't know what, some kind of individuals "in" society, whatever that means. Such a view is dangerous because it must result in a few people being society makers and exercising power over the rest.[19]

Peace educators can instruct students to exert influence in public affairs by teaching them how to be competent citizens so they can communicate effectively in spoken and written language, collect and interpret information on problems of public concern, describe political-legal decision-making practices, justify personal decisions on controversial public issues, and implement strategies for action to promote principles of justice and democracy. Through internships and other community-based activities, students can test out what they learn in a classroom to gain a better understanding of the political processes through which concerned citizens can express their moral impulses.

• **Promoting critical thinking.** Hannah Arendt once wrote, "Thinking is the urgent work of a species that has responsibility for its survival."[20] It could be argued that the problems of war that threaten human existence have reached their current crisis level precisely because certain human beings, mainly those who hold power, are not thinking straight. For example, what possible event or cause could justify blowing up the whole planet through the massive use of nuclear weapons?

Educators have for a long time supported the development of critical thinking skills in the classroom. Reflective thinking, divergent thinking, reasoning, inferential skills, or analytic thinking can be promoted by giving students problems to think through. In critical thinking, there is an enormous difference between the technical problems dealt with in mathematics, science, or engineering, and the human-social problems dealt with in reasoning about human behavior. Solutions to technical problems can be determined in self-contained logical realms. In contrast, real-life problems are rarely settled in a rational manner because of opposing points of view, contradictory lines of reasoning, the realities of power, and value-laden assumptions. Because of this ambiguity that exists in the real world, the type of critical thinking promoted in peace education classes must be dialectical, where students are encouraged to reason with other people's ideas and think through belief systems, moving back and forth between different points of view. The distinguished American anthropologist William Sumner described well the kind of developed critical thinking faculty that should be encouraged in peace education classes:

> The critical habit of thought, if usual in a society, will pervade all its mores, because it is a way of taking up the problems of life. People educated in it cannot be stampeded by stump orators and are never deceived by dithyrambic oratory. They are slow to believe. They can hold things as possible or probable in all degrees, without certainty and without pain. They can wait for evidence and weigh evidence, uninfluenced by the emphasis and confidence with which assertions are made on one side or the other. They can resist appeals to their dearest prejudices and all kinds of cajolery. Education in the critical faculty is the only education of which it can be truly said that it makes good citizens.[21]

Participants in peace education classes must be encouraged to evaluate current policies of their governments, their own belief systems, and their action or inaction in relation to injustice. The skills for doing this can be taught through social inquiry, a process which involves the following steps: (1) present and clarify a puzzling situation, (2) develop hypotheses from which to explore the problem, (3) define hypotheses, (4) explore assumptions, implications and logical validity of hypotheses, (5) gather facts and evidence to support hypotheses, (6) form solutions. In this model,[22] the teacher helps move students from stage to stage by sharpening discussion, by focusing student questions and interests, and by providing advice. Teachers can provide resources and access to expert opinions when required. When handled successfully, this way of conducting peace education classes helps people negotiate and come to grips with different values that provide the basis for conflicts. By developing hypotheses, students get to test the consequences of their own value judgments.

In everyday life, peace education students will talk to people who look at events in a variety of ways. Their parents and peers will often see situations differently from them, and students will be frustrated at their inability to come to terms with these conflicts and dilemmas. In order to learn how to deal with such situations, they can in class construct points of view, place ideas in a logical relationship and listen to someone else's point of view — how another person organizes his or her ideas, and not dismiss those views as blind, irrational prejudices. Edward DeBono, a professor from Cambridge, England, who has promoted cognitive thinking skills, says that teachers interested in teaching such skills need to promote two distinct aspects of perception: breadth and change.[23] Breadth implies looking widely and more deeply at a given situation, trying to create a perceptual map that includes all pertinent factors. Change implies trying to see things in a different way to shed light onto some problem. Such an approach broadens a person's ability to see things in more complex ways and increases students' abilities to solve problems creatively.

Students in peace studies classes are attempting to understand one of the most vexing problems confronting human beings — the use of violence. Teachers in these classes help students understand that problem solving is not a purely cognitive process. Successful problem solving involves feelings, intuitions and hunches. In learning how to be a problem solver, a student needs to recognize his or her own feelings, tune in on his or her intuitions, and follow up on hunches in ways that either confirm or deny them. The affective side of human behavior, therefore, plays an important role in helping people solve problems. Furthermore, effective problem solving takes place in groups. Problem solving is an inherently cooperative process in which several individuals get together to accomplish shared goals. Thus, a teacher's attempt to create a democratic classroom can help provide the basis for effective problem-solving.

• **Promoting self-esteem.** Peace education hopes to overcome powerlessness so people can address problems created by violence. Each individual experiences a complex series of events within family and environment which determines his or her own self-concept, mental health, leadership ability, and interpersonal skills. Research shows that certain skills and attributes contribute to the creation of altruistic individuals who have the capacity to change the world. The experiences that help individuals realize their own power are successful past experiences with problem solving; the ability to cope with stress; feelings of optimism about society; confidence in self; feelings of responsibility for the well-being of others; experience of emotional warmth; and reward for helping behavior.

At the heart of peace pedagogy lies the interpretation of our lived experiences:

The first point is what everybody would assume will be included in a peace education program: analysis of our present, real world, describing its basic facts to the extent they are relevant for peace problems.[24]

People experience in their daily lives feelings of fear that make them feel powerless. Sharing these feelings in peace education classes helps validate their perceptions and can build strength as learners realize these problems aren't unique to themselves. Others may feel the same way. Sharing these feelings can become the basis for action to resolve the feelings of inadequacy that arise from violence in people's lives.

In a democratic classroom everybody's opinion is valued. Building class lessons around student experiences of peace and violence helps involve students in the lesson and teaches them to value their experiences. By examining the social reality of people's lives, students can name and understand a world that through violence creates so much misery. Thus, in peace education classes, teachers establish a continuous process of questioning, challenging, acting, and reflecting upon behaviors conducive to peace. Such examination of daily experience will help students articulate and commit themselves to an ethical stance in the world that should heighten their own self-esteem and sense of what they can accomplish in the world.

Setting up a classroom according to Montessori principles implies letting learners explore at their own pace what they want to learn. Dr. Montessori believed that human beings have a fundamental desire to work, that it is instinctual for the human species to produce things through work and receive feelings of well-being from productive activity. Accomplishing tasks well helps students increase their self-esteem; therefore, teachers in peace education classes should provide students with concrete tasks they can accomplish that will reward initiative and creativity. Research on cooperative classrooms indicates that students in democratic environments take greater risks, which helps prepare them to be peacemakers.[25]

Positive self-esteem comes from action. Peace education students need to try out in practical situations their hunches and ideas about how to bring peace to the world.

Self esteem is derived from significant others and from some kind of achievement. Although the significant others are primarily parents, teachers, and respected others, students who have been engaged in service programs consistently report how much the experience has helped their self esteem.[26]

Translating their thoughts about peace into action will help students gain a more realistic understanding of the nature of violence in this world. This can be done through field placement and supervised internships where students can experience the daily reality of working to make the world more peaceful. Although some of these field experiences can be frustrating, with group support and proper supervision, students can gain insights into their own behavior and learn realistically about their own strengths and weaknesses as peacemakers.

Affirmation is essential to nurturing a sense of competence and high self-esteem. Unfortunately, most students live in a "put-down" culture where sarcasm and downgrading are common, even as signs of affection. With so much negative reinforcement, it is easier to give up and accept others' judgment than to struggle both against criticism and against the difficulty of learning new things. Affirmation builds confidence. It comes from ongoing feedback about human behavior. Hearing that we are doing well encourages us to continue to do so. Teachers should use affirmation activities that will help students feel they are liked and appreciated.[27] Being comfortable with and believing in affirmation and thinking clearly about each individual in the group are key elements in establishing an affirming atmosphere.

Other things that teachers can do to promote self-esteem in their classes include peer tutoring, advising, and counseling. When students help each other learn, their own knowledge of subject matter increases, as do their feelings of competence. In some peace studies programs at the university level, students serve as peer counselors, helping other students make decisions about what courses to take and helping them search for what type of career might best fit their interests. Faculty are often too busy to spend large amounts of time counseling students full of doubts about their future. Peer counseling can fill an important gap in peace studies programs, providing students with affective support in dealing with a frightening and confusing world.

For many teachers, daily disputes in the classroom are the most pressing challenge to their conflict management skills. Teaching students the techniques of nonviolent problem-solving will give them the opportunity to take responsibility for their own conduct. Teachers who have used cooperative skills that involve students in classroom management have discovered a reduction in inappropriate, nonresponsive and obstructive behavior on the part of students.[28] In some schools, such as the Open School in St. Paul, Minnesota, an advisory board of students and faculty determine school governance procedures. Working closely with faculty helps students' self-esteem by giving them actual roles in decision-making with authorities. Student participation in governance builds democratic classes and schools, while it helps students acquire a real taste for the problems and challenges of working cooperatively with others. The influence of students upon each other results in more peer encouragement for achievement and greater attention to classroom tasks which students themselves have had a chance to develop. Cooperative use of students, where classroom management is shared, releases pressures on teachers to motivate, counsel, and discipline all students.

Principals and school administrators can contribute to the achievement of democratic behavior in schools by making decisions regarding instruction and appropriate school direction in consultation with other staff members and students. Principals can model the democratic behavior they are seeking to foster, and they can make clear to all people in a school building their plans for democratic governance. They can promote involvement in school problems and provide an awareness of areas for shared concern. Supervisors and administrators can also provide resources such as in-service sessions on cooperative learning activities, summer salaries for staff to revise curriculum to include peace and justice activities, praise for teachers' activities to promote cooperative learning, and the opportunity for teachers to visit other teachers' classrooms to learn more about relevant teaching techniques. They can also help establish professional support groups for teachers interested in peace education. Through activities such as these, principals and school administrators can help establish a school climate that will reinforce the learning of peaceful behavior.

Large schools tend to be impersonal and alienating environments, where teachers work according to a rigid schedule and students are submitted to impersonal routines. In recent times, many educators have broken out of these huge plants and have set up alternative schools which foster more of an atmosphere of cooperation and experimentation. The Cluster School in Cambridge, Massachusetts, is an example of one such alternative high school. At this school, students and teachers have instituted a community meeting as a governing body where rules and policies are set for the school. No major decisions are made without consulting the whole school community. At first, staff members chaired meetings, but after time, students learned the skills, and they now chair the community meetings. Each meeting's agenda is circulated in advance, and all significant issues are discussed in advance in groups of not more than twelve. In this way students are personally involved in issues and a sense of community is developed.

Setting up classrooms, governing schools, clarifying issues, taking leadership roles, and making decisions help students learn how to participate within democratic societies. These learnings all become part of a person's behavioral disposition, so that regardless of how a person may feel about a particualr war or peace issue, that person would be committed to a democratic process to resolve the problems of violence. Students raised in this manner can help make the world more peaceful as they become adults and transfer these learnings into their families, workplaces, neighborhoods, and community organizations. These skills are not easily taught and must be reinforced to become a part of a person's behavioral repertoire. Approaching peace education by focusing on teaching methods will not bring about a sudden revolution where a violent world is instantly transformed into a peaceful kingdom. Rather, it might imply a gradual evolution where citizens who deeply value democratic traditions will work to see that they are maintained in their families, in their workplaces, and in their countries. Adoption of democratic procedures will bring about a respect for diversity, the value of each individual, and the general well-being of communities and nations. With such values, political actors might start promoting peaceful and respectful behavior of others, rather than reinforcing the current world system based on competition, greed, and violence to pursue profit and gain.

8. Developmental Issues

The individual takes part in the course of the development of mankind at the same time as he pursues his own path in life.

Sigmund Freud, *Civilization and Its Discontent*

Peace educators confront the difficult question of what it means for individuals to grow up in a world threatened by war and other forms of violence. How can individuals cope with the awesome threat of nuclear destruction and the threats of violence they confront in their daily lives? Older people are scared to leave their homes. Taxpayers are angered by huge outlays for national defense. Women fear sexual assault. Adults lovingly want to protect young children from harm, but vivid and disturbing images of violence threaten children's well-being and psychological health. Recent psychological studies have determined that expectations of violence and nuclear destruction are more widespread in children than many adults realize. Just because children may not appear to be outwardly anxious does not mean that they are unconcerned about being beaten up in their neighborhoods, lack fear about attacks in school, or are undisturbed by the nuclear threat. An American Psychiatric Association study reported in 1982 that 50 percent of high school pupils in the United States reported that the threat of nuclear war had affected their plans for the future.[1] A more recent study found that 58 percent of eleven- to nineteen-year-olds "worried" or were "very worried" about nuclear war.[2] Another study done on children in the United States and in the Soviet Union indicated that children in the United States begin to worry about nuclear war at approximately eight years of age and children in the U.S.S.R. at about seven.[3] Other studies have indicated that the majority of children in the advanced countries in the world fear nuclear annihilation.

The anxieties children feel about violence in their lives exert a malignant influence:

Most children are aware of the nuclear threat at a young age but, unlike adults, children cannot easily deny their fears. Psychiatrists say fear for the future can be especially crucial to the developmental stages where adolescents begin to picture themselves as they will be adults, where they

139

develop their "ego ideal." When their fears prevent or hinder this development, psychological maturity may be delayed or stunted. Youngsters may choose to live for the moment; they may be more prone to sensation seeking and less likely to make long term commitments. All of these results have important consequences for education.[4]

Psychologists researching the impact of the development of nuclear weapons upon the psyches of young people fear that some may develop a sense of themselves as helpless and incompetent. Children need to hold a vision of the future as relatively stable but their trust in adults can be undermined as they feel overwhelmed by fantasies of a world out of control where everything they hold dear may be obliterated. Children who have no faith in the future can replace things like acedemic effort, career planning, and family goals with a "live for today" attitude, manifested in many ways — including apathy, irresponsibility, promiscuity, alcohol and drug abuse, and turning to cults or fundamentalist beliefs to reconcile feelings that the world is doomed.

Erik Chivian, a staff psychiatrist in Cambridge, Massachusetts, has interviewed many people, young and old, in his "nuclear age" research for Educators for Social Responsibility.[5] His findings about young people's fears of nuclear war suggest that at the third grade (age eight) there is a marked sense of confusion, hopelessness and fear of abandonment. Children at this age are often troubled by nightmares involving destruction of their homes, the world around them, or their parents. By the fifth grade a young person has more information and may become obsessed by the medical consequences of war and violence. By adolescence young people begin to experience anger at the adult world and erect defenses which are expressed as indifference or defiance. Some of this anger turns into cynicism or gallows humor. (Punk culture expresses the despair that some youth feel about the violent nature of contemporary life.) In their teenage years choices between career, family, and college increase anxiety and further complicate reactions. At this point in life young adults may first experience *psychic numbing,* tuning out emotional feedback through immersion in family life, job, material gains, or other personal achievements. Instead of reacting to cognitive dissonance created by a clash between ideals and reality, teenagers often ignore global strife and instead concentrate on more immediate concerns. Some psychiatrists have even suggested that the spectacle of adult society "sitting back and doing nothing as we prepare to blow ourselves up"[6] increases young people's despair, their belief that nothing lasts and that therefore all is meaningless.

Research indicates that children are most reassured when adults attempt to do something about children's fears. Children have many different reactions to violence. Possessing a minimum of information, young people are likely to ask difficult questions of teachers, parents, and government leaders. Adults who respond to these questions in ways that respect human growth and maturation can reassure young people growing up in a violent world.

Human beings have needs and insecurities at different ages that can influence how they react when confronted by violence.

> Instead of simply condemning violence we should think very seriously about it from an early age on and all through life: about what causes violence in ourselves and in others; what could be done to prevent these causes from occurring, or from resulting in violent actions; how energy aroused by stimuli which evoke violent feelings could be channeled into constructive behavior.[7]

Being able to address people's concerns about violence requires that peace educators construct learning environments that reflect an understanding of how human beings grow and develop through the life cycle. People have different needs and insecurities at different ages that influence how they react to studying about violence. This chapter will first discuss different development theories and then point out salient points that need to be taken into account when constructing peace education programs for the family, for young children, for pre-teens, for adolescents, for college students, for adults, and for older citizens.

Theories of Growth and Development

An understanding of when to teach certain topics is established according to the way in which humans learn and develop. Individuals continually construct their notions of self and the world around them. They fine-tune their senses, sharpen their awareness, and develop cognitive, behavioral, social and psychological skills which alter their perceptions and provide the tools necessary for survival in a world of ever-increasing information and skyrocketing technology. Human development does not stop when a person leaves school. Role models influence choices about how to behave by providing alternative ways of responding to life situations. Individuals continue to change through emotional crises and physiological growth as they advance through the life cycle. Career choices, family planning, political involvement, and aging are a few of the developmental challenges all people face in their struggle for self-actualization. During critical periods of development it is essential for certain learning to take place in order for an ability to be acquired. Readiness to engage in specific learning tasks or acquire certain concepts refers to the point in time when an individual has matured sufficiently for specific learning to take place. Researchers agree that people develop at different rates and that development is both orderly and gradual.

The psychologist Abraham Maslow described a hierarchy of needs, where an individual first has to meet certain necessities like food, water, clothing, and shelter before that person can work for the betterment of others. Peace education has to consider these conflicting needs when constructing peace education programs. If a pupil lives in miserable circumstances, he or she may not be willing to focus on the arms race or violations of human rights — issues that seem very distant to someone who has to devote energy to find food and shelter. Maslow posits that all people strive for a state of self-fulfillment where they can improve the world, but teachers have to be sensitive to different needs before expecting students to be interested in making the world more peaceful.

Jean Piaget, a Swiss psychologist, constructed complex theories about cognitive, or knowledge-acquiring, development, by combining his broad knowledge of biology, philosophy, logic and psychology with observations of his children.[8] As a result of his observations he created a theory of cognitive development concentrating on internal processes and actions based upon the manner in which human beings make sense of the world. According to Piaget each person has a set of mental tools, or *schemata,* which can change either radically or slowly during the time from birth to maturity. As humans adapt to their environments, changes occur in attitude, values, and knowledge. These changes are determined by maturation, activity, or social experience. Further research in the intellectual development of humans indicates that at different stages of growth a person has a characteristic way of viewing the world and explaining it to her/himself. (See Table 3.)

Erik Erikson, a psychoanalyst interested in society's influence on the developing personality, developed theories stating that crises mark the stages of development indicating a turning point in psychosocial awareness.[9] Young children are concerned with achievement in school and with pleasing their parents. Peer relationships cause anxiety for many adolescents as they struggle to identify with or belong to a desired group. Adults in their twenties and thirties are typically torn between choosing self-actualization and isolation or a love relationship and intimacy. People in middle age strive to achieve competence and generativity, as opposed to self-absorption. Senior citizens struggle with their fears and concerns of death. Providing information that helps answer the puzzling questions of human existence during various life crises can stimulate psychosocial growth. (See Table 4.)

Psychologist Lawrence Kohlberg defines three levels of moral development from childhood to adulthood based empirically on a study of 84 boys whose development he followed for a period of over 20 years.[10] Kohlberg's stages of moral judgment trace a progression from an egocentric understanding of fairness based on individual need, to a conception of fairness anchored in the shared conventions of societal agreement, and

Table 3. Piaget's Stages of Cognitive Development

Stage	Approximate Age	Characteristics
Sensorimotor	0–2	Begins to make use of imitation, memory and thought
		Explores environment through senses
Preoperational	2–7	Gradual language development
		Has difficulty seeing another person's viewpoint
Concrete Operational	7–11	Understands laws of conservation and reversibility
Formal Operational	11–15	Thinking becomes more scientific
		Able to use logic when solving abstract problems
		Develops concerns about social issues and identity

finally to a principled understanding of fairness that rests on the free-standing logic of equality and reciprocity. He terms these three views of morality *preconventional, conventional* and *postconventional* to reflect the expansion in moral understanding from an individual to a societal to a universal point of view. A key component in moving from one stage to another is the capacity to take the perspective of another person. In the preconventional stage individuals evaluate their actions only in terms of their effects on themselves and on no one else. Children move towards higher levels of moral reasoning when they come to grips with viewpoints different from theirs. (See Table 5.)

In an effort to address the repeated exclusion of women from critical theory-building studies of psychological research, Carol Gilligan conducted research which explored identity and moral development in females. In her book *A Different Voice,* she challenged Kohlberg by stating that moral judgments of women differ from those of men. Women grow up seeing the world as composed of relationships rather than of people standing alone, a world that coheres through human connections rather than through a system of rules. Men appear to have an increasing fascination with the legal elaborations of rules, and little boys tend to place the world in relation to themselves, as it defines their character.[11] Men and women may experience attachment and separation in different ways, and each sex may perceive a danger that the other does not see—men in connection, women in separation. Gilligan hypothesizes that this difference stems from

Table 4. Erikson's Stages of Personal and Social Development

Stage	Approximate Age	Needs
Trust *vs.* Mistrust	0–1	food, care, human contact
Automony *vs.* Doubt	1–2	self-control, goal-directed activity
Initiative *vs.* Guilt	2–6	confidence, support for completion of tasks
Industry *vs.* Inferiority	6–12	attention, conquer goals of school
Identity *vs.* Role Diffusion	Adolescence	competence, define continuity of life Who am I?
Intimacy *vs.* Isolation	Young adulthood	establish quality relationships
Generativity *vs.* Self-absorption	Young and middle adulthood	productivity, notion of maintaining world
Integrity *vs.* Despair	Late adulthood	acceptance of life cycle

infancy. Since women are usually the primary caregivers, little girls form their identity through attachment to the mother. Little boys form their identity through separation from mother. She also suggests that women base their moral decisions on networks of caring and a sense of being responsible to the world, in contrast to men, who often base their moral behavior on abstract principles or laws.

Parenting for Peace

Educators can and should teach peace to students of all ages. The role of educators in creating peaceful children and adults, however, is limited by children's experiences outside the classroom, most specifically in their homes. Parents play a key role in raising peaceful children. Peace education, to be effective, begins in the home, where children first develop a sense of trust, learn about their own capacities, and acquire social skills.

> Probably in the childhood of every activist peacemaker there were one or many experiences of being trusted and attended to by an adult. Such experiences build up a reservoir of competence and inner security that makes it possible to take risks on behalf of what one believes.[12]

Table 5. Kohlberg's Stages of Moral Reasoning

Stage	Approximate Age	Characteristics
Preconventional	until age 5 or 6	Judgements based on own needs and perceptions and on the physical power of the rule makers
Conventional	until adolescence	Judgement based on social expectations and the belief that one must be loyal to one's family, group, or nation, and maintain the social order
Postconventional	young adulthood (not all people reach this state)	Judgement based on principles that go beyond specific laws or the authority of the people who make the laws

If children experience the possibility of peace through nonviolent conflict resolution at the family level, their faith in the possibility for peace and willingness to work for it at different levels grows.[13] Young people must be hopeful. They need assurance from their parents that the world will be all right. They need to learn through experience that change is possible and that they can help bring about change. Parents can teach their children methods of survival and strategies for change in a society filled with injustice and exploitation. Parents need to articulate a consistent set of humanistic values and then struggle to live by them as they transmit them through social modeling.[14]

Parents need to keep informed so they can provide accurate information to their children about news events dealing with terrorism, war, and violence. Parents should not force discussions of violent events upon young children but should rather listen carefully to children's fears and respond in a sensitive manner to their children's anxieties about violence in the world. Parents may not always have answers for why certain violent events occur, but responding to children's emotional fears can help allay some of the deep-seated concerns young people have about violence.

Educators for Social Responsibility offers a suggestion to families interested in improving family communication:

> One structure which some families have established to facilitate communication among its members is the family meeting. It is a time set aside regularly each week, or called when necessary, when family members come together to discuss plans, problems and misunderstandings. It is a place for airing differences, for hearing things out. It is also a place to express appreciation and acknowledge jobs done well.[15]

Such meetings help teach children cooperation and help them learn nonviolent ways to resolve conflict. Even for parents who can find the time to construct a cooperative system at home, though, it becomes difficult to maintain this structure within the social context of life in the 1980s. While living in an era of exploitation and dominance, parents who want to raise peaceful children can provide peaceful models by never using personal violence, e.g. spanking, but rather by taking the time to explain the natural consequences of certain actions. Spanking teaches children to use physical violence to resolve disagreements. Because conflict is an inevitable part of life, children need to learn in their families how to take other people's feelings into account in order to deal constructively with conflict. Adults should help young people talk out conflict, rather than allowing or encouraging such behaviors as kicking, biting, or hitting.

"Violence is nurtured by excessive competition. Nonviolence, on the other hand, springs from cooperation."[16] By sharing family chores, involving children in adult activities, playing group games and reading to each other, parents can teach important skills about peaceful living, while allowing each family member to experience each other as individuals in relation to the family. In promoting children's self-esteem and relating to the needs and interests of all family members, parents help children develop as caring persons, which will help children to deal with life's changing situations. They should neither encourage children to abandon hard tasks nor insist that children "do things right." Children in their early years can learn a sense of accomplishment by cooking, shopping, and contributing to the daily maintenance of family life.

Parents can play an important role in developing skills and techniques to manage conflict nonviolently. They can model caring and help their children talk through violent situations to learn alternative behaviors and nonviolent responses to events in children's lives. Parents can show their children that being concerned about others is a natural extension of concern about themselves. Adults hoping to promote a more peaceful world should impart to children the social considerations of courtesy, generosity, and fairness even to people with whom they disagree. Parents, by supporting children even though they disagree with them, can teach children that they can change their minds without loss of respect or love. Parents should remain open to their children in spite of fundamental disagreements.

Children who grow up to become active in nonviolent social change come from homes where there is an emotional closeness. They have successful experiences with problem-solving, the ability to cope with stress, feelings of optimism about society, confidence in themselves, and feelings of responsibility for the well-being of others. Warm home relationships, with intellectual stimulation and a knowledge of current events, provide experiences that enable children to face the world with confidence.

There are many obstacles to creating an affirmative, cooperative and accepting family environment. It takes time for problem-solving and shared decision-making with children so that everyone in the family learns communication skills. The payoffs for creating such a family system are considerable: Greater harmony, motivation, efficiency, children and parents sharing life together, happiness, communication, discovery of one's worth and potential. "People's potential can only be realized to its fullest when all human beings are confident of thei worth to the society in which they live."[17]

Childhood

Peace educators can best meet the needs of all children, not by focusing on the horrors of violence, but by including ways of resolving disputes in the broader context of values, skills, and classroom practices. A peace education curriculum should help children develop a sense of mastery and control, teaching problem-solving skills and an appreciation of cultural diversity. Children's fears about their safety in the world can be counteracted by a curriculum which stresses cooperation and personal efficacy.

An understanding of Piaget's work helps teachers decide when and how to present war and peace concepts to children. Infants and toddlers tend to think in concrete terms limited to the here and now. Their thought is characterized by inability to anticipate the future, and the lack of ability to consider events which might be happening outside the immediate environment. Infants are also egocentric. They have an awareness of self which doesn't recognize the different perspectives, needs, and interests of others.

Erikson's theory of personal/social development defines the crisis of early childhood as initiative versus guilt. The child-part of each person tries new things and tests new powers, while the part of the personality struggling to become adult constantly evaluates motives and actions. Young children have a rigid consciousness or superego, an internalized set of rules from family and environment about expected behavior that enables them to distinguish between right and wrong.

The years from two to six seem to harbor the greatest number of new fears, such as fears of being lost, bitten or injured. Children are exposed to frightening images on television, in books and in their own lives. Initial experiences with war movies can terrify children. Their wild imaginations worry about being attacked by ferocious animals, being in the dark, losing their parents, being bombed, being abandoned, or going up to high places.[18] Children are most successful when they find practical ways to deal with their own fears. Parents, teachers and siblings can instill fear in young children by modeling negative reactions to frightening situations, or they can provide positive role models by providing accurate information, encouragement, and helping children think through creative responses.

Because young children are particularly vulnerable to the process of identification, the example of peaceful behavior established by teachers, parents, and other significant role models can play an important role in helping then develop as peaceful people. A child will not only imitate the actions of another person but will acquire the person's characteristics.[19] Children believe that they share particular physical or psychological attributes with the model; they experience vicarious emotions similar to those the model is feeling; they want to be like the model; and they behave like the model and adopt the model's opinions and mannerisms. Behaviors indicative of this period include hero-worship.

Teachers and parents choose songs, fables, films, etc., to expose a child to peacemakers, real or imagined, in an effort to counterbalance the macho hero-images of TV and history books. Strong men using weapons to kill other people often become the worshipped role models of youth exposed to Western culture. Thoughtful consideration of the messages implied in children's books can counterbalance "a hidden curriculum" of competition, aggression, or violence which children get from television, movies, peers, schools, etc.

Early childhood teachers should use props and visual aids, because the manipulation of concrete materials helps children express ideas and seek solutions for their concerns. Teachers in child care centers and kindergartens should not expect pupils at this age to see the world from another person's viewpoint and therefore should avoid social studies lessons about worlds far removed. Teachers can offer children choices about what to do in the early childhood classroom. At first, this may be difficult for young children who tend to think of one thing at a time and cannot think ahead about the implications of a choice, but starting with simple choices between two or three options will help children learn to predict the consequences of their actions.

When considering peace studies appropriate to this age group, educators, psychologists and psychiatrists stress the importance of finding out what children already know and making sure they have correct information.[20] Children four to six years of age may be scared about what they hear on the news or read in comic books or watch on cartoons, while not really comprehending it fully. These young people need to be reassured that adults care about the future and are involved in making the world safe. They should not be misinformed, but at this age they cannot understand the magnitude of such things as the nuclear dilemma. Behavioral scientists, however, are no longer surprised that children as young as five and six fear that a nuclear war is likely.[21] Teachers working with pupils at this age should not emphasize the horrible consequences of war. Children need reassurance from adults and can't cope with visions of a doom-filled world out of control.

The vulnerability of children to social modeling suggests that the most appropriate method to integrate peace education in elementary school would be to create a cooperative, affirmative environment in which children can appreciate who they are and what they are capable of doing. Teachers who display consistent treatment of all children and accept divergent thought or styles of life plant seeds of peaceful, cooperative living, the ability to love oneself and the capacity to accept other people despite their differences. Children in their early school years need to accept diversity by learning about different cultures and figuring out their own backgrounds. They should discuss stereotyping and name-calling. Why are people different? Meeting children from different countries can teach them that people throughout the world have needs similar to theirs, and that it's all right to be different.

An awareness and appreciation of the diversity of individual and collective values the world over can lead to nonviolent resolution of conflict. Children can develop empathy with others by becoming aware of similarities and differences of other people. If they realize that cultures are neither superior nor inferior, they may be inclined to view discussion and dialogue as better means of resolving conflict that the use of force or withdrawal. Developing an understanding of the interdependence of people the world over will help promote the value of cooperation as a means of human welfare, sharing with others the common resources of planet Earth. Knowledge of how people depend upon each other for their basic needs may foster the development of a sense of community and cooperation on a global basis.

Children entering the concrete operational level of thinking may still have difficulty seeing another person's point of view, but diminishing egocentrism enhances their ability to make moral judgements that take into account the interests of others. At about the age of six, children start to consider more that one aspect of a situation when drawing conclusions. The middle childhood years are characterized by a unilateral respect for authority which leads to feelings of obligation to conform to adult standards and obey the rules. By the time a child reaches the age of eight or nine, s/he will begin to leave a rigid moral stage and enter into a morality of cooperation. A mutual respect for authority and peers allows the child to value his or her own opinion and abilities more highly and to judge people more realistically. The child's view of punishment also changes. Where once s/he would favor severe, expiatory punishment, the young person will instead prefer milder, reciprocal punishment that leads to restitution of the victim and helps the culprit recognize why an act was wrong. Perceptions of rules also change during this time from a belief that rules must be obeyed because they are sacred or unilateral to the recognition that rules were made by people and can be changed. Children who are going to be successful change agents need to consider themselves just as capable of changing rules as anyone else. This would be an ideal time to discuss international institutions, world order, cultural differences, civil rights, and human rights. A discussion of individual attitudes and beliefs that present different points of view will help promote critical thinking.

Children in their middle childhood years can benefit from values clarification exercises that help analyze the values that underlie beliefs and actions. Certain skills will help them examine values: (1) Seeking alternatives when faced with a choice; (2) looking ahead to probable consequences before choosing; (3) making choices on one's own, without depending on others; (4) being aware of one's own preferences and valuations; (5) being willing to affirm one's choices and preferences publicly; (6) acting in ways that are consistent with choices and preferences; and (7) acting those ways repeatedly, with a pattern to one's life.[22] These skills help people understand the differences between the values people hold and the values they actually live by. Values clarification exercises can help children aged eight to ten express their changing attitudes and establish their beliefs about peace and justice issues.

By the age of eleven most children have acquired conceptual tools which enable them to organize their environment meaningfully and to make a distinction between their society and other societies. "Children from nine to twelve are often extremely interested in facts. They are collectors of facts, always eager to add to their store."[23] This is the ideal time in life to introduce students to the interdependence of the global community. Research studies done on this age of childhood indicate that children of about ten years of age are receptive to foreign people and cultures but that this open-mindedness declines after this time, so that by fourteen years of age there is a tendency to stereotype people from different cultures.[24] Discussions of import and export items, films of other cultures, and literature from different countries will further expand the child's growing awareness of the world. Middle school students are sensitive to peer pressure and begin to look critically at adults. Teachers can build a more sophisticated understanding of the world by bringing in speakers to present different points of view. At this age children can develop sensitive attitudes towards other people. Before and after the ages of seven to fourteen children's attitudes are much more rigid. Adults working with children at this age have to think about how to make them aware of the problems that the world faces:

> Young children need help in understanding the complexity of the world order so that they may have a basis for reacting intelligently to its problems as they grow older.[25]

As students enter their teenage years they don't want to be told what to think, but want to make up their own minds. At this point they also are developing a capacity for a long-term future orientation and for a wider world view. This is the beginning of the age of idealism. Teachers can complement this interest by getting students to think about the kind of world they want to inhabit. Pupils in the middle school years are ambitious and optimistic. It is important for children at this age to adopt caring values which will help them devote their lives to humanitarian causes. Teachers can stress the contributions of people like Dr. Martin Luther King, Jr., or Dorothy Day, who dedicated their lives to peace and justice. If they acquire at this age an orientation towards making the world better for others, they have the potential to mature into adults deeply concerned about peace and justice.

Adolescence

Puberty marks the onset of adolescence. Erik Erikson identified adolescense as a crisis of identity versus role confusion.[26] Identity confusion may result in impulsive or poorly thought-out actions. The young person may resort to regression into childishness to avoid resolving conflicts. During this period some adolescents may form cliques or foster an intolerance to divergent lifestyles, defenses against identity confusion. Teenagers from cultural or racial minority groups are thrust into a particularly intense identity crisis. They have to deal with the same life changes as other teens, but they have other problems caused by their minority status.

Development during this time is uneven. The rate of growth doubles for about two years, and sexual maturation begins. Teenagers are concerned with how they appear to others, as well as being concerned about their identity, as they search for continuity. In spite of all the difficulties during this period in life, Otto and Healy have listed some personality resources and strengths of adolescence. They are: (1) considerable energy or drive and vitality; (2) a real concern for the future of the United States and the world (idealism); (3) exercising their ability to question contemporary values, philosophies, ideologies and institutions; (4) heightened sensory awareness and perceptibility; (5) courage; and (6) feelings of independence.[27]

Peace educators can take advantage of the developing concerns about social issues manifested during adolescence. An examination of existing social, political and economic systems would be appropriate at this age. Considerations of alternative societies and future worlds are exercises which can both enhance the students' ability to accept differing lifestyles and provide hope for the future which is necessary for the healthy personality development of human beings. According to Robert Jay Lifton, author of *The Broken Connection,* by the time that a child today reaches thirteen, s/he has been struggling for some time to cope with the issue of mass destruction.[28] His or her appetite for understanding and intuitive grasps of fundamental ethical and moral dilemmas may never be as profound as during early adolescence. The realization of the importance these teens will have in the creation of the future can facilitate an appreciation for the topics of peace education. "Many people believe that adolescents' normal growth depends on a social structure which grants young people a place in society."[29]

To help teenagers' struggle to establish their identities, peace educators should suggest that students keep a journal to express fears, to clarify values, and to provide a forum for personal issues that can't be shared comfortably with parents or in a public setting such as a classroom. People at this age are developing complex peer relations and need acceptance. Teachers should set a tone of tolerance for different points of view. Many high school pupils who already have well-established notions about the world need facts and information to form enlightened opinions about peace and justice issues and the complicated nature of international relations. As they enter adulthood, teenagers need both a sense of autonomy and authority that can be fostered by letting students plan activities and units. Students can be asked to define their concepts of strength or power. Teachers should assure students that they don't know all the answers, but rather are discussing issues in order to develop a broader understanding of them. This is a period of self-introspection and analysis. Teenagers should be encouraged to think about the way the world is and the way they would like it to be.

In school settings peace educators can create an atmosphere of empathy where students are encouraged to place themselves in other people's positions and see themselves through other people's eyes. They can promote positive self-images on the part of the learners, teaching self-confidence and an understanding that each person is responsible for his or her style of life. Students should learn both at home and in school that they have some responsibility for the world and that they can do something to influence their environment. In order to do this, parents and teachers of children at all levels have to set up learning environments where responsibility and independence are stimulated, where there is room for experiments with behavior and where cooperation is emphasized rather than competition. Adults in these environments should not attempt to preach values, but rather set an example by their own behavior of activities of peacemaking and nonviolence.

Young Adults

As teenagers graduate from high school they either enter the work force, join the ranks of the unemployed, enlist in the armed forces, or attend college. Those who acquire full-time jobs spend their time mastering the demands of work and establishing a network of supportive relationships. Those unable to find work who don't join the armed forces or attend college have to struggle to survive. The daily demands of finding food, shelter, clothing, and money consume these individuals so that they may have little energy for peace causes. Those who join the military probably will not be interested in the activities of the peace movement. Therefore, those early adults most likely to express interest in peace education are college students. Some college students who are working full-time to support themselves will have little time for peace activities. Others will have clear career goals in fields such as engineering that exclude electives not relating directly to their major. Other students will come from families, communities, and schools where they have received no introduction to the peace movement, and consequently may not actively seek peace education classes. In spite of these obstacles, college students can be very idealistic. They want to make a mark on the world and are often attracted to the idealistic nature of peace studies. This group of students may feel revulsion at huge arms expenditures which deny them financial aid. They will be concerned about conscription and military service, and some will be eager to understand better why their countries place such a strong emphasis on defense. Many youth who want to work for freedom and justice or desire careers in human service occupations soon discover the limited nature of these careers because their governments prefer to fund the military. These students, who tend to major in liberal arts, education, nursing, or social welfare, are the young adults most ripe for peace studies. They will be taking courses that raise questions about the nature of human societies, and their natural curiosities can be complemented by queries into the nature of violence. Their desire to make the world better will attract them to peace education courses, which have become on many college campuses the reservoir for students' idealism. Peace studies can allow young adults to acquire commitments to adopt careers oriented towards improving the world.

Adulthood

Adulthood is a time of growth, change, and continued development underscored by the realization of one's own mortality. Life experiences form patterns of behavior, which affect readiness to learn. Each adult goes through a series of developmental tasks that include selecting a mate, becoming competent, starting a family, managing a home, finding a congenial social group, and taking civic responsibility.[30]

Life crises are caused by periods of disequilibrium which signify the onset of a turning point. A decision must be made to either regress or progress into the next passage of life. The first turning point of adulthood occurs in the twenties, when individuals move out on their own and realize they are alone. No one can make them safe. Up until then, a person has had the family to rely on for strength and support. Some adults handle this by what Gail Sheehy refers to as the "Piggyback Principle," where they choose to merge with another human being and attack life as a duo.[31] Aspiring employees bond with mentors who help them work through the complex hierarchies of modern bureaucracies.

Once an adult has made a commitment to explore a certain facet of existence — college and on to a career, employment in hopes of substantial earnings, marriage in hopes of a family, whatever — the person will probably spend a good ten years engaged in this or related events. These are the years in which an individual "finds" him or herself. Ambitious individuals climb corporate ladders. The demands of finding and getting established in a career and building some kind of family will be all-consuming, with little time or energy to work for peace. Exceptions come from those students who, through the idealism of their youth, form a commitment to work for peace and justice in their careers by joining the Peace Corps or performing some kind of service in poor communities. Some will enter public life, support political candidates who desire to end the arms race, or may even run for office themselves. The vast majority of people in their twenties will be consumed with finding a niche for themselves in the social order.

The thirties are characterized as a time for developing competence. At this point an individual will refine the skills and knowledge needed to perform successfully the tasks taken on in the earlier period when individuals locate their place in the social order. At this point teachers become competent in running their classes and may be secure enough in their daily routines that they would be willing to take some risks by branching out to include peace and justice concepts in their lessons. Teachers who have earned a degree of respect within their schools can start exerting leadership to promote within a school setting awareness of peace and violence.

Usually in the late thirties or early forties individuals will start to question what they have accomplished thus far in their lives. Seemingly all at once, they will call into doubt the various positions they have reached. How happy am I in this marriage or profession? Do I want to be tied to this spouse or this boss for the rest of my life? What has seemed such a perfect life becomes confining, boring, questionable. By the time a person reaches the age of 38 or 39 s/he may be disillusioned by a series of jolts. As s/he works to fulfill his or her dreams, s/he becomes less of a dreamer.

A sexual panic is common in the forties, as individuals realize they are not the sensuous creatures they fancied themselves to be years ago. Women and men alike will experience trying times, which often result in switching sex roles. At this time in the mysterious passage leading to our second season we confront the sexually opposite side of our nature. Men may become more nurturing, and women more assertive to make their mark upon the world. At this point some adults become concerned about threats to the planet, choosing to devote their lives to the struggle for peace. According to Erikson generativity is the central stage of adult development, encompassing "man's relationship to his production as well as to his progeny."[32] Defining generativity as "the concern in establishing and guiding the next generation," Erikson centers adulthood on relationships and devotion to the activity of taking care of others and making sure there will be a secure future.[33] Daniel Levinson sees the ultimate tasks of adulthood as defining a life that brings self-fulfillment and a sense of meaning.[34] At this point some individuals make drastic life shifts to work on peace and justice issues. Some may decide that the "rat race" is not worth all the strain and drop out to join a peace group, dedicating their lives to bettering humanity. Teachers may at this point in their careers become alarmed about the threatening nature of the world and become involved in peace education.

Despite these tendencies, few adults are actively seeking to change the current direction of political and social institutions. Many feel that the problems of violence are too great and adopt material goals or hobbies that stimulate their interest. Through psychic numbing,[35] many resist working on the problems of war and peace. Because many adults have repressed their fears, they neither have the awareness nor the desire to act to change catastrophic situations. Human denial of the terrors of nuclear war makes it hard for adults to respond to the life-threatening situation created by the escalating arms race. Many adults ignore the complex problems of the world while living in a highly specialized, segmented society dominated by material concerns and individual needs. Very few points of contact are made with the larger world. Through "selective inattention" many people maintain peace of mind.

Adults must work to change the existing status quo if there is to be peace on earth. The responsibilities of educators to the adult community are to inform the population about the problems of violence; to acquaint people with the present system of government; to enhance their ability to participate in public life; and to provide hope by brainstorming alternatives which will promote nonviolent options.

Adults need information about a constantly changing world. Community education classes held in schools after hours, in churches, and in neighborhood centers can help provide information about public policy and help adults understand social reality. A 1984 survey of newspaper readers' interest notes a change in interest from local news to international news:

> "We've had international crises upon crises, inflation, recession, unemployment, and a growing concern about the country's ability to compete in foreign markets," Clark said. "People today are worried — about the real possibility of nuclear war, the economy, the environment."
>
> As a result there is an increased demand for more foreign and national news compared with that expressed in an earlier survey, Clark found. She said that over a 10 year period some years ago the desire was for domestic (local and national) news over foreign news by a 10-1 margin. The 1984

survey found that readers now want 60% domestic and 40% foreign news
in their papers.[36]

Adults need to communicate with others in order to clarify their
understanding of public events. Some adults set in their ways accept the
status quo. Because these adults resist change, peace educators have to
listen carefully to their concerns in order to introduce new concepts about
peace. Adults will resist learning things they fear or things that provoke
painful emotions. The skills of active listening and one-on-one communication can help overcome this resistance. No one can change another person.
A teacher's expertise lies in the ability to create an environment in which
another will be encouraged to discover and try new skills, knowledge, and
attitudes. One important goal in working with adults in peace education is
to get them to solve problems themselves and to understand that they can
become effective change agents. Peace educators working in adult communities need to develop tangible goals for making the world more peaceful
and introduce adult learners to organizations working on peace issues.
Since peer acceptance and involvement is an important part of the change
process, adults concerned about war and peace issues need to be introduced
to others who share their concerns. Together they can discuss what kind of
world they want to live in and leave to their children.

There are basically four steps to peace studies in adult education: (1)
examine the formation of attitudes towards peace, conflict, and justice; (2)
envision a peaceful and just world, because society cannot move in a direction until there is a goal; (3) define peace as a process involving all people
at the personal, familial, interpersonal, societal and global level; and (4)
discuss how we can be peacemakers at home, at work and in the community. Peace educators teaching adults can help citizens relearn patterns of
behavior that contribute to violence. Adults need to tell their own stories
about their own individual "journeys for justice," so they can share with
others experiences with violence and attempts to achieve peace. Such
discussions should be frank, allowing people to unearth frustrations and
painful moments that help form the psychological limits of an individual's
behavior. Each adult will have a complex set of reactions to specific situations based on past experiences and patterns of reinforcement. Men, particularly, are taught to be strong and courageous and to fight to protect their
honor, behavior that can get them in trouble if they strike out at ones they
love or alienate people at work. In close-knit affinity groups adults can examine how their patterns of behavior spur violent reactions. Such an understanding can become the basis for learning new behaviors, especially in
small learning groups where a sense of trust allows people to discuss experiments with nonviolence. Peace educators can focus on life crises and help
adults learn from them when they serve more as therapy group facilitators
than traditional educators providing information and facts about violence.

Since studies indicate that IQ performance increases at least until the mid-fifties, middle-agers are capable of learning new facts and skills. Creative productivity reaches a high point during middle age.[37] Middle-age individuals tend to be in good health, and some even experience financial security. During the middle years most people experience a change in time orientation. Instead of thinking in terms of the years they've already lived, suddenly they begin to think in terms of the time they have left.[38] Because many people desire to use their remaining years to create a better world for future generations, middle age is an ideal time to work for peace.

Like others in every age group, older people thrive by demonstrating their competence. Erikson terms this last stage of psychosocial development as ego integrity versus despair, where the challenge is to achieve an acceptance of life, without despair about how life has been spent. At this stage people review their lives and acquire satisfaction from how they have conducted their affairs. If a person does not gain a sense of satisfaction, that person may fear death.

As most people approach retirement, they can finally rest from concentrating on achieving their goals set by others and can concentrate on goals of their own choosing.[39] During this wonderful period of life individuals can pursue their lifelong passions. Some may be inclined to volunteer at peace and justice organizations. This generation can contribute to the peace movement in many ways. They have knowledge and skills to share with others. Retired people have extra time, and through the concern they show for future generations, can demonstrate their competence by becoming actively involved in peace education endeavors. Many people facing retirement have up to thirty years during which they can work to make the world safe for future generations. In their desire to leave a better world for their progeny, grandmothers and grandfathers can become an important force for peace. Their wisdom about the ways of violence and the struggle for peace can provide important leadership for efforts to make the world less violent.

Conclusion

Peace studies can be introduced at the primary level of schooling and can continue in an appropriate fashion throughout the course of an individual's life. Injustice is a fact of life that persists throughout the lifespan and can be approached in a wide variety of ways. Perhaps the most important place to address violent behavior is the home, where individuals first learn values and communication skills. The years when children form their ideals of the world and their relationships to other people present an ideal time to begin a humanistic socialization process to promote a consciousness of individual existence in relation to others.

Peace education rests on the assumption that the way to change social systems riddled by violence and committed to war is to change oneself. Until people change one by one they are not going to change by the thousands. Not even the most powerful leader of the most powerful nation in the world can order profound changes in individual beliefs and behaviors. In considering how to construct peace education programs in families, schools, and adult learning communities, it is crucial to understand the process of individual change so that peace educators can assess the readiness of their pupils to confront the terrifying topics that must be addressed in peace education classes. Individuals don't necessarily change in orderly, precise, rational, or direct manners. Often it takes a severe crisis to jolt an adult out of one belief system into another. Individuals regress to previous stages and need to develop higher levels of moral reasoning in order to appreciate the complexity of peace and justice issues. Peace educators can best become change agents by paying attention to the changes they themselves go through as they address the issues of war and peace and listening carefully to the concerns of others. Understanding the dignity and worth of humankind and feeling good about oneself can facilitate individuals striving for peace on the personal and social level.

9. Educational Issues

I want to express the utmost sympathy with the people who have to grapple with this problem (the invention of nuclear weapons) and in the strongest terms to urge you not to underestimate its difficulty.

J. Robert Oppenheimer

Peace educators encouraging healthy growth and development in children and adults have to overcome psychological barriers to learning about peace. Throughout the world the wholesale use of terror, weapons, and state policies that promote the use of force weakens people's faith in the possibilities for the future and thereby threatens the legitimacy of educational endeavors. The primary task of education for peace is, therefore, to reveal and tap all those energies and impulses that make possible the full human capacity for a meaningful and life-enhancing existence.

Peace educators have to help people overcome their cynicism about violence by challenging the impact of violence upon people's lives. Because of the terrifying nature of the threats of violence to human security, teaching about the problems of war and human violence raises deep emotions in both teachers and students. People trained in the ways of violence resist learning nonviolent alternatives. Peace education, by confronting commonly held assumptions about the violent state of reality, has to figure out how to reach people from a wide variety of backgrounds. Topics brought up in peace education classes present special considerations for peace educators.

The foremost educational issue confronting peace educators concerns the differing developmental needs of peace students (discussed in the previous chapter). In addition to designing age-appropriate curricula, peace educators should be sensitive to various psychological barriers that resist learning new information, the emotional aspects of peace studies, and the challenges of reaching different people.

Psychological Barriers

At the basis of the pedagogical relationship between teacher and students lie their own mental capacities—the various psychological histories that individuals bring to discussions of war and peace, and the skill of teachers to respond to those histories. In teaching about conflict peace educators have many psychological obstacles to overcome. All human beings desire security, and, as mentioned earlier in this book, different views of security influence how an individual will approach war and peace problems. These psychic and mental histories, which include ignorance of violence, resistance to learning about war, and fear of change—must be overcome if peace educators are to play a role in transforming violent behavior to peaceful action.

Discussions of war and violence can be extremely difficult. In countries like Northern Ireland where violence touches everybody's lives, peace education courses can tap deep feelings of grief. In other countries citizens are ignorant of the terrors of war. A major war has not been fought on United States soil since the Civil War. People in Europe, on the other hand, experienced the horror of both modern wars, and have a much more accurate sense of its terror. The catastrophe of atomic weapons occurred on Japanese soil, but millions of people in other countries have little knowledge about the awesome destructiveness of these weapons and are ignorant of the horrors of a nuclear holocaust. For many, the threat of war is intangible, and their psychic energies are taken up with more concrete issues of survival.

Furthermore, human beings have strong resistances to overcoming their ignorance of the horror of nuclear weapons and the awesome threats of war. People are incredulous that such threats exist. They don't want to accept the fact that these perils are a part of their conscious lives and resist knowing that something this terrible has been created:

> This second kind of bad news about the nuclear threat is that we created it ourselves, that it is the outgrowth of our own individual and collective fear and hostility, amplified by a technological, genocidal exuberance that is peculiar to the last four decades of the present century.[1]

Confronting the human commitment to violence forces us to look at the irrational and aggressive aspects of our own personalities. Many educators do not know how to deal with the dark side of the human psyche, but they should be prepared to delve into how people form their attitudes towards violence. This can be done in a trusting atmosphere where a teacher shares with students his or her own experiences with violence. This cannot be done quickly and requires teachers and students over time to develop trusting relationships with each other. The author of this book allows at least fifteen minutes at the beginning of each of his peace education classes to allow any member of the class to bring up concerns related to peace or violence. Those students constantly bring up events in their lives that provide fruitful discussions about deep-seated fears and insecurities.

Another way that fear of the unknown makes peace education difficult is that many people feel ignorant of the complex issues surrounding the arms race. Without access to "secret" information, the average citizen delegates issues of national security to "experts" who supposedly have informed understandings of these issues. Governmental secrecy about national security policies contributes to a feeling that ordinary citizens don't know the "true" issues and therefore can't make informed judgements about security matters:

> Many people who recognize the significance of the nuclear threat are bewildered by the complexity of the issues, by the esoteric jargon used by "experts" to discuss the issues, and by the fact that equally qualified "experts" hold diametrically opposed views on many of the issues. Often, when the president announces a new policy or deployment, the papers are filled with voices of authorities, some defending the decision and others challenging it. The average citizen is driven to despair with feelings of intellectual futility and helplessness. Citizens reason that the problem lies beyond their intellectual abilities and that they must therefore defer to experts and let them determine policy.[2]

These feelings of ignorance and being overwhelmed by the complexity of national security issues quickly remove from the average citizen the desire to influence defense policy. Peace education, by providing information about national security, can raise the level of awareness about foreign policy matters and help citizens feel informed enough to engage in debate about war and peace issues.

People who trust leaders believe that their government has their best interests in mind and do not question a system that takes care of them. Many feel that government leaders have moral sensibilities that would keep them from "pushing the button," and therefore don't believe that a holocaust could happen. Some people receive a sense of security from knowing that they live in a garrison state that other countries would fear to attack. Because of these feelings of trust for the state many are reluctant to unsettle the patterns that provide them security by challenging the status quo.

Peace education promotes changes in the way human beings think about violence and security. Moving towards a world that abandons war will require enormous changes in both the structures of the world and the way people think about their involvement as citizens. Some, because they can't predict the outcome, fear the unknown. The world is so heavily armed, and militarism has become so deeply ingrained throughout societies, that many people resist moving toward a world that seeks alternative security systems.

> People in general seem to have difficulty in envisioning a disarmed world, and therefore fear what they cannot describe to themselves as a reasonable set of living circumstances.[3]

A sharp reduction in arms threatens people used to an arms race. Human beings are creatures of habit, and, bolstered by the public relations campaigns that support expensive armament systems, trust that the current state of affairs provides security. With these beliefs they hesitate to rush towards the largely unknown nature of an unarmed world, or at least a world that spends less on defense capabilities and searches for new methods to achieve security.

Peace education runs into all the psychic barriers that make social change difficult to achieve. People are cynical about the prospects for change and feel powerless to effect change. They would just as soon let someone else take the risks involved in working for peace. Living in a frightening world beset by violence makes it hard to challenge existing systems. Government repression of peace movements contributes to a sense of powerlessness. A basic human desire to be respected by peers keeps many who fear criticism from being radical. It is hard to change other people's opinions, to fly in the face of accepted wisdom, and to confront biases. People who feel overwhelmed about confronting state policies supporting militarism will despair that anything can be done to create a more peaceful world. Whole segments of the population feel they cannot get involved in social change efforts because their jobs would be threatened or because they are confounded by the difficulty of confronting the war system. Furthermore, to work for change implies a belief in the future, i.e., if I learn about nonviolent alternatives I may want to see them occur to help secure a future for the world. While many people are seeking to implement less violent scenarios for the future, more and more people in advanced technological nations are living in the present. Seeking immediate gratification, they belong to a "now" generation that doesn't plan for the future. The existence of nuclear weapons has shattered their belief in the future and created a sense of urgency so that they hurry to live their lives before they are "nuked." Living in the present, many modern citizens have little faith that there will even be a future and can't commit themselves to working for something that, at a deeply subconscious level, they believe will never happen.

Given the difficulties in trying to bring about changes in the social order, people withdraw inside themselves. Some who are concerned about violence try to transform their private lives into more peaceful patterns. Pessimism about changing reality leads to a situation where some feel the only thing they can really change is their own attitudes and behavior. Others concerned about the threats of war feel they have to present a "together" picture of themselves to the world; they are afraid to admit their deep-seated fears and worries about the future. Acknowledging ignorance or impotence about these issues reveals weakness.

Further difficulties in learning about peace and war come from the nature of child-bearing practices. Childhood conditioning plays an important role in a person's ability to accept new ideas or work towards a world based on trust rather than fear. In extremely authoritarian households where young people are physically abused, screamed at, or denied respect, children can have neither opportunities to learn responsibility nor confidence in their ability to change the world.[5] In some households parents raise children with psychological patterns that rely on authorities to provide answers. Many of these children often aren't willing to accept the ambiguity that goes with trying to change a reliance on militarism. In extreme cases where children are victimized, they seek scapegoats for the frustration they feel and act out their frustrations destructively. Being raised in a climate of cruelty, they do not readily confide their feelings to others. Since the path to safe, verbal communication based on a feeling of trust was blocked for them, they live in a suspicious world dominated by enemies and lack the self-esteem necessary to question military dogma. Children who have been lied to, beaten, humiliated and deceived grow into angry adults with deep-seated hatred towards the world that makes it difficult for them to participate in the trusting climate necessary for peace education classes.

Given these psychological barriers peace educators have to teach realistic possibilities for change and confront the fears and ignorance that dominate views on these issues. By establishing a peaceful classroom they can create an atmosphere of trust that will provide positive experiences for students as peacemakers, which will help convince them that their own efforts can help the world move towards a less threatening modus operandi.

Dealing with Emotions

Many tend to think that education provides facts and theories and consequently is concerned solely with cognitive development. Such a view of pedagogy leaves little or no room for the emotional aspects of human development. A traditional view of education says that teachers should be uninvolved with subject matter and strive to present materials without showing emotion. Such a dry and emotionless view does not belong in peace education. Peace educators deal with subjects that evoke powerful feelings. Studying ways in which extinction of our way of life could come about involves deep and complex emotions which peace educators should provide opportunities to discuss. Unless these fears are dealt with, peace education students can become confused and bewildered. It is therefore crucial that peace educators help their students confront feelings generated by discussions of war and violence in order for students to move beyond a state of terror to a state where they can positively act upon strong emotions.

> It is true that much negative, critical teaching on war and the nuclear threat can induce a sense of fatalism and impotence. The response is paralysis, anxiety, neurotic escape from apparently awesome and insuperable problems.[5]

Without confronting such emotions peace educators may contribute to a sense of cynicism about the threatening nature of the world.

Students faced with terrifying images of war and destruction have a natural tendency to deny them. This process of denial has been extensively discussed by Robert Jay Lifton[6] and others, who describe it as psychic numbing. Because certain topics, such as the destruction of life after a nuclear holocaust, are threatening and overwhelming, many people would prefer to ignore them. Who wants to discuss the circumstances whereby the world, as we know it, could end in one half-hour? The tendency of people faced with such horror is to block it out or displace it in such a way that fear and terror don't constantly dominate their psyches.

The challenge for the peace educator, then, is to break through these processes of denial by confronting the horrors of violence directly with a systematic approach similar to what people go through when dealing with death. Many people might imagine somehow that they will escape a nuclear conflagration, but recent studies about nuclear winter imply that for humans on the planet Earth, there may be no such thing as an escape from the consequences of a nuclear war. Therefore, the study of war in contemporary times means that students and teachers must confront the specter of their own deaths, as well as what Jonathan Schell calls the unimaginable concept of planetary extinction.

Researchers such as Elisabeth Kubler-Ross[7] have determined that the grieving cycle involved with confronting death implies going through five stages—denial, anger, bargaining, depression, and acceptance. Understanding how these stages help people deal with violent threats to their lives will help peace educators deal with some of the powerful emotions that may come forth in their classes. When people are given information too difficult to handle, their first response is to deny it. This response is automatic and unemotional. In this way most people lead their lives not thinking about nuclear extermination or thinking that if there were a nuclear war that they would somehow escape. This helps cushion the terror under which we live. The irony of modern technology demands that people confront the logical implications of going to war, because any war has the possibility of erupting into a nuclear exchange, which could extinguish the human species. Teachers can help students get through the denial stage by giving them information about nuclear winter scenarios.

After the denial stage comes anger and rage. Why must this happen to me? This isn't fair. The anger stage can be a potent mobilizer of energy. People threatened by violence have a natural response to save themselves. Their anger spurs them to become active in attempts to overcome what threatens them. This stage can be characterized by fear for oneself and concern for the fate of all living things. Such fears can cause doubts for people raised with patriotic notions that their country can do no wrong. Individuals at this stage have a hard time figuring out whom to get angry at and how to channel their rage.

The next stage is bargaining. If I do this, will I be saved? People in this stage attempt to reduce dangers by taking precautions. This is an important phase in the death cycle because individuals at this stage settle with their friends and relatives. In this stage people try to reach compromises that will extend their lives. In relation to the threat of war, this stage may also give rise to political involvement. If I work hard to end the threat of war, then perhaps my life and life on this planet will be saved. Peace activists who go through this stage in their awareness about the nuclear threat feel a great sense of urgency and are zealous about peace.

The next stage of dealing with death involves depression and grief, incredible sorrow for what might happen both to ourselves and to our earth:

> Until now, every generation throughout history lived with the tacit certainty that other generations would follow. Each assumed, without questioning, that its children and children's children and those yet unborn would carry on — to walk the same earth, under the same sky. Hardships, failures, and personal death were ever encompassed in that vaster assurance of continuity. That certainity is now lost to us whether we work in the Pentagon or the peace movement. That loss, unmeasured and immeasurable, is the pivotal psychological reality of our time.[8]

Helping students at this stage can be hard for teachers, especially in a culture that doesn't condone the expression of feelings. Students who view movies about the effects of a nuclear blast or read books like *The Fate of The Earth,* by Jonathan Schell, can be overcome with grief and sadness about the potential horror brought on by the technology of modern weapons. This stage can be characterized by withdrawal and a sadness that can be an important catalyst, because with it, students and teachers can share a grief for life that has within it a deep respect for the planet and for all living things. In this way owning and acknowledging these feelings can put peace educators in touch with what Joanna Macy calls the "Web of Life."[9] Through these feelings, people can grow to appreciate the value of life and the horror of anything that threatens it.

Fear can be healthy for living organisms. If a child playing on a street sees a truck coming and senses fear, that child will get up and run out of the way of the truck. Fear produces reactions that lead to survival. The feelings of fear and despair experienced by studying the total effects of war can contribute to a life-embracing energy, both in the desire to do something to change the state of affairs that causes that fear and in the identification with other human beings and life forms that are similarly threatened.

The final stage of acceptance brings a certain clarity about life and its importance. At this stage people feel resolved about their lives. Peace educators accept the threats of violence as a part of the human condition. They realize that they must continue with their lives and are not overwhelmed by feelings of panic which characterize the earlier stages of dealing with death. They appreciate with great sadness that the world is threatened, and, knowing that people need to better understand the danger that confronts all of us, use their skills and techniques to inform people about this crisis. Joanna Rogers Macy has written a valuable book that contains different exercises to help people work through the despair and anxiety associated with the nuclear threat.[10] These exercises can both help avoid the sense of powerlessness that comes from feeling overwhelmed by forces that threaten existence and help clarify emotions raised by contemplating something as awful as a nuclear holocaust.

The grieving cycle can provide a useful guide to understanding what each of us goes through when faced with the horrors of nuclear war. Although it is natural for individuals confronting their own death or the extinction of life on this planet to have within them deep feelings of grief, these individuals construct defenses that keep them from looking at national defense policies. Surrounded by fears, they are scared to challenge official policies. They fear that to question official policy would be to make them vulnerable to the terrible anxiety and dread associated with the topics of war and nuclear annihilation. Working through these stages of grief with the help of educators can result in a kind of clarity:

> If we listen carefully to students and explore their questions and concerns without trying to impose a particular point of view, students respond with a great deal of openness and depth of feeling. They no longer feel alone and powerless in a solitary world of unshared fears. They are glad for the chance to talk, and they begin to find some basis for hope in the recognition that their concerns about the future are shared by others — adults as well as peers.[11]

Yes, these emotions are terrifying, but they can contribute to building a sense of moral concern for the future of the planet.

Suffering helps people tear down their defenses. Teachers are often afraid to confront emotional issues in classrooms because they are afraid they will fall apart and don't want to exhibit emotions to students. Years of conditioning have constructed defenses that are hard to undo. But it is these very defenses that must be undone in order for people to transform themselves into effective peacemakers. Feelings of despair, confusion, grief, anger, and helplessness all come up in peace education classes. In reality, when people confront these issues they don't break, fall apart, or become destroyed. They become healthier. The deep-seated feelings of despair and sadness that people hold within them are released; it is a catharsis. People need permission in peace education classes to talk about their distress about the world. Peace educators have to be bold in expressing their own emotions so they can set an example to students of loving, caring human beings concerned about the fate of the earth. We all live in a world of dispassionate leaders who talk calmly about "mega-deaths" and the "survivability" of nuclear war. Emotional reactions to these terms contribute in important ways to producing citizens who are neither craven nor silent, but rather are prepared to confront that terror in an attempt to create a safer future.

The arms race, where destructive weaponry can not only kill every individual on earth, but do it many times over, presents a challenge to the human conscience. Why build such weapons if they have such frightening capacities? What would possibly justify their use? Why are precious resources being wasted on building more of these weapons when that money could go towards eliminating the poverty and injustice that often cause wars in the first place? To study these issues in depth involves the study of collective madness:

> Human existence itself may be absurd, as many have claimed, but I think we live right now in a very special realm of absurdity; we're haunted by something we can't see or imagine. We are afraid of something we call "nuclear holocaust" and at the same time are removed from, and have little awareness of that threat. So our absurdity has several layers, and that's where I think we have to start.[12]

Addressing these issues in a peace course can help remove deep-seated defenses and provide an uplifting feeling that energizes people for the important challenge of changing patterns of violent behavior. The classroom is a good place to start analyzing these deep-seated fears. The emotional nature of these discussions will mean that classes will have deep meaning and significance for students.

Challenging commonly held assumptions about war and peace can raise additional educational issues for peace educators. When a mind comes in contact with new ideas or notions that challenge strongly held beliefs, a situation is created which is called cognitive dissonance. In these situations students are often confused and bewildered:

> Cognitive dissonance or the challenge to one's existing cognitive structures regarding right and wrong are essential to growth in moral maturity.[13]

Claims made by peace educators often defy commonly held notions of national security. They go against what national leaders and major media state as being in the best interests of the national state. Students' views, which they learn through these media, are therefore challenged, and a situation of dissonance is established, but this dissonance can lead to important growth. As Carl Jung said, "There is no birth of consciousness without pain."[14] The difficulty of having commonly held assumptions challenged forces students to think through national defense policies and provides important moral dilemmas for intellectual and moral development.

Peace education is a matter of the heart. People have to look carefully at themselves and decide where they stand. The topics of peace education draw out of both students and teachers feelings of concern for life on this planet. Students who start to question national policies cannot return to a state of innocence where the world will seem safe and secure. They must learn to live with the omnipresent threat of violence. The topics covered in the study of war and peace are themselves intimidating. There is so much that has to be learned in order to understand why human societies contain such destructive power, and students often feel paralyzed because they feel they don't know enough about this material. Acknowledging these feelings is the first step to an awareness that helps people gain control over confusing emotions they have about violence in their lives.

Understanding Different People's Backgrounds

Teaching about peace can be confounding because while everybody wants peace, each person has a different view about how to achieve it. Thomas Belmonte, in a lead article of a special edition of *The Bulletin of Peace Proposals* dedicated to peace education,[15] discusses how each human has a notion of a peaceful garden of Eden — a place where people live in harmony, security, freedom, and economic well-being. Students in a peace education class for adults taught by this author described their images of peace in the following ways: "Being outdoors, a part of the universe"; "meditating"; "working with other people to achieve a peaceful world . . . this image is not exactly peaceful because it involves confronting the power structure"; "living in a world where all people have food, clothing, shelter, and dignity"; "a community working together"; "thinking globally, but acting locally"; "living in a farm community, taking care of one's own needs"; "the family, living together in a caring community . . . growing together"; "peace is a dynamic process . . . me accepting myself, accepting people around me, and growing together"; "starting internally with myself . . . peace is an attitude of accepting other people's points of view"; "a tall tree next to a rippling brook . . . thinking of nature as an escape from the immediate"; "each person communicating thought . . . after something is festering, working it through by communication, and experiencing peace afterwards." These different images reflect the life experiences of each of the students in the class. Some of them contain common characteristics of cooperation and communication, but others contain wholly different themes.

The following wishes for a peaceful world come from young children in Sheboygan, Wisconsin.

Karen Schmitt (age 12)

I wish all countries would share peace with each other. I want Russia and the U.S. to stop making bombs and start talking over their difficulties.

I wish for peace among all people, no matter what color, race, or religion they are. They should learn to become friends. I also want the crime rate to end. I wish for the killing and destruction to stop.

I wish the unemployment to stop so all people will be happy and at peace with each other. I wish the poor and lonely may find happiness where ever they may be.

I think that if we want to be able to be peaceful we have to work together and stick up for what we really believe in.

Paul Gartman (age 12)

My hope for peace in the world is that all the nations should get together and stop all the fighting in the world.

I hope for peace so all the killings and injuries will stop.

No one really wants war. Besides, all war gets you is death.

I really don't know why there is war. Neither side really wins. They both lose in life and love.

I feel war is useless. It does not get you anywhere but where you started from.

Melissa Morton (age 11)

I hope the dreams of war and hunger ending will one day soon come true. Everyone prays day after day and hoping deep down it will. You can look at yourself, see how wealthy you are, as there are people out there starving, dying, and hoping that it would all stop. You hear so much about war and hunger, thinking that one day one of these people could be you. It's all very frightening! Think of young children. They need to know and feel the feel of being able to see the sun set peacefully on the fresh smell of flowers blooming. I know you have dreams and hopes of your own that you would like to see happen one day. We should all get a chance to see a dream happen at one time or another.

This last wish for a peaceful world has been uttered by millions of human beings throughout history—the dream of a world without hunger or war. These peaceful images portray a gentler world than the one most people inhabit and form the basis for many religious myths. Even though images of peace belong to all human beings, there is great diversity in opinion about how they should be achieved. Likewise, as Betty Reardon has mentioned,[16] individuals have different notions about how to achieve security. For some people security comes through disarmament, while others believe that the road to security is paved with munitions. "Peace with honor" motivates political leaders, while peace through contemplative withdrawal motivates Eastern religions. A common need for human security underlies these different notions but is manipulated by munitions suppliers in their unending demand for increased armaments, "to make the world more secure."

Peace educators should start out their classes discussing these different notions so that students can understand commonly held notions of peace that grip human consciousness, as well as the important differences that exist in ideas of how to achieve peace.

A discussion which took place at the World Congress on Disarmament Education at UNESCO, Paris, 13–16 June, 1980, provides an illustration of this diversity. The question arose between African and European participants as to what kind of disarmament education each was undertaking. For the European, the main issue was the problem of nuclear armaments and the search for ways to abolish these weapons. The African opposed this view, pointing out that more Africans are killed with conventional arms or die as a result of poverty and starvation than because of nuclear weapons.[17]

All human beings have a basic need for peace and give their allegiance to states to secure that peace. States and governments support expensive defense systems in hopes of guaranteeing their citizens a peaceful existence. Without a realization of this right to peace[18] all other rights remain uncertain, unfulfilled, or precarious. Peace education teaches people how to preserve that right. In some countries nuclear weapons threaten the right to peace; in others underdevelopment and political oppression deny people a right to a peaceful existence; still other countries face wars of liberation. These differences must be taken into account when constructing peace education programs.

Understanding your students is a basic principle of education. For traditional teachers and schools this often means understanding their reading and writing ability as well as their past educational experiences.

Students have differing religious backgrounds and values that will influence how they react to the topics of peace education. Students raised in different generations and cultures will have varying attitudes about how to achieve security. Peace educators should have students work in small groups to expose those differences and, by sharing different opinions, create an atmosphere of respect for different beliefs about these issues.

> Peace education must begin where people find themselves, must begin with what is real for them; and it must proceed by enabling them to test their understanding of reality in a kind of dialogue with the experienced world.[19]

Peace education, therefore, helps people evaluate their notions of security, power, dependence, violence, and peace—notions which are formed by everyday realities and impressions they receive from the culture. The effectiveness of peace educational endeavors depends, to a large degree, upon discovering the barriers to new ways of thinking about peace and national security and then helping people break down those barriers. In this way peace education requires sensitivity to the different agendas that students bring to peace education classes:

> Peace education starts with the individual and the right of each person to lead his or her own life taking destiny into his or her own hands; and therefore according to modern day peace education, it is up to the individual to define what his or her own basic needs are and how to satisfy them. The function of peace education has been to investigate the causes and processes that lead to the non-fulfillment of basic needs.[20]

Just as different nations have separate notions of what peace education should be, people from different classes and ethnic backgrounds within a given society will have different needs for peace and levels of support for peace education efforts. Working with these differences becomes an important part of peace education:

> Education for peace must begin with our everyday experiences and immediate fears, not with mere models of peaceful world order or of a peaceful social life.[21]

Peace educators should construct with their students proposals, programs, and projects that are based on students' needs and interests. Because of the controversy surrounding the topics, peace education classes discussing war and peace will often run into conflicting points of view even though people who differ about the way to achieve peace often share similar goals. The best way to deal with this conflict is to listen carefully to different perspectives, try to understand them, and appreciate their origins.

    Similarly, the teacher should share with students his or her own biases about how to reach peace. In a discussion where teachers and students are honestly delving into how they formed their attitudes about violence and searching for answers to violent behavior, students and teachers can learn to respect each other's opinions. By challenging assumptions in peace education classes, the educational endeavor helps students learn important skills of accepting the validity of other people's points of view. Accepting the legitimacy of other perspectives helps create a learning environment conducive to handling the diverse opinions that are brought to peace education classes.

10. What Difference Does It Make?

Education is that process by which we learn new ways of thinking and behaving, a very significant component of the transition-transformation processes. Education is that process by which we glimpse what might be and what we ourselves can become.

Betty Reardon

Human beings are used to thinking about violence and war as problems to be controlled rather than thinking positively about peace as an achievement, as a state of being within their control. Peace education rests on an active vision of peace where skilled individuals, who have been trained in the ways of nonviolence, intervene in conflict situations to manage them without using force. Peace education hopes to realize the vision of *shalom* presented in the Hebrew Bible, where people in communities use their individual and collective resources to care for each other and promote social well-being. For too long human beings have used violent means to achieve their goals. Peace educators have to help counter this reliance on violence by building visions of the future different from a current pattern of bigger and better armaments, hoping they will never be used. As the Book of Proverbs says, "Without a vision, the people perish."

Although the future is under nobody's control, currently small groups of power elites make important decisions that have far-reaching consequences for coming generations. At the same time, the great masses of people all over the world face the future concerned, uncertain, and powerless. The Dutch sociologist Fred L. Polak presents the image of the future as a driving force in history:

> As long as a society's image of the future is positive and flourishing, the flower of culture is in full blossom. Once the image of the future begins to decay and lose vitality, however, the culture cannot long survive.[1]

Rather than creating a culture that contains beautiful, optimistic images of the future, modern societies are creating a hideously deformed image of the future with environmental poisoning and nuclear destruction looming in people's minds. Arms races have become addictive. Countries

173

are borrowing heavily and stealing in order to maintain their habit. They are mortgaging the future of their youth in order to maintain expensive defense budgets that rob valuable resources from social programs. This addiction affects the minds of citizens as they contemplate with terror a civilization that has the power to destroy itself in its own search for dominance. Drug addiction and rising rates of teenage suicides are just a few indications of the effects of these policies upon contemporary life.

Peace education represents a celebration of life rather than support for the death-bearing values implied in militaristic cultures. Peace education confronts these horrors by presenting a vision of a nonviolent world. Peace education does not so much tell people *what* to think about the future but rather *how* to think about the future. Peace educators should ask their students about their visions for a nonviolent world and help them realize what will have to happen in order for that world to occur. They should point out to students the peace-loving aspects of human civilization and emphasize the dreams of those trying to create a better future. This type of education does not build upon one vision for the future but rather attempts to create a multiplicity of visions, to restore utopian thinking, and to encourage imagination. In peace education classes students examine how to take control of their own lives to work for a more humanistic society based on social justice and human rights with equality for all. They should ask the question, "What kind of world do we really want and what will it take to get there?"

Peace education allows teachers to use their creative energies to build a better world. The limits to human imagination are what people impose through cultural beliefs. Peace educators have to crash through the boundaries of existing beliefs to encourage people to believe peace is possible, that the current violent state of reality can be altered to a more peaceful condition. Reality is a matter of perception. To a large extent people's expectations determine the nature of their reality. Human beings have always faced scourges of different kinds. They have lived through plagues, survived wars, outlasted food shortages, and existed in periods of drought. In spite of these calamities the power of fantasy and the human will for survival has charted courses for improvement. Violence will never disappear from human communities, but its level can be decreased by actively confronting violent situations. A proper goal for human existence is to improve the human species. Peace education helps students realize this goal by seeing the world in different ways, by examining what it means to be human, by developing a peaceful consciousness, and by exploring more peaceful scenarios of a less violent state of affairs.

Many people concerned about nuclear weapons feel they can no longer trust governments to make decisions about their future. The state owes its origins to the subjugation of large masses of people by a small group of men using force. Under the nuclear threat the state no longer becomes a well-meaning protector, but rather the bad father who no longer guarantees the survival of its citizens. With this sentiment many concerned citizens feel the need to plan a future different from what their government represents with its heavy reliance upon weaponry. Peace education, then, helps people withdraw their allegiance from states that threaten destruction and encourages people to feel personally responsible for violence and hence for its elimination.

This book has basically relied on a three-part framework for peace education — formation, information, and transformation. Helping people understand how they are personally responsible for violence and how they have formed their own violent behaviors contributes to an understanding of how we all depend upon the use of force. Information about peaceful alternatives as well as the violent undergirdings of social reality will help people imagine new scenarios that become the basis of transformative visions that provide an antidote to current violent practices. This final chapter will describe the role of peace education in promoting those visions and conclude with a discussion of the effectiveness of peace education in making the world more peaceful.

The Transformative Vision

A transformative scenario for the future has been named the "Apollo vision" after the first human space flights which exhibited the Earth as a blue sphere hurtling through space. It assumes that the Earth is a spaceship with limited resources, that human beings depend on each other, that they will work together to change their values, and that they can build a better future for the vast majority of people on this planet. This transformation vision of the future has been discussed by Willis Harman,[2] who states that many people throughout the world are starting to question the traditional industrial thinking based on growth and materialistic progress. This process of assimilating new global values is being facilitated by electronic communications that make it easier for people to relate to other human beings throughout the globe. Evidence of this transformation has been provided during the 1960s with the resistance to the war in Vietnam, during the 1970s with the advent of the environmental movement, and during the 1980s with an increased concern about the future of the world as evidenced by the growth of peace movements and by local groups getting together to plan for the year 2000. In Europe, evidence of this transformation comes from Green parties that are questioning industrial and social policies throughout the continent. Further evidence that individuals are trying to create new visions to transform their life circumstances comes from a wide variety of liberation movements opposed to tyranny and patriarchy, such as the feminist movement, which has made many important contributions to peace education. Individuals involved in these efforts seek a transformation that implies a change in thinking and a fundamentally different way of acting upon the planet Earth. It relies on human beings moving from compulsion to compassion. It assumes that people can adopt a common goal to live together. In the transformation vision war would be considered outmoded:

> If one genuinely wants to reverse the arms buildup, one must make a commitment to fundamental changes that will enable one to break the military completely. This means a decision at the outset to work for abolishing both national military arsenals and the war system that brought them into being. Without that commitment for abolition, selected weapons systems may come and go, as arms control agreements rise and fall, but recurring buildups of arms, like the craving for a fix by an addict will always return.[3]

The transformation scenario notes that in past times civilizations that have not adapted to changing circumstances have become extinct. Civilizations that reach their climax start to lose their vitality and decline because of the hardening of ideas. An essential element in cultural breakdown is lack of flexibility and the use of military might to strengthen a decaying value system. But history also shows that human beings have at times changed their behavior. They have abolished slavery and colonialism. Transformationists hope to probe deeply into the human psyche and instill a belief that violence can be replaced with humane behavior. As opposed to a Marxist point of view, which tries, by changing the nature of social relations, to alter human consciousness, the transformation approach to the future hopes to create new images of reality which will then provide support for changing social institutions.

In order to challenge the existing patterns that have created such a violent world, leading "futurists" are calling for a radical change in human belief systems: "What we need, then, is a new 'paradigm' — a new vision of reality; a fundamental change in our thoughts, perceptions, and values."[4]

This "Aquarian Conspiracy"[5] looks for a turnaround of human consciousness in a critical number of individuals to bring about a renewal of society. The new values promoted by these "new age" thinkers include nonviolence, economic well-being, social justice, participation in decision making, feminism, spirituality, and ecology. Such a change in consciousness would provide distinctly new ways of thinking about old problems and provide creative solutions to the problems that face human beings on this planet. "A new world, as the mystics have always said, is a new mind."[6] The hope is that a widespread change in people's attitudes would provide political support for changes in major policies and practices that have brought the world to this juncture.

Spirituality has also become an important part of a new value system promoted for a peaceful future. Here "spirituality" refers to the strength of the human spirit to use care and moral concerns to transcend particular oppressive circumstances, unify with others, resist aggression, and struggle against evil, which Albert Schweitzer defined as that which threatens life. Within a background of violence, the human spirit has always resisted evil. Human beings in touch with their spiritual sides worship life and abhor violent behavior which threatens life.

An important part of the new values promoted through transformation theory is the image provided by Teilhard de Chardin of the planetization of human beings, where, as they become closer through increased communication, they will share the same image of a peaceful planet. Under this image, unbridled nationalism will give way to the love of humanity. Spiritual instincts that allow for the love of other human beings generate a wider loyalty to a unified world that will abandon national sovereignty in order to adopt a collective security. This spiritual image of unity promotes world citizenship, where all the world's people belong to the same family.

Disunity is seen as a danger that nations and people throughout the earth can no longer endure. With spiritual energy and commitment, human beings can show mercy, compassion, and kindness towards all people. The spiritual mission of human beings promotes an ever-advancing civilization that will oppose warfare and self-aggrandizement. Such spiritual beliefs help people withstand the terror of violence and create alternative belief systems that will create a better future.

Deep within the human psyche lies certain archetypes. One of these is the belief in peace. Such a belief is manifest in all the religions of the world and motivates human behavior to seek to reduce violence. This deep belief in peace forms part of the spirituality behind the transformation scenario. It is a vision of all human beings working together to make the planet a safe place to live. It is a concern for the well-being of other human beings. These spiritual beliefs may be lost in a technological world based on material gain, but they are a deep part of the human condition and lie at the heart of the various peace movements.

In some ways the transformation vision asks us to return to the spirituality of native people. Native Americans believed that the earth is our mother, and we wouldn't despoil our mother, would we? To achieve a peaceful future requires understanding the natural realm and attempting to live in harmony with it. Our very existence depends upon a healthy environment. If our environment is poisoned, we will be poisoned, too. The future of ourselves, as well as of other life forms on this planet, depends upon respecting the natural environment, treating it in ways that will help it flourish, and retaining its ability to nourish life throughout the millennia of history.

The Role of Peace Education

Peace education can play an important role in helping people clarify their existing values and explore the implications of new values:

> Realizing that hope for the future lies in the young people who will soon be decision makers holding the world's destiny in their power, one comes to hope that the value systems they are forming are directed towards peace. How can children and youth learn to become creative, nonviolent social agents in a complex world if they are not forming sound values based on peaceful priorities.[7]

Through an educational process, peace educators can help affirm transformative values, even though those values may contradict the stated policies of their governments. One of the leading thinkers in the new age conspiracy, Marilyn Ferguson, has said:

> The future is in the hands of those who can give tomorrow's generations valid reasons to live and to hope. The message of the Aquarian Conspiracy is that there is ripeness for a Yes.[8]

Peace educators, by teaching about the problems of violence and helping students think about alternatives to violent behavior, can become part of the solution to the problems that beset the modern world. The key to changing the future relies upon the flow of information and communication between human beings who are increasingly having their consciousness and imaginations formed by media and state-controlled images of the future. There is no one blueprint for the future. Every visionary will have his or her own images, and the government will have its own. (In typical fashion the Reagan administration has proposed an expensive technological path to a world where the threat of nuclear weapons would be reduced—"Star Wars.")

It is up to citizens throughout the world to meet with their peers, colleagues, friends, and neighbors, to discuss transition scenarios to build a less violent future. Peace education can play a key role in that process by giving people skills to pull together other concerned adults to address questions about the role of violence in their lives and to formulate visions for a less violent future. These small affinity groups provide a source of identity for peacemakers who often lose faith in their governments because of governmental violence. People can feel a sense of pride and allegiance to a small group. Shifting allegiances from national governments to causes supported by small groups provides individuals with a sense of direction in life. Peace education can play an important role in this process by helping people determine where their allegiances lie.

Elise Boulding has suggested the following exercise, which can be done in a classroom or with a group of adults.[9] Set a 200-year framework by thinking back 100 years to what life was like and then imagine 100 years into the future. What changes have taken place in the past hundred years? What changes can you imagine taking place in the next hundred years? Regarding the past hundred years, it is important for peace educators to understand not only the violence in the world and how it came about but also what has been done to reduce levels of violence. How successful have peace activities been? Which have failed and which have succeeded? Why? In this way peace educators themselves become action researchers, putting theories into practice and testing them to see what works and what doesn't. How do people learn about nonviolence? How do they unlearn the ways they are taught to be violent? Do their attitudes about violence change as they grow older? What are some factors that stimulate students to work for peace? What are some of the best ways to teach peace topics to people of different ages? These are some of the questions that peace educators must address in order to improve their techniques. Peace educators who try in methodical ways to answer these questions contribute to peace by adding to the general theory of how to bring peace to this world.

Peace educators often have an important role to play in helping people create an image of a better future and how to get there. Part of the exercise mentioned above is to imagine yourself some specific time in the future and imagine what the world would be like at that time. Then subtract ten years and imagine what the world must be like at that time in order for the world to come into the fruition that was originally imagined. In this way go back every ten years to the present and posit at each ten-year interval what changes should take place in order to bring the desired future into existence. This exercise can last for a whole day and allow people to concretize their hopes for a better world by imagining how to create a less violent and more just world. If individuals can realize a desirable and realistically obtainable world, they can devise strategies to achieve it.

People in power will not initiate changes in the existing order because they benefit from that order. Change must come from outside existing power structures. When individuals in peace movements, nonprofit organizations, planning groups, neighborhood associations, professional associations, church communities, and self-help groups understand their common needs, they can articulate their desires, and advocate change by providing new input into the decision-making systems that control wealth and power. As peace education assists this process of awareness about violence, people awaken from their complacent slumbers and demand reforms that lessen the possibilities of violence.

Peace education can contribute to building a consensus about how to reduce violence in this world. By raising individuals' consciousness about problems that exist in the world, peace educators help form notions of what can be done about those problems. Although they themselves should not tell students what to do, they need to encourage students to develop their own images of a less violent, more wholesome future.

> Bypassing the traditional channels of top down decision making, our objective centers on reaching public opinion, mobilizing it, and transforming it into an effective instrument of global politics.[10]

Consensus building depends upon developing compelling images that will motivate people to work for a better world. Peace education hopes to change fundamentally the way that people look at the world and contribute to a process where individuals agree on what the problems are and what must be done to solve them. Students in peace education classes should have both a sobering sense of how difficult it will be to alter established patterns of violence and an optimistic sense about the role they can play in determining the future.

Peace education can also play an important role in making the world less violent by teaching the skills of nonviolence, skills that can be used in the home, on the job, in school, and in social life. Peacemakers need to learn how to negotiate and compromise. They have to be able to identify their own feelings and the feelings of others. In order to change their lifestyles they need to understand ecology and learn how to live more attuned with nature. They have to become good listeners and have the courage to act upon their convictions. If the vast majority of people in this world adopt these skills, the power structures of nations might not change, but the daily lives of individuals would be more peaceful.

The achievement of peace on this Earth and the elimination of structural violence is a matter of more than mere wishing. At some point individuals who want peace will have to start participating in affairs of the world in order to bring about desired changes. At this stage individuals should define locally achievable goals and undertake limited tasks where they can experience success, because such achievements bolster self-esteem and help provide the confidence necessary to bring about more difficult changes in complex structures. When people can't achieve their goals they feel helpless, burned out, and often express despair. Peace educators should improve their students' capacities for problem-solving and do it in ways that maintain high levels of energy. In addition to teaching topics related to war and peace, peace educators have to keep morale high, help plan and implement strategies, and build and maintain educational organizations. Ultimately, the hope is that students in peace education classes, workshops, and forums will intervene in the violent nature of reality and will be able to use their influence to create policies and programs that make the world more peaceful.

It will take an enormous effort to change the war mentality. Many individuals on this planet earn their living working for the war machine.

Peacemaking must move from an avocation, where people volunteer their time, to a full-time vocation and career. People working for peace who achieve their goals create a sense of hope about the future. They need to develop a science of peace commensurate with the science of war that now attracts so much energy within nation-states. Societies are geared up to wage war. Peace education has to help societies gear up to wage peace.

The Long-Term Nature of Peace Education

Many peace educators feel a sense of urgency, exemplified by the letterhead used by the Bulletin of Atomic Scientists, which contains an image of a clock to indicate that it is three minutes to midnight, and at midnight an atomic conflagration might destroy the world. People who turn to education as a strategy to help develop a consciousness to prevent war and other ecological catastrophes assume that citizens who become alarmed will do something to change political systems that promise war and environmental destruction, and that those actions will make a difference. Peace education has been practiced for over 100 years by concerned citizens, churches, and enlightened educators. In spite of their efforts and the activities of millions of people who have joined and actively supported peace movements during this time, the world has grown more violent. (One hundred and twenty "small" wars between 1945 and 1976 have accounted for 25 million deaths—more than twice the death rate during the First World War.) Many well-meaning individuals who turn to peace education sense an increasing reliance on militarism to manage human affairs and despair of ever bringing peace to the world. Feeling that their efforts will not be able to stem the flood of militarism, they often become burned out and cynical about the prospects for peace.

Education implies, at best, a change in consciousness. In most cases it merely implies learning of facts and theories—information that may or may not result in a change of consciousness or a desire to work for peace. Even if peace education persuades students about the nature of war threats and instills a desire to do something about those threats to alter the current state of affairs, those students may not have the will, the capacity, the knowledge, the skills, or the power to take action that would result in a more peaceful world. Therefore peace educators face an important quandary: How effective are they in bringing peace to the world?

Questions of teacher effectiveness raise the specter of educational evaluation. Teachers do not *cause* students to do anything. They plant seeds in pupils' minds and cannot know whether or not those seeds will grow into plants that ultimately bear fruits. "To bear a fruit" for a peace educator would be to have a student become so concerned about the fate of the earth that the student does something to make the world more peaceful; however, teachers do not follow their students around to see whether they initiate efforts to bring peace to the world. Therefore, they cannot evaluate the effectiveness of their work by seeing whether their students become peace activists or the world grows more peaceful. Theoretically, such questions could be answered with detailed longitudinal studies into the peace activities of graduates of peace classes, but in actuality, teachers should evaluate themselves according to more immediate criteria. What effect has their teaching had upon their students' minds? Do pupils understand various peace issues or have a more sympathetic attitude towards peace?

Even if a peace educator effectively motivates students to work for peace and those students follow through on those commitments, such actions may not produce results for many years. Randall Forsberg, the founder of the freeze movement in the United States, has estimated that it will take a couple of hundred years to educate United States citizens about the importance of a freeze on the production of nuclear weapons. Because any such changes in the world will take years to come about, peace education does not appear to be an effective way to stop the immediate threats of war.

> Presumably we want peace studies to contribute toward peace and less war, but peace educators seldom if ever have any control over world events such as war and peace. The most we can do, as a general rule is to influence the minds of students who attend classes.[11]

Peace education hopes to create in students a disposition to promote economic well-being, peace, and justice. Peace educators can look to their students to see if these attitudes have been produced as a result of their teaching endeavors. Whether or not these students actually work to change the world is another question. Peace educators cannot control all the complex variables that may contribute to whether or not a particular student works for peace. But teachers can control both the information given students and the manner in which it is presented. Peace educators can evaluate at the end of educational programs whether students have acquired more peaceful attitudes. The effectiveness of peace education, therefore, cannot be judged by whether it brings peace to the world, but rather by the effect it has upon students' thought patterns, attitudes, behaviors, values, and knowledge stock.

Very little research on the effects of peace education classes has been conducted. According to one study by William Ekhardt,[12] peace education itself does not produce changes in personality that might result in more peaceful behavior. Such changes in personality might lead to more compassion and less fatalism. However, this study (with a very small group of twelve students) does show attitude changes in the areas of ideology, morality, and philosophy. These changes can occur in a classroom, but nobody can predict whether they will last over time. For example, a graduate of a peace education class could be drafted and exposed to a military lifestyle, or as often happens, that student's country could go to war, which could produce a shift where the whole population could become more approving of militaristic values. Such a cultural shift in beliefs about war or peace could negatively influence any nonviolent or nonmilitaristic tendencies students may have acquired in peace education classes.

Peace educators are, therefore, engaged in a frustrating enterprise. Living in a violent world, they teach peace education courses because they want to make the world less violent, but the most they can do is change some students' attitudes or dispositions towards violence:

> The prospects for peace education are thus not very encouraging. The patterns of violence in the international system, in individual societies, and in the minds of people are so ingrained that one needs to have a kind of neurotic stubbornness to hold fast to the concept of peace. Sigmund Freud once depicted the weakness of reason in the face of madness, unreasonableness, and the superiority of instincts. Yet, as he indicated, there is something special about this weakness: "The voice of the intellect is low, but it doesn't rest until it is heard. Finally, after countless repeated impulses, it is heard. This is one of the few points where one may be optimistic for the future of mankind." Education for peace can and must trust this low voice of reason.[13]

Peace educators resemble prophets, crying out against the madness of violence and human slaughter, who are often ignored. Seeing threats to the world, they predict doom but are denounced as being crazy, utopian, or unrealistic. They disseminate the findings of peace researchers about how to create a more peaceful world. Research advances a body of ideas that may or may not become part of public policy. Insights gained from peace research can provide information that might develop important strategies to create alternatives to present policies pursued by nation-states. However, whether those strategies ever become official policy remains a function of political activity.

In order to avoid frustrations about the lack of their direct ability to make the world more peaceful, peace educators have to understand the complex nature of their endeavors. They sow seeds that may germinate in the future to produce new degrees of consciousness about the problems of violence that plague human existence. In teaching about peace and violence they take one small step towards creating a less violent world, and they should appreciate the importance of that step. Apropos is a Buddhist saying that a journey of a thousand miles starts with the first step. Peace educators may not be changing the social structures that support violence, but they are attempting to build a peace consciousness that is a necessary condition for creating a more peaceful world.

A particular student, stimulated by a peace course, who talks to his/her friends or family, might provoke others to think more carefully about the commitment to militarism that governs political affairs. Often students who take peace education classes become peace educators themselves by organizing forums on war and peace issues. When these forums stimulate others to think through the problems of violence, they create a ripple effect, where people who learn new knowledge and insights share them with others, who in turn share them with still others, and the message spreads. These activities lie outside the control of the original peace educator who started this chain of events, but the important point is: If that educator had not had the courage to denounce the violent state of the world, none of those people subsequently affected by that message may have ever been challenged to think about alternatives to violence. Peace educators make important contributions to peace by building upon the peaceful instincts of students and creating a space for discussion of the problems of violence. These educational activities are not a sufficient condition for achieving peace, but they are necessary. People's traditional patterns and ways of thinking need to be challenged in order to overcome the culture of violence that dominates the world. Graduates of peace education classes can, in turn, use similar methods to teach others about the problems of war and peace. (One student in a peace education course taught by the author of this book was a director of a summer camp who attended meetings with other directors of summer camps throughout the state of Wisconsin. He suggested at one of these meetings that he was going to do a week of peace activities at his camp. Consequently, other directors endorsed this idea, and throughout Wisconsin during the summer of 1984 campers were declaring their camps nuclear free zones, writing letters to elected representatives, viewing movies about the problems of war and peace, discussing how to create a more peaceful world, etc.)

Peace education activities can help create the kind of consciousness described by Teilhard de Chardin—where the world is becoming more self-aware of itself as a limited planet, and where individuals need to trust others to build a safe and healthy planet. Without that consciousness, we are all doomed to wars, pestilence, and struggles for scarce resources.

"The challenge of peace" calls for transnational perspectives on disarmament, new forms of international cooperation and exchange, the development of the arts of diplomacy, negotiation, and compromise, the fashioning of the economics of disarmament, and the shaping of policy in congruence with the conditions of global interdependence. If the world is to move away from the brink of terror, then new approaches, new combinations of reality, new risks must occur. Higher education should play a vital role in the evolution of such an imaginative spirit.[14]

Education for peace has to build a belief in the future by creating in students a sense of hope that the world will be better and that the differences that peace educators bring about through creating a peace consciousness are important. People work for peace in a variety of arenas — in the highest reaches of power, in their homes, in the streets, in church sanctuaries, in clandestine meetings, and in classrooms. Educational activities of peace educators allow them to use their professional skills to contribute to the dialogue to create a safer world. They may not see immediate results, but they have to appreciate the importance of taking that first step, of doing something about the violent threats that dominate modern life, and of using their training to build a consensus for peace.

> Peace education does not pretend radically to change the pupils' attitudes in the course of a few lessons. It considers itself as one of the factors on a long-term process of transforming ways of thinking. And it will only produce any real effect if an attitude of international solidarity is advocated by politicians or at any rate by important and influential groups within society.[15]

Political action will be necessary to change human behavior from reliance on violent means to settle disputes, solve conflicts, and conquer those opposed to a particular perspective. Peace educators may at some time participate in peace movement activities or support particular causes, but as educators, they should focus primarily on teaching activities, appreciating the importance of educating others to help build the consensus that will provide a breeding ground for a peaceful future. The path to peace is a moral road. This world will not become more peaceful until citizens develop a moral revulsion to current violent practices and the moral will to change reality in more peaceful directions. Education, by influencing students' attitudes and ideas about peace, can help create in human consciousness the moral strength necessary to move towards a more peaceful future.

Important questions need to be asked about the outcomes of peace education activities. How could it be determined if the world is less violent because of the efforts described in this book? During the 1930s leading educators and intellectuals, alarmed about the dangers of a growing militarism, turned to peace education to oppose fascism. Maria Montessori lectured extensively throughout Europe about the need to learn how to solve conflicts nonviolently and the need to keep children from being fascinated by war. "Establishing a lasting peace is the work of education; all politics can do is keep us out of war."[16] Thousands of other educators at the same time inveighed against the use of force and promoted democracy. Fifty years later, fascist regimes no longer exist in industrialized democracies in the Western world. Are we to attribute this success in overcoming fascism to the efforts of peace educators? Were they successful in instilling in human minds a respect for human rights and for democratic processes that ultimately triumphed over the forces of fascism? This is a very difficult question to answer and points to the need for complicated research studies to determine the effect of peace education. Clearly, the Second World War, with its use of violent means, played a key role in overthrowing the fascist governments in Japan, Italy, and Germany, but perhaps it could be argued that visions of human rights and democracy inspired the soldiers fighting in those wars. Were the efforts of educators central to producing those visions, which motivated forces on the Allied side to produce the tremendous effort necessary to overthrow the Axis powers?

Similarly, teachers in Japan have played a leading role in promoting awareness about the horrors of the atomic bomb. No nuclear weapons have actually been detonated in acts of aggression since the bombing of Nagasaki in 1945, and forty years later millions of citizens throughout the world are opposing any use or production of nuclear weapons. Have these citizens heard the cries of teachers in Japan pleading with humanity to never again resort to such barbarism? What roles have these teachers in Japan played in building the burgeoning consensus that is appearing on this planet opposed to nuclear weapons? It could be stated that these teachers have been supremely successful in their efforts to alert the human community to the dangers of nuclear weapons, but it would be hard to establish a chain of causality from their teaching efforts to the aversion to nuclear weapons that currently exists on this planet.

Teachers from Japan have held conferences on the horrors of nuclear weapons, lobbied within their country to teach "A-bomb" education within the schools, and traveled throughout the world with their message of peace. Although these efforts have no doubt stimulated many others to think about the consequences of nuclear policies, they cannot be said to cause nuclear disarmament (should such an event ever occur), but they can be credited with playing an extremely important role in helping the world community understand the ramifications of nuclearism. Similarly, educational activities—courses, teach-ins, speak-outs, public forums, marches, demonstrations—helped halt the war the United States was waging in Vietnam. In Argentina the actions of mothers whose children disappeared have helped educate citizens in that country (and the world) about the repressive characteristics of a military junta. These events demonstrate that peace education can help change patterns of violent behavior.

Bringing peace to this world is a complex activity that ranges in scope from political leaders negotiating arms agreements to lovers amicably settling disputes. Influencing politics seems outside the classroom realm. Teachers have certain cognitive and affective goals for their students. Teachers may want their students to become aware of the role of violence in their lives, but awareness does not necessarily lead to action. What happens as a result of a particular instructional act is quite outside a teacher's control. Most peace educators have fairly traditional goals—hoping that their students will become more informed, think critically, learn the skills of conflict management, and use their rights as citizens—and are not sure what results their peace education activities will have. The activities of peace educators do not seem so much to be changing political structures as creating both a belief system and a way of life that embraces peace. These beliefs help build a consensus against the use of force. The hope is that peaceful life styles and beliefs will influence others, and the effects will spread, slowly transforming violent actions into peaceful behavior.

Appendix A. Religious Resources for Peace Education

Periodicals

Baptist Peacemaker, Deer Park Baptist Church, 1733 Bardstown Road, Louisville KY 40205.
Catholic Worker, 36 E. First St., New York NY 10003.
Christianity and Crisis, 537 W. 121st St., New York NY 10027.
Fellowship, Fellowship of Reconciliation, 523 N. Broadway, Nyack NY 10920.
The New Internationalist, 113 Atlantic Ave., Brooklyn NY 11201.
The Peacemaker, P.O. Box 627, Garberville CA 95440.
Sojourners, 1309 L St. NW, Washington DC 20005.

Research and Lobby Groups

Center for Theology and Public Policy, 4400 Massachusetts Ave. NW, Washington DC 20016.
Friends Committee on National Legislation, 245 Second St. NE, Washington DC 20002.
Institute for Peace and Justice, 2913 Locust Ave., St. Louis MO 63103.
National Interreligious Service Board for Conscientious Objectors, 550 Washington Building, 15th and New York Avenues NW, Washington DC 20005.
New Call to Peacemaking, Box 1245, Elkhart IN 46515.
Shalom Education, an Ecumenical Task Force on Christian Education for World Peace, 67 E. Madison St., Suite 1417, Chicago IL 60603.

Books and Pamphlets

Christian Attitudes Towards War and Peace: A Historical Survey and Critical Reevaluation. Roland Bainton. (Nashville: Abingdon, 1960).
The Christian Witness to the State. John Howard Yoder. (Newton, KS: Faith and Life, 1964).
Darkening Valley: A Biblical Perspective on Nuclear War. Dale Aukerman. (New York: Seabury, 1981).
Education for Peace and Justice. Padraic O'Hare, ed. (New York: Harper & Row, 1983).
An Ethic for Christians and Other Aliens in a Strange Land. William Stringfellow. (Waco TX: Word, 1973).
Jesus and the Nonviolent Revolution. Andre Troeme. (Scottsdale PA: Herald, 1973).

A Just Peace. Peter Matheson. (New York: Friendship, 1981).

Living Towards a Vision: Biblical Reflections on Shalom. Walter Brueggeman. (New York: United Church, 1982).

Making Peace in the Global Village. Robert McAfee Brown. (Philadelphia: Westminster, 1981).

A Matter of Faith: A Study Guide for Churches on the Nuclear Arms Race. (Washington DC: Sojourners, 1981).

The New Testament Basis of Pacifism and the Relevance of an Impossible Ideal. G.H.C. MacGregor. (Nyack NY: Fellowship, 1954).

New Testament Basis of Peacemaking. Richard McSorley. (Washington DC: Center for Peace Studies, 1979).

Nuclear Holocaust. Ronald Sider and Richard K. Taylor. (New York: Paulist, 1982).

Peace Is Possible. Shirley Heckman. (New York: United Church, 1982).

Preventing the Nuclear Holocaust: A Jewish Response. Rabbi David Saperstein. (Washington DC: The Religious Action Center, 1982).

The Politics of Love: The New Testament and Non-Violent Revolution. John Ferguson. (Greenwood SC: Attic, 1980).

The Risk of the Cross: Christian Discipleship in the Nuclear Age. Christopher Grannis, Arthur Laffin, and Elin Schade. (New York: Seabury, 1981).

Sermon on the Mount. Clarence Jordan. (Valley Forge PA: Herald, 1982).

Visions of Peace. Shirley Heckman. (New York: Friendship, 1983).

War and the Gospel. Jean Lasserre. (Scottsdale PA: Judson, 1952).

Waging Peace: A Study of Biblical Pacifism. John Lamoreau and Ralph Beebe. (Newberg OR: Barclay, 1980).

Appendix B. Curricular Materials

Alternatives to Violence: A Manual for Teaching Peacemaking to Youth and Adults by Kathy Bickmore. This resource manual explains the history, traditions, and practices of nonviolence. It contains a variety of readings as well as exercises appropriate for twenty 45-minute sessions. ($9.95) Alternatives to Violence, Cleveland Friends Meeting, 10916 Magnolia Drive, Cleveland OH 44106.

An Approach to Peace Education by Sissel Volan. Provides classroom activities and fact sheets to teach intermediate and secondary students about international understanding, cooperation, and peace. Obtain from ERIC Document Reproduction Service on microfiche or paper — ED 213 645. Write to ERIC, P.O. Box 190, Arlington VA 22210.

The Arms Race: Opposing Viewpoints by David L. Bender. This book includes four to six viewpoints on each of four questions: Why is there an arms race? Do nuclear weapons provide security? Are nuclear weapons immoral? How can the arms race be stopped? ($5.95) Greenhaven Press, 577 Shoreview Park Drive, St. Paul MN 55112.

Choices: A Unit on Conflict and Nuclear War. Includes 40 worksheets designed for reproduction as student handouts for the junior high level and up. ($9.95) National Education Association Professional Library, P.O. Box 509, West Haven CT 06516.

Crossroads: Quality of Life in a Nuclear World. This collection of high school curricula in social studies, science, and English contains worksheets, and is designed to explore reasons for the nuclear weapons buildup, to understand the effects of a nuclear explosion, to discuss the effects of military spending, and to encourage students to form rational opinions and act on them as productive citizens. Jobs with Peace, 77 Summer Street, Room 1111, Boston MA 02110.

Decision Making in a Nuclear Age by Roberta Snow and Elizabeth Lewis. Delves into nuclear war issues that are relevant to developing social insights, interests, and decision-making skills that encourage young people to participate in a democracy. ($12.50) Educators for Social Responsibility, 23 Garden St., Cambridge MA 02138.

Defense. Reprints of a series of articles that help explain United States defense policy. Available from Social Issues Resources Service, Inc., P.O. Box 2507, Boca Raton FL 33432.

Dialogue: A Teaching Guide to Nuclear Issues. A 250-page manual containing suggestions on how to introduce nuclear education into schools; sample letters to faculty, parents, and school administrators; guidelines for age-appropriate ways to talk to young people about nuclear issues and for presenting different points of view; K-12 curriculum ideas in all subject areas; an adult study guide; and an extensive annotated bibliography. ($12.95) Educators for Social Responsibility, 23 Garden St., Cambridge MA 02138.

191

Educating for Global Responsibility: Teacher Designed Curricula for Peace Education, K–12 by Betty Reardon. A collection of curricula from the United States presented in a book format. Teachers College Press.

Education for Peace and Justice: A Manual for Teachers by James and Kathleen McGinnis. Four volumes contain teaching strategies for elementary, secondary, and college levels, as well as classroom activities, student readings, and bibliographies. Vol. I: National Dimensions, Vol. II: Global Dimensions, Vol. III: Religious Dimensions, Vol. IV: Teacher Background Readings. The first three volumes are $9 each and volume IV is $5. The Institute for Peace and Justice, 2747 Rutger St., St. Louis MO 63104.

The Friendly Classroom for a Small Planet by Priscilla Prutzman. This is a handbook on creative approaches to living and problem-solving for children. Included are affirming activities which attempt to promote living and working cooperatively with others. Children's Creative Response to Conflict Program, Avery Publishing Group, Wayne NJ 07470

Learning Peace: Ain't Gonna Study War No More by Grace Abrams and Fran Schmidt. A resource unit intended for teachers in grades 7–12, it is an effort to educate students to "wage peace." ($3) Jane Addams Peace Association, 1213 Race Street, Philadelphia PA 19107.

Let's Talk About Peace, Let's Talk About Nuclear War: A Peace Curriculum by Teaching in the Nuclear Age. The authors of this K–12 curriculum guide promote open communication about the subject of nuclear war and have suggestions for age-appropriate exercises and activities. A section devoted to addressing the thoughts and feelings of students is included. ($10) Bananas, 6501 Telegraph, Oakland CA 94609.

A Manual on Nonviolence and Children. Edited by Stephanie Judson. The resource book contains classroom activities, games, bibliographies and many suggestions for how to create a nonviolent classroom or home environment for children. ($9.95) New Society Publishers, 4722 Baltimore Ave., Philadelphia PA 19143.

The Nuclear Age: A Curriculum Guide for Secondary Schools. Five consecutive lesson plans covering the history of nuclear weapons, the effects of nuclear weapons, and the history of US–USSR attempts to limit such weapons. Fifty pages of factual outlines, quotations, bibliographies, and a glossary. Ground Zero, 806 15th Street N.W., Suite 421, Washington DC 20005 ($2.50).

Nuclear Arms. A collection of articles providing different viewpoints of the nuclear arms race. Greenhaven Press, 577 Shoreview Park Road, St. Paul MN 55112.

Nuclear Disarmament: Debating the Issue. This series features editorial commentary and analysis from the nation's press. The unit includes 12 editorial opinions, nine cartoons and three discussion activities. ($9.95) Gary McCuen Publications, Inc., 411 Lailaieu Drive, Hudson WI 54016.

Peace Child: A Study Guide for Schools by David Woollcombe. *Peace Child* is a musical about two children who become friends and bring peace to the world. This study guide is divided into ten lessons—one lesson for each scene of the story. It is suggested for use with fourth through twelfth graders. The Peace Child Foundation, P.O. Box 33168, Washington DC 20033.

Peace Is in Our Hands by Grace C. Abrams and Fran C. Schmidt. This resource unit for teachers of kindergarten and grades 1 to 6 is offered as a response to the challenges of a confused and violent world. It is a guide for teachers wishing to introduce important concepts included in peace education. ($5) Jane Addams Peace Association, 1213 Race Street, Philadelphia PA 19107.

Peace Studies Project Report. This preliminary report describes existing high school curricula materials on nuclear war and disarmament. A list of organizations and publications on the topic are included. ($1) National Council for the Social Studies, 3501 Newark St., NW, Washington DC 20016.

Perspectives: A Teaching Guide to Concepts of Peace. A 400-page K–12 curriculum to guide teachers in discussions of concepts of peace and the means by which peace can be promoted and preserved. It examines enemy images, considers individuals and groups that have helped to work for peace, and ways to begin creating that world. ($12.95) Educators for Social Responsibility, 23 Garden St., Cambridge MA 02138.

Teaching Nuclear Issues: Nuclear Dangers, A Resource Guide for Secondary School Teachers, by Paulette Meier and Beth McPherson. Guide provides annotations of background reading for teachers, classroom materials, books for independent student reading, peace groups, safe energy organizations, and audiovisual resources. ($5.00) Nuclear Information Resource Services, 1345 Connecticut Ave., NW, 45th Floor, Washington DC 20036.

War or Peace in the Twentieth Century. This curriculum developed and tested by teachers provides a review of the causes and effects of war in the twentieth century. Contains readings and vocabulary intending to provide students with an understanding of modern war. Greenhaven Press, 577 Shoreview Park Road, St. Paul MN 55112.

Watermelons Not War! Kate Cloud, Ellie Deegan, Alice Evans, Hayat Iman, and Barbara Signer. This book provides many straightforward suggestions for teachers and parents who are concerned about the nuclear threat. Provides useful facts and information helpful to people concerned about young people's reaction to nuclear terror. ($9.95) New Society Press, 4722 N. Baltimore Ave., Philadelphia PA 19143.

Who Builds the H-Bomb by Mark Levy and Helene E. Oppenheimer. An illustrated pamphlet which raises, in a provocative but objective manner, some fundamental questions about individual citizen responsibility. Suitable for 9–12. Peace Education Project, P.O. Box 559, Felton CA 95018.

World Military and Social Expenditures by Ruth Sivard. Compares global expenditures on military preparedness and development with those for social and economic needs. Especially useful are the maps of nuclear world. ($4.50) World Priorities, Box 1003, Leesburg VA 22075.

Appendix C.
Books to Encourage Discussion of Conflict, Conflict Resolution, War and Alternatives to War

Primary Grades

Armstrong, Louise. *How to Turn War into Peace: A Child's Guide to Conflict Resolution.* Harcourt, Brace, 1979. Uses pictures of children in conflict while playing at the beach to explain terms dealing with making war and peace.

Baker, Betty. *The Pig War.* Harper & Row, 1969. *I Can Read.* The rivalry between two groups, each of whom thinks an island belongs to them.

Benson, Bernard. *The Peace Book.* Bantam, 1981. A tale of how young people convince world leaders to embrace peace.

Bolognese, Don. *Once Upon a Mountain.* Lippincott, 1967. A modern fable about a shepherd boy who enlists the aid of the army to respond to an insult.

Cowley, Joy. *The Duck in the Gun.* Doubleday, 1969. A general is unable to wage war because there is a duck resting in his gun.

Emberley, Barbara. *Drummer Hoff.* Prentice-Hall, 1967. A children's story about the destructiveness of war weapons.

Fitzhugh, Louise, and Scoppetone, Sandra. *Bang, Bang, You're Dead.* Harper & Row, 1969. Two groups of children battle for control of a hill and learn how terrible war can be.

Flory, Jane. *We'll Have a Friend for Lunch.* Houghton Mifflin, 1974. Determined to learn how to catch birds, Peaches the cat and her friends embark on a study of bird habits, with surprising results.

Foreman, Michael. *The Two Giants.* Pantheon, 1967. Two giants who used to argue become friends and learn how to cooperate.

————. *War and Peas.* Harper & Row, 1974. When a king asks his rich neighboring country to help his starving subjects, a food-throwing battle ensues.

Kohn, Bernice. *One Sad Day.* Third, 1972. Stripes decides Spots would be happier living in a highly developed society. A battle ensues where both sides lose.

Leaf, Monro. *The Story of Ferdinand.* Viking, 1938. Classic story of the bull who didn't want to fight.

Lionni, Leo. *Swimmy.* Random House. 1963. Shows how cooperation in a school of fish can keep it safe from big fish.

Ringi, Kjell. *The Winner.* Harper & Row, 1969. A wordless book showing two people in competition — both lose.

Seuss, Dr. *The Butter Battle Book.* Random House, 1954./*The Sneetches and Other Stories.* Random House, 1961./*Horton Hears a Who.* Random House, 1954. Humorous books, written in verse, which can serve as springboards for discussions of the arms race, prejudice, size, differences, etc.

Steele, William. *The War Party*. Harcourt, 1978. Despite his preparations, a young Indian warrior's first battle is not what he expected.

Udry, Janice. *Let's Be Enemies*. Harper & Row, 1961. Two little boys in a power struggle.

Wahl, Jan. *How the Children Stopped the Wars*. Farrar, 1969. Camelot/Avon. One lone shepherd boy leads a pilgrimage of children to bring their fathers home from the wars.

Wiesner, William. *Tops*. Viking, 1969. Tops, a giant, is placed at the head of the army. Fortunately, he discovers that the other giant leading the opposing army also prefers to play rather than fight.

Wondriska, William. *All the Animals Were Angry*. Holt, 1970. The chain reaction of hostile feelings.

Zolotow, Charlotte. *The Hating Book*. Harper & Row, 1969. The childhood problem of hating one's friend.

―――――. *The Quarreling Book*. Harper & Row, 1963. A story about people taking out frustrations on each other by picking on the next smaller person.

Intermediate Grades

General Fiction

Bosse, Malcolm. *79 Squares*. Crowell, 1979. A teenager, on probation, befriends a convicted murderer. In the course of events, he becomes victimized by his friends.

Briggs, Raymond. *When the Wind Blows*. Shocken, 1982. A cartoon book tells the moving story of a British couple preparing for a nuclear holocaust according to government instructions.

Collier, James. *My Brother Sam Is Dead*. Four Winds, 1974. Recounts the tragedy that strikes the Meeker family during the American Revolution when one son joins the rebels while the rest of the family tries to stay neutral in a Tory town.

O'Dell, Scott. *Sarah Bishop*. Houghton, 1980. A novel about the American Revolution in which the line between the "good guys" and "bad guys" is blurred.

Cooper, Susan. *Dawn of Fear*. Harcourt, 1976. Boys learn fear when they come face to face with grown-up hatred.

Degens, T. *The Game on Thatcher Island*. Viking, 1977. Harry is flattered when a group of older boys invites him to participate in their game of war, but his elation disappears when the game takes a terrifying turn.

O'Brien, Robert. *Z for Zacharia*. Atheneum, 1974. Portrays a young girl who was the only human left alive after nuclear doomsday, or so she thought.

Schlee, Ann. *The Vandal*. Crown, 1981. An orderly society of the future in which citizens are taught that "nothing lost matters." An interesting approach to the importance of history.

Autobiographical Accounts

Frank, Anne. *Diary of a Young Girl*. Modern Library, 1952. The diary of a thirteen-year-old Jewish girl in hiding from the Nazis.

Hautzig, Esther. *The Endless Steppe*. Cowell, 1968. The experience of being exiled to Siberia.

Kherdian, David. *The Road from Home*. Greenwillow, 1979. The dislocation of an Armenian family.

Koehn, Ilse. *Mischling, Second Degree.* Greenwillow, 1977. A young girl growing up in Nazi Germany.

Osada, Arata, comp. *Children of Hiroshima.* Oelgeschlager, Gunn & Hain, 1981. Collected in the early 1950s, these essays documenting children's remembrances of the Hiroshima blast create a strong impression.

Reiss, Johann. *The Upstairs Room.* Crowell, 1972. Two sisters in hiding from the Nazis.

Siegel, Aranha. *Upon the Head of the Goat.* Farrar, 1981. A childhood in Hungary 1939–1944.

Books About World War II — Focus on Japan

Coerr, Eleanor. *Sadako and the Thousand Paper Cranes.* Putnam, 1977. Story of a twelve-year-old girl who dies from leukemia after the bombing of Hiroshima.

Davis, Daniel S. *Behind Barbed Wire.* Dutton, 1982. The imprisonment of Japanese Americans during World War II.

Lifton, Betty. *Return to Hiroshima.* Atheneum, 1970. Photographs indicate the havoc caused by the bomb.

Nakamoto, Hiroko. *My Japan.* McGraw, 1970. A child's view of Japan from 1930 to 1951.

Takashima, Shiziuje. *A Child in Prison Camp.* Morrow, 1974. Life in a Japanese internment camp in Canada.

Uchida, Yoshiko. *Journey Home.* Atheneum, 1978. After Pearl Harbor, a Japanese-American girl and her family are forced to go to an "alien" camp, where they experience suffering and humiliation. *Journey Home* is the sequel in which the family tries to reconstruct their lives after their release.

Books about World War II — Focus on Germany

Davies, Andrew. *Conrad's War.* Crown, 1980. A bizarre book of a young boy's fantasies about war, killing and guns.

Degens, T. *Transport 7-41-R.* Viking, 1974. A powerful statement on the devastation of war and how misguided patriotism can impose on the human spirit.

Greene, Bette. *The Summer of My German Soldier.* Dial, 1973. The unlikely friendship between a Jewish girl and a German soldier.

Haugaard, Eric. *Chase Me, Catch Nobody.* Houghton Mifflin, 1980. A young boy becomes involved in the activities of anti–Nazi underground.

————. *The Little Fishes.* Houghton Mifflin, 1967. A tale of war and its effects on the children who must live through it and learn to love mankind in spite of it.

I Never Saw Another Butterfly. McGraw, 1964. Children's drawings and poems from Theresienstadt Concentration Camp, 1942–44.

Levoy, Myron. *Alan and Naomi.* Harper & Row, 1977. A powerful portrait of Naomi, who has been traumatized by having witnessed Nazi brutality to her father in France during the war.

Meltzer, Milton. *Never to Forget.* Harper & Row, 1976. Personal accounts reveal everyday life in the Nazi ghettos and the labor and death camps.

Orgel, Davis. *The Devil in Vienna.* Dial, 1978. This is a story of individual acts of bravery and love in a world characterized by mass indifference and betrayal.

Richter, Hans. *Frederick.* Holt, 1970. The friendship of two boys in Germany from 1929 to 1942.

Tunis, John. *His Enemy, His Friend.* Morrow, 1967. A story about the brutality of war.

Van Stockum, Hilda. *The Borrowed House.* Farrar, 1975. A German girl, member of the Hitler Youth, goes to live in Amsterdam.

High School: War and Conflict

General

Ardley, Neil. *Future War and Weapons*. (World of Tomorrow Series.) Warwick, 1982. Speculates about future weapons systems based on current advances in weaponry.

Barnaby, Frank, ed. *Armed Conflict in the Next Decade*. Facts on File, 1984. Discusses the dangers of modern developments in warfare technology.

Bender, David L., and Leone, Bruno, eds. *War and Human Nature: Opposing View Points*. Greenhaven, 1983. This anthology presents such issues as "Are humans aggressive by nature?" "What causes war?" "Is nuclear war justifiable?" "What is a war crime?" and "Are peace movements effective?"

————. ed. *Nuclear War: Opposing Viewpoints*. Greenhaven, 1984. A collection of articles on key aspects of the nuclear debate.

Carr, Albert H. *A Matter of Life and Death: How Wars Get Started or Are Prevented*. Viking, 1966. This book discusses how wars get started and takes the point of view that understanding how wars begin might help avert conflicts between nations turning into disasters.

Cohen, Bernard L. *Before It's Too Late*. Plenum, 1983. Presents a scientific view on the dangers and risks of nuclear power.

Colby, C.B. *Two Centuries of Seapower: 1776–1976*. Coward-McCann, 1976. The story of naval warfare.

————. *Two Centuries of Weapons: 1776–1976*. Coward-McCann, 1975. A detailed examination of the technology of war.

Cormier, Robert. *The Chocolate War*. Pantheon, 1974. A high school freshman discovers the devastating consequences of refusing to join in the high school's annual fund raising drive and arousing the wrath of the school bullies.

Dziewanowski, M.K. *War at Any Price: World War II in Europe*. Harcourt, Brace, 1987. Covers strategic and political issues of World War II in Europe.

Fincher, Ernest B. *Vietnam War*. Watts, 1980. Presents the background and the ensuing complications of this "war without end."

Lifton, Betty Jean. *Children of Vietnam*. Atheneum, 1972. Introduces several Vietnamese children with varying backgrounds: Orphans, hippies, city and rural dwellers—all victims of war.

Maynard, Christopher. *War Vehicles*. Lerner, 1980. All kinds of vehicles, from motorcycles and jeeps to tanks and aircraft carriers, are pictured and described in this book.

Meltzer, Milton. *Never to Forget: The Jews of the Holocaust*. Harper & Row, 1976. Tells the story of the Jews during Nazi Germany.

Williams, Brian. *Exploring War and Weapons*. Warwick, 1979. Highlights techniques of warfare from Roman times to the present day.

The Nuclear Arms Age

Ardley, Neil. *Atoms and Energy*. Warwick, 1982. The story of atomic fission and fusion.

Asimov, Isaac. *How Did We Find Out About Nuclear Power?* Walker, 1976. Traces the work of many scientists over more than 100 years in developing knowledge of nuclear weapons.

Chester, Michael. *Particles: An Introduction to Particle Physics*. Macmillan, 1978. An introduction to the world of atomic and sub-atomic particles, including positrons, kaons, anti-protons, quarks, and others.

Cox, John. *Overkill: Weapons of the Nuclear Age*. Crowell, 1978. Presents the scientific and historical background of today's incredibly powerful and destructive weapons and makes a plea for complete disarmament as our only hope for survival.

Engdahl, Sylvia, and Roberson, Rick. *The Sub-Nuclear Zoo: New Discoveries in High Energy Physics*. Atheneum, 1977. An introduction to high energy physics, including a description of sub-atomic particles and a discussion of current theories in the field and areas for future research.

Ground Zero. *Nuclear War. What's in It for You?* Pocket, 1982. Everything you wanted to know about nuclear war but were too scared to ask.

Hawkes, Nigel. *Nuclear*. Watts, 1981. Discusses the scientific and technological background and the advantages and disadvantages of the controversial form of energy released through splitting the atom.

Hersey, John. *Hiroshima*. Bantam, 1946. A novel about the first time an atomic bomb was dropped on a civilian population.

Lens, Sidney. *The Bomb*. Dutton/Lodestar, 1982. Details the race between the U.S. and the Soviet Union for superiority in atomic weaponry since the inception of the Manhattan Project in 1939.

Pringle, Laurence. *Nuclear Power: From Physics to Politics*. Macmillan, 1979. Provides an overview of the story of nuclear energy and attempts to clarify major issues in the controversy surrounding nuclear energy.

Schell, Jonathan. *The Fate of the Earth*. Knopf, 1982. Details the immense destructive power of the current nuclear arsenals maintained by the superpowers.

Weiss, Ann. *The Nuclear Arms Race: Can We Survive It?* Houghton Mifflin, 1983. Discusses the history of the post–World War II arms race and the arguments for and against the further development and stockpiling of nuclear weapons.

————. *The Nuclear Question*. Harcourt, Brace, 1981. Discusses the development of nuclear power, its benefits, dangers, and future, and the controversy surrounding it.

Zuckerman, Edward. *The Day After World War III*. Viking, 1983. Discusses prospects for survival in the United States after a nuclear war.

War and Peace Literature

Babel, I. *The Collected Stories*. Meridian, 1974. A Russian Jewish writer tells stories about the Russo-Polish campaign of 1920 and life in Jewish communities.

Barry, J., and Ehrhart W.D. *Demilitarized Zones: Veterans After Vietnam*. East River Anthology, 1976. Poems and stories by Vietnam veterans.

Bova, B. *Millenium*. Random House, 1976. A novel about people and politics in the year 1999.

Burdick, E. *Fail-Safe*. McGraw-Hill, 1962. A novel about the nuclear weapons system that challenges the assumption that these weapons have effective fail-safe devices.

Collins, Larry & Lapierre Dominique. *Fifth Horseman*. Simon and Schuster, 1980. In this novel Colonel Muammar al-Quaddafi holds the city of New York in terror by threatening to use an atomic weapon unless an independent Palestinian state is created.

Dos Passos, John. *Nineteen Nineteen*. Houghton Mifflin, 1946. Award-winning novel about the First World War.

Follett, Ken. *Triple*. New American Library, 1979. A novel about superpower rivalry in the Mideast, focusing on Israeli production of nuclear weapons.

Frank, Pat. *Alas, Babylon*. Bantam, 1976. Post-holocaust survivalist novel about how a small town in Florida survives the bomb.

Freeling, Nicholas. *Gadget.* Cox & Wyman, 1977. A story of nuclear terrorism. "Gadget" refers to a nuclear device.

Golding, William. *Lord of the Flies.* Capricorn, 1962. A metaphor about the degeneration of the human race. Tells a story of the barbarity of a group of English school boys abandoned on an island in the Pacific Ocean.

Heller, Joseph. *Catch-22.* Simon and Schuster, 1961. Set in the European theatre during World War II, this novel emphasizes the absurdity of war.

Hoban, Russell. *Riddley Walker.* Summit, 1980. A terrifying look at a generation that grew up after a nuclear holocaust.

Ibuse, M. *Black Rain.* Kodansha, 1980. A Japanese novel about the bombing of Hiroshima.

Lagerkrist, Pav. *The Eternal Smile.* Hill and Wang, 1971. Three stories by Nobel Prize-winning author about the role of evil in human communities.

MacLean, Alistair. *Goodbye, California.* Doubleday, 1978. A terrorist group kidnaps scientists and nuclear reactors from a nuclear power plant and threatens the state of California with destruction.

_____. *Ice Station Zebra.* Doubleday, 1980. A spy novel about American and Soviet submarines interacting under polar ice.

Mailer, Norman. *The Naked and the Dead.* Rinehart, 1971. World War II combat novel based on author's own experiences.

Maxwell, A.E. *Steal the Sun.* R. Marek, 1981. A novel set in Los Alamos, New Mexico, 1945, where people try to steal uranium used to produce nuclear weapons.

Miller, Walter M. *A Canticle for Leibowitz.* Lippincott, 1973. A story set in a monastery in the Southwestern part of what was the United States, many centuries after a nuclear holocaust.

Pohl, F. *Man Plus.* Random House, 1976. Sometime in the future as the world nears nuclear war, top United States scientists race to colonize Mars.

Remarque, E.M. *All Quiet On the Western Front.* Little, Brown, 1958. Classic novel about the horrors of trench warfare in France during the First World War.

Rhinehart, Luke. *Long Voyage Back.* Delacorte, 1982. People on a sailboat on Chesapeake Bay try to survive a nuclear attack on Washington, D.C. They end up traveling to Straits of Magellan.

Shute, Nevil. *On the Beach.* 1957. The memoirs of the final days of the human race, cast in Australia after a nuclear holocaust.

Sjorgren, Peder. *Bread of Love.* University of Wisconsin Press, 1965. A novel by an award-winning novelist based on his experiences as a volunteer in the Finnish Continuation War 1941–44. The speaker of the entire story is a soldier who has the task of reporting to a mother the death of her two sons.

Snow, C.P. *The New Men.* Penguin, 1959. Fictional account of the exploitation of atomic fission and the development of the atomic bomb.

Tolstoy, Leo. *War and Peace.* Modern Library, 1931. Classic war novel about Russian strategy and behavior during the Napoleonic wars.

Vonnegut, Kurt. *Cat's Cradle.* Dell, 1971. A novel about a scientific invention which, despite the best intentions of its inventors, destroys the world.

West, M. *Clowns of God.* Hodder and Stoughton, 1981. Pope Gregory XVII abdicates papacy because of his radical, humane ideas.

Wiesel, Elie. *Night.* Bantam, 1982. A terrifying account of the Nazi death camp horror that turns a young Jewish boy into an agonized witness to the death of his family.

Appendix D. Organizations Providing Resource Materials for Peace Studies

The Grace Contrino Abrams Peace Education Foundation, Inc. Box 1153, Miami Beach FL 33110. Offers teacher-training workshops, leadership seminars, classroom presentations, consultant services and a resource library. Has developed *Creative Conflict Solving for Kids* and publishes newsletter, *Peace Ed News.*

Alternatives, Inc. 1924 E. Third, Bloomington IN 47401. A public, nonprofit organization providing publications dealing with disarmament, transnational operations, security, hunger, justice, and conflict resolution.

American Friends Service Committee. 1501 Cherry St., Philadelphia PA 19102. The Quaker AFSC carries on its programs as an expression of beliefs in a faith in the power of love and nonviolence to bring about change. Has 10 regional offices.

Association for Childhood Education International. 3615 Wisconsin Ave. NW, Washington DC 20016. Concerned with children, their education and their needs around the world. Members in more than 70 countries look to ACEI for support as they work to improve the quality of life for children everywhere. Publishes *Childhood Education.*

Association for Supervision and Curriculum Development. 225 N. Washington St., Alexandria VA 22314. Has published *Global Studies: Problems and Promises for Elementary Teachers* and *Education for Peace: Focus on Mankind.*

Association for World Education. P.O. Box 589, Huntington NY 11743. Studies world issues through problem-oriented and experiential approaches; promotes intercommunication among colleges, universities, and post-secondary institutions for research centers which are working toward a global view in education. Publishes *Journal of World Education.*

Brethren Service Committee. 1451 Dundee Ave., Elgin IL 60120. The service committee of one of the three historic peace churches; staff has produced adult educational material.

Cambridge Commission on Nuclear Disarmament and Peace Education. 57 Inman St., Cambridge MA 02138. Has published *Issues of War and Peace: An Annotated Bibliography of Books for Elementary and Junior High School Students.*

Canadian Institute for International Peace and Security. 307 Gilmour Street, Ottawa, Ontario, Canada K2P 0P7. A government-sponsored institute that promotes dialogue in Canada on peace and security issues; publishes occasional papers and a quarterly journal, *Peace and Security.*

Canadian Peace Research and Educational Association. c/o Brandon University, Brandon, Manitoba, Canada R7A 6A9. Founded in 1966, this association holds annual conferences and regional conferences in Canada; subsidizes the journal *Peace Research,* and the *Canadian Peace Research Education Association Newsletter,* both of which are provided to members.

Carnegie Endowment for International Peace. 11 Dupont Circle, NW, Washington DC 20002. A nonprofit, nonpartisan, public interest organization dedicated to making available continuing, objective information and analyses of our national defense—information which is free of the special interest of any government, military, political, or industrial organization.

The Center for International Cooperation of the National College of Education. 2840 Sheridan Rd., Evanston IL 60201. Established a peace issues bibliography service in 1984. The bibliography is computerized, listing resources on a wide range of peace-related topics for elementary and secondary school teachers and parents.

The Center for Peace and Conflict Studies, Wayne State University. 5229 Cass Avenue, Detroit MI 48202. Conducts institutes, seminars and in-service workshops designed to impart knowledge, strategies and skills necessary for understanding and resolving domestic and international conflict. It has available *World Order Values Bibliography: Books and Audio-Visual Materials for Children.*

Center for Multinational Studies. Ste. 980, 1625 I St., Washington DC 20006. An economic research organization studying the effects of multinational corporations on production, employment, trade, finance and development. Publishes findings and recommendations.

Center for War/Peace Studies. 218 E. 18th St., New York NY 10003. Publishes *Global Report,* which seeks to apply a global perspective to issues involved in the U.N. Law of the Sea Conference and U.N. activity on disarmament.

The Citizens Committee on Interdependence Education. Ste. W-219, 1011 Arlington Blvd., Arlington VA 22209. Supports community partnerships between citizens and school personnel so that students may learn more about the world in which they live.

The Consortium of Peace Research, Education and Development (COPRED). c/o Center for Conflict, George Mason University, 4400 University Drive, Fairfax VA 22030. Publishes *The Peace Chronicle;* has a *Global Education Packet* of curriculum evaluation materials, a *Peace Education Packet* which provides a general introduction, and *A Repertoire of Peacemaking Skills,* an illustrated book for teachers; holds annual conferences in the field of peace studies.

Ecole Instrument de Paix. 5 rue du Simplon, 1207 Geneva, Switzerland. This nongovernment association publishes a newsletter in French, *Ecole & Paix,* which is distributed in France and Switzerland.

Educators for Social Responsibility. 23 Garden Street, Cambridge MA 02138. Helps teachers and parents deal with peace and nuclear-age issues. Organizes workshops and curricula for teachers and publishes a quarterly newsletter, *Forum.*

Fellowship of Reconciliation. Box 271, Nyack NY 10960. A worldwide ecumenical organization devoted to the peaceful resolution of international conflict, advancement of human rights, solutions for world hunger and disarmament; a major voice of Christian pacifism.

Global Education Associates. 475 Riverside Drive, No. 570 New York NY 10915. Facilitates the efforts of concerned people of diverse cultures, talents, and experience in contributing to a more human and just world order. Quarterly magazine *Breakthrough.*

Global Learning, Inc. 40 S. Fullerton Ave., Montclair NJ 07042. Dedicated to furthering a global perspective in education—primarily elementary and secondary. Professional staff and extensive network of consultants to conduct workshops, in-service courses and institutes on global perspectives, peace, social injustice and ecological concerns.

Global Perspectives in Education. 218 E. 18th St., New York NY 10003. Has published a collection of K–12 classroom materials on a wide range of topics under the general heading *Perspective.* Also publishes a newsletter.

Institute for Defense and Disarmament Studies. 251 Harvard St., Brookline MA 02146. Studies the factors which deter serious consideration of a world without nuclear weapons and advocates a freeze on strategic delivery systems and nuclear warhead production.

Institute for Peace and Justice. 4144 Lindell, No. 400, St. Louis MO 63108. The institute is committed to the ideal of peace through justice as stated by Pope Paul VI, "If you want peace, work for justice." Publishes a teachers' curriculum, *Educating for Peace and Justice.*

Institute of International Education. 809 UN Plaza, New York NY 10017. Seeks to build understanding and advance a more peaceful and productive international order through the interchange of students and scholars, knowledge and skills.

Institute for Global Education Equity. 415 Ethel S.E., Grand Rapids MI 49506. Publishes a newsletter, *Equity,* that promotes public dialogue on matters of peace and justice.

The International Association of Educators for World Peace. c/o Norman Marcus, University of Wales Institute of Science and Technology, Cardiff CF1 3EU, Wales, United Kingdom. A nongovernment organizational member of the United Nations that relates to the Economic and Social Council of the U.N. and to UNESCO. Publishes an annual journal, *Peace Progress.*

International Peace Research Association. IPRA Secretariat, IEPERJ/SBI Rua Paulino Fernandes 32/30, Rio de Janiero RJ Brasil. Encourages research into the conditions of peace and the causes of war and other forms of violence; publishes a newsletter that describes ongoing peace educational and research activities through the world.

Jane Addams Peace Association. C/o Marghi Dutton, 63501 Bell Springs Rd., Garberville CA 95440. Sponsors educational programs of the Women's International League for Peace and Freedom (WILPF). Among these programs are the International Disarmament Fund, international seminars, and the Nuclear Information Committee. Publishes a bimonthly newsletter of WILPF's Committee on Education.

Lutheran Colleges Task Force on Peace and Justice Education. c/o Karl Mattson, Gettysburg College, Gettysburg PA 17325. Supports peace studies efforts at Lutheran colleges and universities and publishes *Peace and Justice Education Newsletter.*

Milwaukee Peace Education Resource Center. 2437 N. Grant Blvd., Milwaukee WI 53210. Publishes a newsletter, *Peacemaking for Children,* which has suggested activities for parents and classroom teachers; serves as a peace education resource center.

Movement for a New Society. 4722 Baltimore Ave., Philadelphia PA 19143. A decentralized, nationwide network of small groups working for fundamental social change by nonviolent means. The small groups work collectively in direct action, training/organizing, and the building of alternative institutions.

Peace Education Commission of the International Peace Research Association. Robin Burns, Executive Secretary, School of Education, La Trobe University Bundoora, Victoria 3083 Australia. A network for peace educators from all corners of the world; publishes a newsletter which lists peace education activities and conferences.

Peace Education Resource Centre. Ministry of Education (Victoria), Second Floor, 234 Queensberry Street Carlton 3053, Victoria, Australia. Provides peace education resource materials for teachers; publishes papers and conducts in-services for teachers in five different countries.

Peace Science Society International. School of Management, State University of NY, Binghampton NY 13901. An international organization for the advancement of peace science and related studies; sponsors two journals—*Conflict Management* and *Journal of Conflict Resolution*.

Peace Studies Association of Japan. Nihon Heiwa Gakkai, P.O. Box 5187, Tokyo International, Japan. Publishes *Peace Studies Newsletter;* promotes global networking for peace studies; and arranges visits with Japanese peace researchers.

Peace Studies Unit, Department of Political and Security Council Affairs. C/o Robin Ludwig, United Nations Secretariat, Room 3235 G, New York NY 10017. Serves as a clearinghouse for nongovernment organizations (NGOs) and academic institutions in the promotion of peace; encourages continued cooperation with the United Nations on peace issues.

The Pembina Institute for Appropriate Development. P.O. Box 839, Drayton Valley, AB Canada TOE OMO. Publishes *Peace Education News* on behalf of the Canadian Peace Educators Network.

Project for Global Education. 1011 Arlington Blvd., Ste. W219, Arlington VA 22209. An effort by four organizations to promote global values and world order education. It is intended to stimulate thought and discussion among students, faculty and campus clergy about world problems and model futures.

Promoting Enduring Peace. P.O. Box 5103, Woodmont CT 06460. Seeks to improve international understanding and goodwill. It distributes educational materials free and annually gives the Gandhi Peace Award to a person who has made significant contributions to peace.

Resource Center for Nonviolence. P.O. Box 2324, Santa Cruz CA 95063. Offers a wide-ranging public education program in the history and theory, methodology and current practice of nonviolence as a force for personal and social change. Publishes occasional newsletter.

Riverside Church Disarmament Program. 490 Riverside Dr., New York NY 10027. Educates the public about the horrors of nuclear war through its publications, seminars, and conferences. Acts as a speakers' referral agency and supports church disarmament programs throughout the country.

School Initiatives Program. 149 Ninth St., San Franciso CA 94130. Develops conflict resolution curricula in cooperation with school personnel. Provides on-site resources for teachers interested in conflict resolution.

Shalom Education. 1448 E. 53rd St., Chicago IL 60615. A Chicago-based group of pastors, seminary professors, Christian educators and local church-school teachers, and a national network of concerned groups and individuals working to find and create resource materials so that Christian education programs might be infused with the best methods, basic values and perspectives that will teach the way of peace (a world without war, hunger or systemic injustice).

Science for Peace. University College, University of Toronto, Toronto, Ontario, Canada M5S 1A1. Has various chapters throughout Canada; holds annual meetings and publishes a bulletin that keeps members informed of their activities.

Student/Teacher Organization to Prevent Nuclear War. 636 Beacon Street, Room 203, Boston MA 02215. Sponsors the Student Day for Peace; has sponsored trips to the Soviet Union for high school students; holds conferences for elementary and secondary students and teachers; and publishes a newsletter, *STOP*.

Swarthmore College Peace Collection. 1384 Massachusetts Ave., Swarthmore, PA 19081. A major depository of peace organizations' records and reference materials on peace and justice themes.

Teachers for Peace. 42 York Rise, London N.W. 5, 15 B England. This organization is the education arm of the Campaign for Nuclear Disarmament and publishes a newsletter which describes peace education activities in the United Kingdom.

Union of Concerned Scientists. 1384 Massachusetts Ave., Cambridge MA 02238. A nonprofit organization of scientists, engineers, and other professionals concerned about the impact of advanced technology on society, UCS has conducted independent technical studies on a range of questions relating to nuclear power plant safety, nuclear arms limitation and natural gas hazards.

United Ministries in Education Peacemaking in Education Prgram. Teachers College, Box 171, Columbia University, New York NY 10027. Regularly offers summer institutes on peace education for teachers.

United Nations Association of the USA. 300 E. 42nd St., 8th Fl., New York NY 10017. Heightens U.S. public awareness and increases public knowledge of global issues and their relation to the United Nations system; encourages, where appropriate, multilateral approaches in dealing with these issues; builds public support for constructive U.S. policies on matters of global concern.

The U.N. University. Toho Seimei Bldg., 15-1 Shibuya 2-chrome, Shibuya-ku, Tokyo 150 Japan. Provides a network of communication for all scholars at the university level, conducts research on global problems, concentrates currently on three areas: world hunger, human and social development, management and use of natural resouces. UNU does not grant degrees or operate within the confines of a central campus.

University for Peace. Apartado 199, Escazu, Costa Rica. Offers a masters' degree in Communications for Peace; publishes assorted materials on world conflict; promotes dialogue on themes of violence, war and peace; and publishes a newsletter describing its activities.

Wilmington College Peace Resource Center. Pyle Center, Box 1183, Wilmington OH 45177. The center makes available films, slide shows and books on the Hiroshima/Nagasaki experience, arms race, nonviolence, and has research files on nuclear testing and fallout, nuclear power, nuclear weapons, disarmament and the peace movement.

Women's International League for Peace and Freedom. 1213 Race St., Philadelphia PA 19107. An international organization working since 1915 by nonviolent means to secure peace, freedom and justice for all, universal disarmament, an effective U.N., an end to racism and sexism, education for peace, and putting people before profits.

World Association of World Federalists. 777 UN Plaza, New York NY 10017. Believes that world problems require world organizations, and seeks to assure peace through disarmament, a just world, and the equitable distribution of resources.

World Council of Churches — U.S. Conference. 475 Riverside Dr., Rm 439, New York NY 10027. An organization of 293 churches in 100 countries which promotes missionary work, aids common activity among churches, and maintains contact with other religious groups.

World Federalist Association. 418 7th Street, S.E., Washington DC 20003. Conducts educational programs aimed at the development of global institutions to deal with global problems such as war, hunger, population expansion, environmental pollution, denial of human rights and economic inequities. Publishes *World Federalist Newsletter.*

World Peace Foundation. 22 Batterymarch St., Boston MA 02109. Advances the cause of peace through research and education in international relations. Specific research in international organizations, U.S.–Canada relations, public opinion and world affairs, and public involvement in international relations. Publishes *International Organization*.

World Policy Institute. 777 UN Plaza, New York NY 10017. Works to formulate practical alternatives to war, social and economic injustice and ecological breakdown. Produces material for college and university level courses and for public education. Sponsor of the World Order Models Project, and of *Alternatives: A Journal of World Policy*.

World Without War Council, Inc. 1730 Martin Luther King, Jr. Way, Berkeley CA 94709. A consulting agency to an enterprise that does not yet exist—a serious and sustained effort to end war. The council affirms the possibility of bringing into existence conditions essential to a world without war; it considers the work of American nongovernmental organizations crucial and focuses on alternatives to violence; research, publications, conferences, intern training, and a quarterly newsletter (free).

Notes

Chapter 1. Goals of Peace Education

1. Quoted in Elizabeth Jay Hollins, *Peace Is Possible* (New York: Grossman, 1966), p. 313.

2. Betty Reardon, *Militarization, Security, and Peace Education: A Guide for Concerned Citizens* (Valley Forge PA: United Ministries in Education, 1982), pp. 16–17.

3. For a more in-depth discussion of the concept "peace," see Johan Galtung, "Violence, Peace, and Peace Research," *Journal of Peace Research* 6 (1969), pp. 167–91.

4. Michael McIntyre, Sister Lake Tobin, and Hazel L. Johns, *Peace World* (Friendship Press, 1976).

5. Ernest Regehr, *Militarism and the World Military Order* (World Council of Churches, 1980), p. 33.

6. Josezet Halaxz, "Some Thoughts on Peace Research and Peace Education," *Handbook on Peace Education,* ed. Christoph Wulf (West Germany, Frankfurt/Main: International Peace Research Association, 1974).

7. R.P. Turco, O.B. Toon, J.P. Ackerman, J.B. Pollack, and Carl Sagan, "Nuclear Winter: Global Consequences of Multiple Nuclear Explosions," *Science* 222 (1983), 1283–1292.

8. J.G. Starke, *An Introduction to the Science of Peace (Irenology)* (Leydn, Netherlands: A.W. Sijthoff, 1968), p. 46.

9. Perrin French, "Preventive Medicine for Nuclear War," *Psychology Today* (September 1984), p. 70.

10. Everett M. Rogers, *Diffusion of Innovations* (New York: Free Press, 1971), p. 176.

12. Gerda vor Staehr, "Education for Peace and Social Justice," *Handbook on Peace Education,* op. cit., p. 308.

13. Kinhide Mushakoji, "Peace Research and Education in a Global Perspective," *Handbook on Peace Education,* op. cit., pp. 3–15.

14. Betty Reardon, op. cit., p. 38.

15. Ibid., p. 40.

16. O.F. Bollnow, *Krise and never Antang* (Heidelberg, 1966).

17. Betty Goezt Lall, quoted in *Peace Is Possible,* op. cit., p. 287.

18. Thornton B. Munoz, "Working for Peace: Implications for Education," *Education for Peace: Focus on Mankind,* ed. George Henderson (Washington DC: Association for Supervision and Curriculum Development, 1973), p. 13.

19. Douglas Sloan, "Toward an Education for a Living World," *Teacher's College Record* 84, no. 1 (Fall 1982), pp. 1–14.

20. Adrian Nastase, "Peace Education in Socialist Countries: Problems and Opportunities," *Bulletin of Peace Proposals* 15, no.2 (1984), pp. 163–170.

21. Adrian Nastase, "Education for Disarmament: A Topical Necessity,"

Teachers College Record **84,** no.1 (Fall 1982), pp. 184–191.

22. H.G. Wells, *Outline of History* (New York: Macmillan, 1927).

23. William Beardslee and John Mack, "The Impact on Children and Adolescents of Nuclear Developments," *Psychological Aspects of Nuclear Developments,* Task Force Report 20, (Washington DC: American Psychiatric Association, December 1981).

24. Jonathan Schell, *The Fate of the Earth* (New York: Avon, 1982), p. 46.

25. Marcia Yudkin, "When Kids Think the Unthinkable," *Psychology Today* (April 1984), pp. 18–27.

26. Jaime C. Diaz, "Reflections on Education for Justice and Peace," *Bulletin of Peace Proposals* **10,** no. 4 (1979), p. 375.

27. Thomas Renna, "Peace Education: An Historical Review," *Peace and Change* **6,** nos. 1 and 2 (Winter 1980), p. 63.

Chapter 2. Empowerment Education

1. Theodor Ebert, "Learning to Work for a Human World," *Gandhi Marg* **6,** nos. 4 and 5 (July–August 1984), p. 294.

2. John Dewey, *The School and Society* (Chicago: University of Chicago Press, 1915), p. 149. (Originally published in 1899.)

3. John Dewey, *Democracy and Education* (New York: Free Press, 1957), p. 82.

4. George S. Counts, *Dare the School Build a New Social Order?* (New York: Day, 1932).

5. Jurgen Habermas, *Knowledge and Human Interest* (Boston: Beacon Press, 1971).

6. Paulo Friere, *Pedagogy of the Oppressed* (New York: Herder and Herder, 1970), p. 61.

7. Paulo Friere, *Education for Critical Consciousness* (New York: Continuum, 1980), p. 96.

8. *Pedagogy of the Oppressed,* op. cit., p. 68.

9. *Education for Critical Consciousness,* op. cit., p.68.

10. Ibid., p. 115.

11. Julius Nyerere, *Freedom and Development* (London: Oxford University Press, 1973).

12. Danilo Dolci, *A New World in the Making* (Westport CT: Greenwood, 1974), p. 30.

13. Ibid., p. 31.

14. Ibid., p. 313.

15. For an interesting discussion of these various educational enterprises see Ruth Propkin and Arthur Tobier, eds., *Roots of Open Education in America* (New York: City College Workshop Center for Open Education, 1976).

16. For a history of Highlander School see Frank Adams, *Unearthing Seeds of Fire: The Idea of Highlander* (Winston Salem NC: Blair, 1975).

17. Frank Adams, "Highlander Folk School: Getting Information, Going Back and Teaching It," *Harvard Educational Review* **42,** no. 4 (November 1972), p. 505.

18. Corinne Kumor-D'souza, "India: Education for Who and for What?" *Education for Peace: Reflection and Action,* ed. Magnus Haavelsrud (Keele, United Kingdom: I.P.C. Science and Technology Press, 1974), p. 110.

19. See Sam Bowles and Herb Gintis, *Schooling in Capitalist America: Educational Reform and the Contradictions of Economic Life* (New York: Basic, 1976).

20. This theory has been substantiated for American schools by Colin Greer, *The Great School Legend* (New York: Penguin Books, 1972), and in England by Paul Willis, *Learning to Labor: How Working Class Kids Get Working Class Jobs* (New York: Columbia University Press, 1981).

21. Jean Anyon, "Ideology and U.S. Textbooks," *Harvard Educational Review* **49** (1979), pp. 361–386.

22. Tipper Gore, "Raising Kids in an X-rated Society," *Engage/Social Action,* May 1987.

23. See Beatrice Gross and Ronald Gross, eds., *Radical School Reform* (New York: Simon and Schuster, 1969).

24. Michael W. Apple, *Ideology and Curriculum* (London: Routledge & Kegan Paul, 1972).

25. Fred W. Newmann, *Education for Citizen Action* (Berkeley CA: McCutchan, 1975), p. 21.

26. Colin Greer, op. cit., p. 63.

27. Svi Shapiro, "Disempowerment or Emancipation?" *Issues in Education* **2,** II, no. 1 (Summer 1984).

28. Henry A. Giroux, *Theory and Resistance in Education* (South Hadley MA: Bergin & Garvey, 1983), p.69.

29. Gene Sharp, *Power and Struggle: The Politics of Nonviolent Action* (Boston: Porter-Sargeant, 1973).

30. Andrew Czartovyski, *Education for Power* (London: Davis-Poynter, 1974), p. 120.

31. For a good discussion of the struggle to create a nonviolent world see Marjorie Hope and James Young, *The Struggle for Humanity: Agents of Nonviolent Change in a Violent World* (Mary Knoll, New York: Orbis, 1977).

32. Magnus Haavelsrud and Robin Richardson, "Peace Education Theory and Praxis," *Bulletin of Peace Proposals* **5,** no. 3 (1974), p. 197.

33. Christian Bay, *Strategies of Political Emancipation* (Notre Dame IN: University of Notre Dame Press, 1981), p. 81.

34. The original midwife metaphor came from Socrates but has been adapted by Danilo Dolci as the "maieutic" approach. See Otto Klinzberg, "The Maieutic Approach: The Plan of a New Education Centre at Partinico," *Prospects* **3,** no. 2 (Summer 1973).

35. Barbara Solomon, *Black Empowerment: Social Work in Oppressed Communities* (New York: Columbia University Press, 1976).

36. Richard C. Remy, *Handbook of Basic Citizenship Competencies* (Washington DC: Association for Supervision and Curriculum Development).

37. John Dewey, *Experience and Education* (London: Collier-Macmillan, 1963).

38. Robert W. White, "Motivation Reconsidered: The Concept of Competence," *Psychological Review* **66** (1959), pp. 297–333.

39. James S. Coleman et al., *Equality of Educational Opportunity* (Washington DC: Superintendent of Documents, Government Printing Office, 1966).

40. For a discussion of community development education, see Ian M. Harris, "An Undergraduate Community Education Curriculum for Community Development," *Journal of the Community Development Society* **13,** no.1 (Spring 1982).

41. For a general discussion of affinity groups see Murray Bookchin, "Spontaneity and Organization," *Toward an Ecological Society* (Montreal: Black Rose Books, 1980), pp. 249–274.

42. Joel Kovel, *Against the State of Nuclear Terror* (Boston: South End, 1983), p. 188.

43. Ervin Lazlo, *A Strategy for the Future* (New York: George Braziller, 1974).

Chapter 3. *Practices of Peace Education*

1. Clinton Fink, "Editorial Notes," *Journal of Conflict Resolution* **16,** no. 4 (December 1972).

2. *A Directory of Peace Studies Programs,* published by the Consortium on Peace Research, Education and Development (COPRED) in 1986, lists 90 such programs in the United States. To obtain a copy, contact Maire Dugan, COPRED, George Mason University, 4400 University Blvd., Fairfax VA 22030.

3. Clinton Fink, "Peace Education and the Peace Movement since 1815," op. cit., p. 70.

4. Jan Berry, "Getting the Government into the Peace Business," *Fellowship* **50,** nos. 4 and 5, p. 11.

5. Robert Jay Lifton, "Beyond Nuclear Numbing," *Teachers College Record* **84,** no. 1 (Fall 1982), p. 15.

6. Michael Washburne, "Peace Education Is Alive — But Unsure of Itself," *War/Peace Report* (New York: Institute for World Order, 1971).

7. See *Mini Directory of Peace Studies Programs,* COPRED (Consortium on Peace Research, Education, and Development).

8. For a more complete discussion of courses offered at universities and colleges, see *Peace and World Order Studies: A Curriculum Guide* (New York: Transactional Academic Program, Institute for World Order, 777 United Nations Plaza, New York, NY 10017).

9. Thomas Renna, "Peace Education: An Historical Overview," *Peace and Change* **6,** nos. 1 and 2 (Winter 1980), p. 63.

10. Bertrand Russell, *Education and the Social Order* (London: Allen and Unwin, 1932, 1972 ed.), p. 90. See also pp. 145 and 152–153.

11. For discussion of disarmament education see *Bulletin of Peace Proposals* **11,** no. 3 (1980), which is dedicated to this topic.

12. Quoted in "Concepts of Peace Education: A View of Western Experience," Robin Burns and Robert Aspeslaugh, *International Review of Education* **29** (1983), p. 330.

13. The reference to "appeasement education" comes from a speech given by Dr. Rhodes Boyson at a young conservative gathering in Folkstone, England, in November 1982. "The Bomb in the Classroom," *The Times,* 28 February 1983.

14. "Preface," *Harvard Educational Review* **54,** no. 3 (August 1984).

15. John E. Mack, "Resistances to Knowing in the Nuclear Age," *Harvard Educational Review* **54,** no. 3 (August 1984), p. 261.

16. Hiromu Morishita, "A View on Peace Education in Japan," *Gandhi Marg* **6,** nos. 4 and 5 (July–August 1984), pp. 357–362.

17. Toshihiku Fujii, "The Task and Structure of Peace Education in Hiroshima," *Education for Peace,* op. cit., p. 117.

18. Eleanor Coerr, *Sadako and the Thousand Paper Cranes* (New York: Dell, 1977).

19. B. Jaye Miller, "The Nuclear Experience: Japan's Unknown Peace Movement," *Socialist Review* no. 78, **14,** no.6, p. 70.

20. The Committee for the Compilation of Materials on Damage Caused by the Atomic Bombs in Hiroshima and Nagasaki, *Hiroshima and Nagasaki: The Physical, Medical, and Social Effects of the Atomic Bombings* (New York: Basic, 1981, p. 599).

21. Ibid., p. 600.

22. Ram Chandra Pradhan, "Education for Peace and Human Rights: Search for an Indian Perspective," *Gandhi Marg* **6,** nos. 4 and 5 (July–August 1984), p. 273.

23. R. Ndubisi Okechukwu, "Cultural Constraints on Peace Education in Nigeria," *Bulletin of Peace Proposals* **10,** no. 4 (1979), pp. 382–388.

24. Mahedra Agrawal, "Peace Education in the Context of Global Crisis," *Gandhi Marg* **6,** nos. 4 and 5 (July–August 1984), p. 287.

25. Ram Chandra Pradhan, op. cit., p. 287.

26. Michael N. Nagler, *America Without Violence* (Covelo, CA: Island, 1982), p. 145.

27. Amrut W. Nakhre, "Peace Action as Peace Education: An Analysis of the Impact of Satyagraha on Participants," *Bulletin of Peace Proposals* **10,** no.4 (1979), p. 206.

28. Jaime Diaz, "Disarmament Education: A Latin American Perspective," *Bulletin of Peace Proposals* **11,** no. 3, p. 274.

29. Jorge Serrano, "Report of the Latin American Council for Peace Research," *International Peace Research Newsletter* **22,** no. 1, 1985 (pp. 2–4).

30. For a discussion of human rights education see the special edition of *Bulletin of Peace Proposals* dedicated to this topic: **14,** no. 1 (1983).

31. "Annex II," *Synopsis of the Interregional Experimental Project on the Study of Contemporary World Problems,* Ed-83/Cont. 403/6 Paris, 8 July 1983, p. 1.

32. Recommendation adopted by the UNESCO General Conference, 18th session, Paris, 19 November 1974.

33. *Synopsis of the Interregional Experimental Project on the Study of Contemporary World Problems,* op. cit., p. 2.

34. Quoted in *Militarization, Security, and Peace Education: A Guide for Concerned Citizens,* by Betty Reardon (Valley Forge PA: United Ministries in Education, 1982), p. 73.

35. Jaime Diaz, "Disarmament Education: A Latin American Perspective," *Bulletin of Peace Proposals* **11** no. 3 (1980), p. 273.

36. See *Bulletin of Peace Proposals* **15,** no. 3 (1984).

37. Derek Heater, *Peace Through Education* (London and Philadelphia: Falmer, 1984).

38. Robin Richardson, "Tensions in World and School: An Outline of Certain Controversies," *Bulletin of Peace Proposals* **5** (1974).

Chapter 4. Key Topics of Peace Education

1. Quoted in *Stop Nuclear War! A Handbook,* David P. Barash and Judith Eve Lipton (New York: Grove, 1982), p. 326.

2. Helen Caldicott, *Missile Envy: The Arms Peace and Nuclear War* (New York: Morrow, 1984).

3. Seymour Melman, *The Permanent War Economy.* (New York: Simon and Schuster, 1974).

4. R.D. Turco, O.B. Toon, T.P. Ackerman, J.B. Pollock, and Carl Sagan, "Nuclear Winter: Global Consequences of Multiple Nuclear Explosions," *Science* **222** (1983), pp. 1283–1292.

5. Ronald J. Glossop, *Confronting War: An Examination of Humanity's*

Most Pressing Problem (Jefferson, North Carolina, and London: McFarland, 1983), p. 179.

6. Teilhard de Chardin, *The Future of Man* (New York: Harper and Row, 1964), p. 115.

7. Thomas Berry, "The Cosmology of Peace," *Breakthrough: Global Education Associates Newsletter* (Spring 1984), pp. 1–5.

8. These values are discussed in Saul H. Mendlovitz, *On the Creation of a Just World Order: Preferred World for the 1990s.* (New York: Free Press, 1975).

9. Richard A. Falk, "Contending Approaches to World Order," *Peace and World Order Studies* (New York: Transnational Academic Program, Institute for World Order, 777 United Nations Plaza, New York, NY 10017), p. 29.

10. Joah A. Stepis, "Conflict Resolution Strategies," *Annual Handbook for Group Facilitators* (San Diego: University Associates, 1973), p. 139.

11. For further information about this approach to conflict resolution contact Martin Luther King Center, 449 Auburn Ave. N.E., Atlanta GA 30312.

12. Roger Fisher and William Ury, *Getting to Yes.* (New York: Penguin, 1983), p. 14.

13. Leonard Berkowitz, "The Concept of Aggressive Drive: Some Additional Considerations," *Advances in Experimental Social Psychology,* Vol. 2, ed. L. Berkowitz (New York: Academic, 1967), p. 302.

14. Konrad Lorenz, *The Territorial Imperative* (New York: Atheneum, 1961).

15. Laurel Holliday, *The Violent Sex: Male Psychobiology and the Evolution of Consciousness* (Guerneville CA: Bluestocking, 1978).

16. Sigmund Freud, *Civilization and Its Discontents* (New York: Norton, 1930).

17. Franco Fornari, *The Psychoanalysis of War* (New York: Anchor, 1974).

18. Klaus R. Schever, Ronald P. Abeles, and Claude S. Fischer, *Human Aggression and Conflict* (Englewood Cliffs NJ: Prentice-Hall, 1975).

19. Robert Nesbitt, ed., *Human Nature and War* (Albany NY: New York State Department of Education, 1973).

20. E.F.M. Durbin and John Bowly, "Personal Aggressiveness and War," *War: Studies from Psychology, Sociology, Anthropology,* Bramson and Goethals, eds., (New York: Basic Books, 1968).

21. William Broyles, Jr., "Why Men Love War," *Esquire* **102,** no. 5 (November 1984), p. 61.

22. Richard Gregg, *The Power of Nonviolence* (New York: Schocken, 1959), pp. 24–25.

23. Thomas Merton, *Gandhi on Non-Violence* (New York: New Directions, 1964), p. 54.

24. David P. Barash and Judith Eve Lipton, *Stop Nuclear War! A Handbook* (New York: Grove, 1982), pp. 66, 67.

25. World Disarmament Campaign, "World Peace Action Programme." (238 Camden Road, London NW1 9HE, England.)

Chapter 5. Getting Started

1. An indication of how large the peace movement is in the United States is that Madison, Wisconsin, a town of 300,000 people in the Midwestern part of the United States, had in 1985 65 different peace and justice organizations, or approximately one for every 5000 citizens.

2. For a more complete discussion of how to organize for public peace

education activities see *Organizing Manual: A Guide for Planning Educational Activities on Nuclear War and Arms Control* (Union of Concerned Scientists, 26 Church St., Cambridge MA 02238).

3. Betty Reardon, *Militarization, Security, and Peace Education: A Guide for Concerned Citizens* (Valley Forge PA: United Ministries in Education, 1982), p. 77.

4. For a presentation on how to conduct adult educational programs in church settings see Connie Johnson, *Living Our Visions of Peace* (New York: Friendship, 1984).

5. John Dewey, *Democracy and Education* (New York: Macmillan, 1916), p. 10.

6. Alfred North Whitehead, *The Aims of Education* (New York: Macmillan, 1929), pp. 10–11.

7. Derek Heater, *Peace Through Education: The Contribution of the Council for Education in World Citizenship* (London: Falmer, 1984), p. 146.

8. For a compilation of essays related to peace and rock music see Mary Ann Philden, ed., *Give Peace a Chance* (Chicago: Chicago Review Press, 1983).

9. For an example of the wide variety of college courses that can contain justice and peace concerns, see Dick Ringler, ed., "Nuclear War: A Teaching Guide," *Bulletin of the Atomic Scientists* (December 1984).

10. Adele Simmons, "A Larger Role for the Undergraduate College?" *Proceedings of the Symposium: The Role of the Academy in Addressing the Issues of Nuclear War* (Geneva, New York: Hobart and William Smith Colleges, 1982), p. 107.

11. Ralph W. Tyler, *Basic Principles of Curriculum and Instruction* (Chicago: University of Chicago Press, 1979), p. 123.

12. William A. Schubert, *Curriculum: Perspective, Paradigm, and Possibility* (New York: Macmillan, 1986), p. 379.

13. Kurt Lewin, *Resolving Social Conflicts* (New York: Harper and Row, 1948).

14. Margaret Lindsey, "Decision-Making and the Teacher," *Curriculum Crossroads,* ed. A. Harry Passou (New York: Teachers College Press, 1962), p. 39.

15. Ronald Lippert et al., "The Teacher as Innovator, Seeker and Sharer of New Practices," Chapter 13 in *Perspectives on Educational Change,* ed. Richard I. Miller (New York: Appleton, 1967).

16. Ibid., p. 308.

17. *Peace and World Order Studies,* 4th ed., ed. Barbara Wien (World Policy Institute, 777 United Nations Plaza, New York NY 10017).

18. *Teaching About War, Peace, Conflict and Change: A Self-Assessment and Planning Process* (United Ministries in Education, c/o Educational Ministries, American Baptist Churches, Valley Forge PA 19481).

19. For a discussion of such an introductory course see Ronald J. Glossop, "The Peace Studies Program at Southern Illinois University at Edwardsville," *Peace and Change* **4,** no.2 (Spring 1977).

20. Joseph J. Fahey, "Parameters, Principles, and Dynamics of Peace Studies," *Education for Peace and Justice,* ed. Padraic O'Hare (San Francisco: Harper & Row, 1983), p. 183.

21. For a listing of these programs see Mary E. Finn, "Peace Education and Teacher Education," *Peace and Change* **10,** no. 2 (Summer 1984), pp. 53–70.

22. Robin Richardson, "The Process of Reflection Workshops and Seminars in Peace Education," *Bulletin of Peace Proposals* **10,** no. 2 (1979), pp. 407–413.

23. Finn, op. cit., p. 54.

24. Stephen H. Balch and Herbert I. Condon, "The Tenured Left," *Commentary* **82**, no. 4 (October 1986).

Chapter 6. Overcoming Obstacles

1. Virgil Elizondo, "By Their Fruits You Will Know Them: The Biblical Roots of Peace and Justice," *Education for Peace and Justice,* ed. Padraic O'Hare (San Francisco: Harper & Row, 1983), p. 48.

2. Dale Spender, *Man Made Language* (London: Routledge & Kegan Paul, 1980).

3. Roy Preiswerk, "Could We Study International Relations As If People Mattered?" *Peace and World Order Studies: A Curriculum Guide* (New York: Institute for World Order, 1981), p. 6.

4. Marc Feigen Fasteau, *The Male Machine* (New York: Dell, 1975).

5. Joel Kovel, *Against the State of Nuclear Terror* (Boston: South End, 1983), p. 64.

6. For an interesting analysis of the terminology see Thomas Merton, "Red or Dead: The Anatomy of a Cliche," *The Nonviolent Alternative* (New York: Farrar, Straus & Giroux, 1977).

7. Robert S. Moyer, "The Enemy Within," *Psychology Today* (January 1985), p. 33.

8. John E. Mack, "The Perception of U.S.-Soviet Intentions and Other Psychological Dimensions of the Nuclear Arms Race," *Preparing for Nuclear War: The Psychological Effects* (New York: Physicians for Social Responsibility, 1982).

9. Seymour Melman, *The Permanent War Economy* (New York: Simon and Schuster, 1974).

10. Henry T. Nash, "Thinking About Thinking About the Unthinkable," *Bulletin of Atomic Scientists* (October 1983), p. 40.

11. John B. Carol, *Language, Thought and Reality: Selected Writings of Benjamin Whorf* (Cambridge MA: MIT Press, 1976).

12. Jaime C. Diaz, "Reflections on Education for Justice and Peace," *Bulletin of Peace Proposals* **10**, no.4 (1979), p. 275.

13. Harold Lasswell, "The Garrison State," *American Journal of Sociology* **46**, no.1 (1941), pp. 455–468.

14. Dale Spender, op. cit., p. 239.

15. Thomas Merton, *The Nonviolent Alternative* (New York: Farrar, Straus & Giroux, 1977), p. 239.

16. Freeman Dyson, *Weapons and Hope* (New York: Harper & Row, 1984), p. 4.

17. Glen D. Hook, "Making Nuclear Weapons Easier to Live With: The Political Role of Language in Nuclearization," *Bulletin of Peace Proposals* **16**, no.1 (1985), pp. 65–77; Glen D. Hook, "The Nuclearization of Language: Nuclear Allegory as Political Metaphor," *Journal of Peace Research* **21**, no. 3 (1984), pp. 259–275.

18. Hook, Ibid., 1984, p. 73.

19. Robert Jay Lifton, "Beyond Psychic Numbing—A Call to Awareness," *Preparing for Nuclear War: The Psychological Effects* (New York: Physicians for Social Responsibility, 1982), p. 60.

20. David P. Barash and Judith Eve Lipton, *Stop Nuclear War! A Handbook* (New York: Grove, 1982), p. 222.

21. For a glossary of Nukespeak terms see Sam Totten, "Orwellian Language in the Nuclear Age," *Curriculum Review* (April 1984), pp. 43–46.

22. Jaime C. Diaz, op. cit., p. 377.

23. Edward S. Herman, *The Real Terror Network: Terrorism in Fact and Propaganda* (Boston: South End, 1982).

24. Mario Borelli, "Integration of Peace Research, Peace Education, and Peace Action," *Bulletin of Peace Proposals* **10,** no. 4 (1979), p. 391.

25. Thomas Belmonte, "A Strategy for the Reclamation of Eden," *Bulletin of Peace Proposals* **10,** no.4 (1979), p. 343.

27. Betty Reardon, "Obstacles to Peace Education," *Bulletin of Peace Proposals* **10,** no. 4 (1979), p. 358.

28. Ibid.

29. *Bulletin of Atomic Scientists* (February 1984), p. 53.

30. Herbert London, "'Peace Studies' Hardly Academic," *The New York Times* 5 March 1985, p. 27.

31. Nick Word, "'Pie-eyed' Peace Courses Accused of Bias," *The Times Educational Supplement* 6 January 1984.

32. Peter Dale Scott, "Introductory Essay," *Peace and World Order Studies: A Curriculum Guide,* 4th ed. (New York: World Policy Institute, 1984), p. 12.

33. Thomas H. Groome, "Religious Education for Justice by Educating Justly," *Education for Peace and Justice,* ed. Padraic O'Hare (San Francisco: Harper & Row, 1983), p. 75.

34. Werner Heisenberg, *The Physicist's Conception of Nature,* trans. from German by Arnold J. Pomerans (Westport CT: Greenwood, 1970).

35. Robin Burns, "Knowledge and Peace Education," *Bulletin of Peace Proposals* **10,** no. 4, (1979), p. 116.

36. Peter Dale Scott, op. cit., p. 13.

37. Michael Silver, *Values Education* (Washington DC: National Education Association, 1976), p. 12.

38. Robin Burns and Robert Aspeslagh, "'Objectivity,' Values and Opinions in the Transmission of Knowledge for Peace," *Bulletin of Peace Proposals* **15,** no. 2 (1984), p. 140.

39. Betty Reardon, op. cit., p. 362.

40. Henry T. Nash., op. cit.

41. Ibid., p. 41.

42. Ibid.

Chapter 7. The Peaceful Classroom

1. Elise Boulding, "The Child and Non-violent Social Change," *Handbook on Peace Education,* ed. Christoph Wulf (Frankfurt/Main: International Peace Research Association, 1974), pp. 101–132.

2. J. Reimer, D. Paolittle, and R. Hersch, *Promoting Moral Growth,* 2d ed. (New York: Longman, 1983).

3. Maria Montessori, *Education for Peace* (Chicago: Regnery, 1972).

4. Quoted in Devi Prasad, *Peace Education or Education for Peace* (New Delhi: Gandhi Peace Foundation, 1984), p. 131.

5. For a discussion of this see Mary O'Reilly, "The Peaceable Classroom," *College English* **46,** no.2 (February 1984), pp. 103–112.

6. Devi Prasad, op. cit., p. 112.

7. Elise Boulding, op. cit., pp. 123–124.

8. Thomas F. Green, *The Activities of Teaching* (New York: McGraw-Hill, 1971), p. 216.

9. David W. Johnson and Roger T. Johnson, *Learning Together and Alone* (Englewood Cliffs NJ: Prentice-Hall, 1975).

10. Ibid., p. 7.

11. Ibid.

12. Bertrand Russell, *The Conquest of Happiness* (New York: Bantam, 1958).

13. Mary A. Hepburn, "Can Schools, Teachers, and Administrators Make a Difference? The Research Evidence," *Democratic Education in Schools and Classrooms,* ed. Mary A. Hepburn (Washington DC: National Council for the Social Studies, 1983).

14. For a discussion of how to establish rules and guidelines for a democratic classroom, see Ian M. Harris, "Boundaries, Set Theory, and Structure in the Classroom," *Education* **93,** no. 3 (February–March 1973).

15. David W. Johnson, Roger T. Johnson, Edythe Johnson Holubec, and Patricia Roy, *Circles of Learning* (Washington DC: Association for Supervision and Curriculum Development, 1984), p. 45.

16. Ashley Montague, quoted in Johnson et al., op. cit., p. 24.

17. Johnson, et al., op. cit., 1984, p. 15.

18. Carol Gilligan, *In a Different Voice* (Cambridge MA: Harvard University Press, 1982).

19. Quoted in Michael True, *Homemade Social Justice* (Mystic CT: Twenty-Third Publications, 1982), p. 34.

20. Quoted in *Harvard Educational Review* **54,** no. 3 (August 1984), p. 271.

21. Quoted in Richard Paul, "Critical Thinking: Fundamentals to Educators for a Free Society," *Educational Leadership* **42,** no. 1 (September 1984), p. 10.

22. B. Massailas and B. Cox, *Inquiring in Social Studies* (New York: McGraw-Hill, 1966).

23. *The CORT Thinking Program* (Elmsford NY: Pergamon, 1984).

24. Johan Galtung, "On Peace Education," *Handbook on Peace Education* ed. Christoph Wulf (Frankfurt/Main: International Peace Research Association, 1974).

25. W. Kegan and M.A. Wallach, "Risk Taking as a Function of the Situation, the Person, and the Group," in G. Mandler, P. Mussen, W. Kegan, and O.A. Wallach, *New Directions in Psychology,* Vol. 3 (New York: Holt, Rinehart and Winston, 1967), pp. 224–66.

26. Margaret Gorman, "Moral Education, Peace, and Social Justice," in *Education for Peace and Justice* ed. Padraic O'Hare (San Francisco: Harper & Row, 1983), p. 166.

27. For a list of affirmation activities, see Stephanie Johnson, ed., *A Manual on Nonviolence and Children* (Philadelphia PA: New Society, 1984).

28. Johnson et al., op. cit. 1975, pp. 174–177.

Chapter 8. Developmental Issues

1. American Psychiatric Association, *"Psychosocial Aspects of Nuclear Developments,"* Task Force Report No. 20 (Washington DC: American Psychiatric Association, 1982).

2. John Goldenring and Ronald U. Doctor, letter, "Adolescents' Fears of Wars," *Lancet* no. 8384 (May 5, 1984).

3. Eric Chivian and John Mack, "What Soviet Children Are Saying About Nuclear War," *Washington Post* 14 October 1983.

4. Mary Finn, "Peace Education and Teacher Education," *Peace and Change* **10**, no. 2 (Summer 1984), p. 55.

5. American Psychiatric Association, op. cit.

6. Dr. Robert Jay Lifton, quoted in Natalie Gittleson, "The Fear That Haunts Children," *McCalls* (May 1982), p. 146.

7. Bruno Bettleheim, quoted in Michael True, *Homemade Social Justice* (Mystic CT: Twenty-third Publications, 1982), p. 66.

8. Jean Piaget, "Intellectual Evolution from Adolescence to Adulthood," *Human Development* **15** (1972), pp. 1–12.

9. Eric Erikson, *Childhood and Society* (New York: Norton, 1963).

10. Lawrence Kohlberg, *The Philosophy of Moral Development* (San Francisco: Harper & Row, 1981).

11. Carol Gilligan, *In a Different Voice* (Cambridge MA: Harvard University Press, 1982).

12. Elise Boulding, *The Personhood of Children* (Philadephia PA: Religious Education Committee, Friends General Conference, 1975), p. 13.

13. Ibid.

14. V. Breitbart and B. Schram, "The Politics of Parenting Books: How to Rock the Cradle Without Rocking the Boat," *Bulletin of the Council of Interracial Books for Children* **9** (1978).

15. Educators for Social Responsibility, *Perspectives: A Teaching Guide to Concepts of Peace* (Cambridge MA: ERS, 1983), p. 28.

16. James and Kathleen McGinnis, *Parenting for Peace and Justice* (Maryknoll NY: Orbis Books, 1983), p. 27.

17. S.E. Dreikurs, "Foreword," *Family Council*, S.E. Dreikurs (Chicago: Regnery, 1974), xi.

18. A.T. Jersild, "Children's Fears," *Child Development Monographs* (1935).

19. Jerome Kagan, *Personality Development* (New York: Harcourt Brace Jovanovich, 1971).

20. Marsha Yudkin, "When Kids Think the Unthinkable," *Psychology Today* (April, 1984).

21. Ibid.

22. S.W. Olds and D.E. Papalia, *Human Development* (New York: McGraw-Hill, 1981).

23. Educators for Social Responsibility, *Dialogue: A Teaching Guide to Nuclear Issues* (Cambridge MA: ESR, 1983), p. 55.

24. Wallace E. Lambert and O. Klineberg, *Children's Views of Foreign People* (New York: Appleton-Century-Crofts, 1967).

25. Judith V. Tourney, "Political Socialization Research in the United States," *Handbook on Peace Education,* ed. Christoph Wulf (Frankfurt/Main: International Peace Research Association, 1974).

26. Eric Erikson, *Identity: Youth and Crisis* (New York: Norton, 1968).

27. H. Otto & S. Healy, "Adolescents' Self-Perceptions of Personality Strengths," *Journal of Human Relations* (1966).

28. Yudkin, op. cit.

29. *Decision Making in a Nuclear Age* (Weston MA: Halcyon, 1983), p. 3.

30. Daniel Levinson. *The Seasons of a Man's Life* (New York: Knopf, 1978).

31. Gail Sheehy, *Passages* (New York: Dutton, 1976).

32. Erik Erikson, *Insight and Responsibility* (New York: Norton, 1964), p. 267.

33. Ibid.

34. Levinson, op. cit.

35. John Gustafson, "Effects of Nuclear Threats on Adults," ESR conference, Madison, Wisconsin, 1984.

36. "Researching the Readers," *The Milwaukee Journal,* 10 June 1984.

37. Olds and Papalia, op. cit.

38. Ibid.

39. C. Buhler and F. Massarek, eds., *The Course of Human Life* (New York: Springer-Verlag).

Chapter 9.   Educational Issues

1. John E. Mack, "Resistances to Knowing," *Harvard Educational Review* **54,** no. 3 (August 1984), p. 269.

2. Erik Markusen and John B. Harris, "The Role of Education in Preventing Nuclear War," *Harvard Educational Review* **54,** no.3 (August 1984), p. 295.

3. Betty Reardon, *Militarization, Security and Peace Education* (Valley Forge PA: United Ministries in Higher Education, 1982), p. 356.

4. For a discussion of the effects of authoritarian child-rearing practices see Theodore Adorno et al., *The Authoritarian Personality* (New York: 1950).

5. Nigel Young, "Some Current Controversies in the New Peace Education Movement: Debates and Perspectives,"*Bulletin of Peace Proposals* **15,** no. 2, (1984), p. 108.

6. Robert Jay Lifton, "Beyond Nuclear Numbing," *Teachers College Record* **84,** no. 1 (Fall 1982), pp. 15–29.

7. Elisabeth Kubler-Ross, *Death: The Final Stage of Growth* (Englewood Cliffs NJ: Prentice-Hall, 1987).

8. Joanna Rogers Macy, *Despair and Personal Power in the Nuclear Age* (Philadelphia PA: New Society, 1983), p. 2.

9. Ibid., Chapter 2.

10. Ibid.

11. Tony Wagner, "Why Nuclear Education?" *Educational Leadership* (May 1983), p. 41.

12. Robert Jay Lifton, "Beyond Psychic Numbing—A Call to Awareness," *Preparing for Nuclear War: The Psychological Effects* (New York: Physicians for Social Responsibility, 1982), p. 53.

13. Margaret Gorman, "Moral Education, Peace, and Social Justice," *Education for Peace and Justice,* ed. Padraic O'Hare (San Francisco: Harper & Row, 1983), p. 157.

14. Quoted in *Despair and Personal Power in the Nuclear Age,* op. cit., p. 19.

15. Thomas Belmonte, "A Strategy of the Reclamation of Eden," *Bulletin of Peace Proposals* **10,** no. 4 (1979), pp. 339–344.

16. Betty Reardon, op. cit.

17. Robin Burns and Robert Aspeslagh, "Concepts of Peace Education: A View of Western Experience," *International Review of Education* (1983), p. 312.

18. See Asbjorn Eide, "The Right to Peace," *Bulletin of Peace Proposals* **10,** no. 2 (1979), pp. 157–159.

19. Charles Chatfield, "Peace Education: An Agenda for the Adult First Word," *Bulletin of Peace Proposals* **12,** no. 2, p. 144.

20. Robert Aspeslagh, "Basic Needs and Peace Education," *Bulletin of Peace Proposals* **10,** no.4 (1979), p. 405.

21. Hans Nicklas and Anne Osterman, "The Psychology of Deterrence and the Chances for Education in Peace," *Bulletin of Peace Proposals* **10,** no.4 (1979), p. 371.

Chapter 10. What Difference Does It Make?

1. Fred L. Polak, *The Image of the Future* (New York: Sythoff, Leyden/Oceana Publications), p. 64.

2. Willis W. Harman, "The Coming Transformation," *The Futurist* (April 1977), pp. 106–112; and Willis W. Harman, "How I Learned to Love the Future," *World Future Society Bulletin* (November/December 1984), pp. 1–5.

3. Robert C. Johansen, *Toward a Dependable Peace: A Proposal for an Appropriate Security System* (New York Institute for World Order, 1978), p. 17.

4. Fritjof Capra, *The Turning Point: Science, Society, and the Rising Culture* (New York: Bantam, 1982), p. 16.

5. See Marilyn Ferguson, *The Aquarian Conspiracy: Personal and Social Transformation in the 1980's* (Los Angeles, Tarcher, 1980).

6. Ibid., p. 36.

7. Michael McIntyre, Sister Luke Tobin, and Hazel L. Johns, *Peaceworld* (New York: Friendship Press, 1976), p. 17.

8. Marilyn Ferguson, op. cit., p. 43.

9. Elise Boulding in an address to the Peace Education Commission of the International Peace Research Association at the University of Sussex in Brighton, England, on 14 April 1986.

10. Ervin Laszlo, *A Strategy for the Future* (New York: Braziller, 1974), p. 87.

11. William Ekhardt, "Peace Studies and Attitude Change: A Value Theory of Peace Studies," *Peace and Change* **10**, no.2 (Summer 1984), p. 79.

12. Ibid., pp. 79–85.

13. Hans Nicklas and Anne Osterman, "The Psychology of Deterrence and the Chances for Education in Peace," *Bulletin of Peace Proposals* **10**, no.4 (1979), p. 372.

14. "The Catholic Bishops' Peace Pastoral and Higher Education," *Harvard Educational Review* **54**, no. 3 (August 1984), p. 319.

15. Chris Bartelds, "Peace Education and Solidarity," *Gandhi Marg* **6**, nos. 4 and 5 (July–August 1984), p. 308.

16. Maria Montessori, *Educating and Peace* (Chicago: Regnery, 1972), p. viii.

Bibliography

Peace Education

Boulding, Elise. *Building a Global Civic Culture: Education for an Independent World.* New York: Teachers College Press, 1988.

Brock-Utne, Birgit. *Educating for Peace: A Feminist Perspective.* Oxford: Pergamon Press, 1985.

Bulletin of Peace Proposals. Special editions devoted to peace education: **10**, no.4; **11**, no. 3; and **15**, no.2.

Bulletin of the Atomic Scientists. **40**, no.10 (December 1984).

Carson, Terrance R., and Gideonse, Hendrik D., eds. *Peace Education and the Task for Peace Educators.* World Council for Curriculum and Instruction, 1987.

The Committee for the Compilation of Materials on Damage Caused by the Atomic Bombs in Hiroshima and Nagasaki. *Hiroshima and Nagasaki: The Physical, Medical, and Social Effects of the Atomic Bombings.* Trans. Eisi Ishikawa and David L. Swain (New York: Basic, Inc., 1981).

COPRED Peace Chronicle. This a a bimonthly publication for members of the Consortium on Peace Research, Education, and Development. Write for information: COPRED, George Mason University, 4400 University Blvd., Fairfax VA 22030.

Dowling, John. *War-Peace Film Guide.* Chicago, World Without War Publications, 1980. (67 E. Madison, Suite 1417, Chicago IL 60603.)

Gandhi Marg **6**, nos. 4 & 5 (July–August 1984). Special Issue: "Peace Education."

Harvard Educational Review **54**, no.3 (August 1984). Special issue: "Education and the Threat of Nuclear War."

Henderson, George, ed. *Education for Peace: Focus on Mankind.* Alexandria VA: Association for Supervision and Curriculum Development, 1973. (125 N. West Street, Alexandria VA 22314-2798.)

Higher Education in Europe **9**, no. 2 (April–June 1984). Special issue on peace studies at the college level in Europe.

Interracial Books for Children Bulletin **13**, nos. 6 and 7 (1982). Special issue: "Racism, Sexism and Militarism: The Links."

Johnson, David M., ed. *Justice and Peace Education: Models for College and University Faculty.* Maryknoll NY: Orbis, 1986.

Judson, Stephanie, ed. *A Manual on Nonviolence and Children.* Philadelphia PA: New Society, 1985.

Kentucky English Bulletin **34**, no.2 (Winter 1984–85). Special issue: "Teaching English in a Nuclear Age."

Kreidler, William J. *Creative Conflict Resolution: More Than 200 Activities for Keeping Peace in the Classroom.* Glenview IL: Scott, Foresman, 1984.

Montessori, Maria. *Education and Peace.* Chicago: Regnery, 1949.

Nuclear Arms Education in Secondary Schools. Wingspread Conference Report. Feb. 1985. (The Stanley Foundation, 420 E. Third St., Muscatine, IA 52761.)

Peace and Change **10,** no. 2 (Summer 1984). Special issue on peace education.
Peace and World Order Studies: A Curriculum Guide. Ed. Barbara J. Wein. World
    Policy Institute, 1984. (World Policy Institute, 777 United Nations Plaza, New
    York, NY 10017.)
Psychosocial Aspects of Nuclear Develpments. Task Force Report #20.
    Washington DC: American Psychiatric Association, 1981. (1700 18th Street,
    N.W., Washington DC 20009.)
Read, Herbert. *Education for Peace.* New York: Harper Colophon, 1955.
Reardon, Betty. *Militarization, Security, and Peace Education: A Guide for Con-
    cerned Citizens.* Valley Forge PA: United Ministries in Education, 1978.
Teachers College Record **84,** no. 1 (Fall 1982). Special issue: "Education for Peace
    and Disarmament: Toward a Living World."
Wulf, Christoph, ed. *Handbook on Peace Education.* Frankfurt/Main: Interna-
    tional Peace Research Association, 1974.

Nuclear Policy

Journals

AEI Foreign & Defense Policy Review
Alternatives
Arms Control Today (each issue includes an excellent bibliography of other
    literature on the subject)
Bulletin of the Atomic Scientists
Commentary
Foreign Affairs (including the book review section at the back of each issue)
Foreign Policy
International Security
International Security Review
Journal of Strategic Studies
Orbis
Nuclear Times
Scientific American
Strategic Review
Washington Quarterly

Books

Adams, Ruth, and Clausen, Susan, eds. *The Final Epidemic.* Chicago: Education
    Foundation for Nuclear Science, 1981.
Aldridge, Robert C. *The Counterforce Syndrome: A Guide to U.S. Nuclear
    Weapons and Strategic Doctrine.* Washington DC: Institute for Policy Studies,
    1978.
Ball, Desmond. *Politics and Force Levels: The Strategic Missile Program of the
    Kennedy Administration.* Berkeley: University of California Press, 1980.
Baugh, William H. *The Politics of Nuclear Balance: Ambiguity and Continuity in
    Strategic Policies.* New York: Longman, 1984.
Beres, Louise René. *Apocalypse: Nuclear Catastrophe in World Politics.* Chicago:
    University of Chicago Press, 1980.
————.*Mimicking Sisyphus: America's Countervailing Nuclear Strategy.* Lex-
    ington MA: Lexington, 1983.
Berman, Robert P., and Baker, John C., *Soviet Strategic Forces: Requirements and
    Responses.* Washington DC: Brookings Institution, 1982.
Bertram, Christoph. *Strategic Deterrence in a Changing Environment.* London:
    Gower, 1981.

Blechman, Barry M. *Rethinking the U.S. Strategic Posture.* Cambridge MA: Ballinger, 1982.

Brauch, Hans Guenter, and Carke, Duncan L. eds. *Decision Making for Arms Limitation in the 1980s: Assessments and Prospects.* Cambridge MA: Ballinger, 1983.

Burt, Richard, ed. *Arms Control and Defense Postures in the 1980s.* Boulder CO: Westview, 1982.

Buteux, Paul. *The Politics of Nuclear Consultation in Nato: 1965-1980.* New York: Cambridge University Press, 1983.

_____. *Strategy, Doctrine and the Politics of Alliance: Theatre Nuclear Force Modernization in Nato.* Boulder CO: Westview, 1983.

Calder, Nigel. *Nuclear Nightmares.* New York: Penguin, 1981.

Chivian, Eric, et al., eds. *Last Aid: The Medical Dimension of Nuclear War* San Francisco: Freeman, 1982.

Clark. *Limited Nuclear War: Politician Theory and War Conventions.* Princeton NJ: Princeton University Press.

Clayton, James L. *Does Defense Beggar Welfare?* New Brunswick: Transaction, 1979.

Cochran, Thomas B; Arkin, William; and Hoenig, Milton M. *Nuclear Weapons Data Book. Vol. 1: U.S. Forces and Capabilities.* Cambridge MA: Ballinger, 1984.

Cohen, Sam. *The Truth About the Neutron Bomb.* New York: Morrow, 1983.

Collins, John M. *U.S.-Soviet Military Balance: Concepts and Capabilities, 1960-1980.* Heightstown NJ: McGraw-Hill, 1980.

Douglass, Joseph D., Jr., and Hoeber, Amoretta M. *Soviet Strategy for Nuclear War.* Stanford CA: Hoover Institution Press, 1979.

Drell, Sidney D. *Facing the Threat of Nuclear Weapons.* Seattle: University of Washington Press, 1983.

Epstein, William. *The Last Chance: Nuclear Proliferation and Arms Control.* New York: Free Press, 1976.

_____, and Webster, Lucy, eds. *We Can Avert a Nuclear War.* Cambridge MA: Oelgeschlager, Gunn and Hain, 1983.

Falk, Richard A. *Nuclear Policy and World Order: Why Denuclearization?* New York: Institute for World Order, 1978.

Feldman, Shai. *Israeli Nuclear Deterrence: A Strategy for the 1980s.* New York: Columbia University Press, 1983.

Ford, Daniel, et al., *Beyond the Freeze: The Road to Nuclear Sanity.* Boston: Beacon, 1982.

Freedman, Lawrence. *The Evolution of Nuclear Strategy.* New York: St. Martin's, 1981.

Frei, Daniel. *Risks of Unintentional Nuclear War.* Totowa NJ: Allanheld, Osmun, 1983.

Garthoff, Raymond L. *Perspectives on the Strategic Balance.* Washington DC: Brookings Institution, 1983.

Goure, Leon, et al., eds. *The Role of Nuclear Forces in Current Soviet Strategy.* Coral Gables FL: University of Miami Press, 1974.

Graham, Daniel O. *High Frontier: A New National Strategy.* Washington DC: High Frontier, 1982.

Gray, Colin S. *The MX and National Security.* New York: Praeger, 1981.

_____. *The Soviet-American Arms Race.* Lexington MA: Lexington, 1976.

Greenwood, Ted. *Making the MIRV: A Study of Defense Decision Making.* Cambridge MA: Ballinger, 1975.

Griffiths, Franklyn and Polanyi, John C. *The Dangers of Nuclear War.* Buffalo NY:

University of Toronto Press, 1979.

Hamilton, Michael P., ed. *To Avoid Catastrophe*. Grand Rapids MI: Erdmans, 1977.

Holloway, David. *The Soviet Union and the Arms Race*. New Haven CT: Yale University Press, 1983.

_____. *War, Militarism and the Soviet State*. New York: Institute for World Order, Inc., 1981.

Huisken, Ronald. *The Origin of the Strategic Cruise Missile*. New York: Praeger, 1981.

Johansen, Robert C. *Salt II: Illusion and Reality*. New York: Institute for World Order, 1979.

_____. *Toward a Dependable Peace: A Proposal for an Appropriate Security System*. New York: Institute for World Order, 1978.

Kahn, Herman. *On Escalation: Metaphors and Scenarios*. Baltimore: Penguin, 1965.

Kaplan, Fred. *The Wizards of Armageddon*. New York: Simon and Schuster, 1983.

Karas, Thomas. *The New High Ground: Systems and Weapons of Space Age War*. New York: Simon and Schuster, 1983.

Katz, Arthur M. *Life After Nuclear War: The Economic and Social Impacts of Nuclear Attacks on the United States*. Cambridge MA: Ballinger, 1982.

Kennan, George F. *The Nuclear Delusion: Soviet-American Relations in the Atomic Age*. New York: Pantheon, 1982.

Kerr, Thomas J. *Civil Defense in the United States: Bandaid for a Holocaust?* Boulder CO: Westview, 1983.

Klessig, Lowell L., and Strite, Victor L. *The Elf Odyssey: National Security Versus Environmental Protection*. Boulder Co: Westview, 1980.

Leaning, Jennifer, and Keyes, Langley, eds. *The Counterfeit Ark: Crisis Relocation for Nuclear War*. Cambridge MA: Ballinger, 1983.

Lifton, Robert Jay, and Falk, Richard. *Indefensible Weapons: The Political and Psychological Case Against Nuclearism*. New York: Basic, 1982.

Lockwood, Jonathan Samuel. *The Soviet View of U.S. Strategic Doctrine*. New Brunswick: Transaction, 1983.

Mandelbaum, Michael. *The Nuclear Future*. Ithaca NY: Cornell University Press, 1979.

_____. *The Nuclear Question*. New York: Cambridge University Press, 1979.

_____. *The Nuclear Revolution: International Politics Before and After Hiroshima*. Cambridge MA: Harvard University Press, 1981.

Martin, Laurence ed. *Strategic Thought in the Nuclear Age*. Baltimore: Johns Hopkins University Press, 1981.

Mayer, Stephen M. *The Dynamics of Nuclear Proliferation*. Chicago: University of Chicago Press, 1983.

Myrdal, Alva. *The Game of Disarmament*. New York: Pantheon, 1977.

Olive, Marsha McGraw, and Porro, Jeffrey D. *Nuclear Weapons in Europe: Modernization and Limitation*. Lexington MA: Lexington, 1983.

Payne, Keith B. *Laser Weapons in Space: Policy and Doctrine*. Boulder CO: Westview, 1983.

_____. *Nuclear Deterrence in U.S.–Soviet Relations.* Boulder CO: Westview, 1982.

Perry, Ronald W. *The Social Psychology of Civil Defense*. Lexington MA: Lexington, 1982.

Polmar, Norman. *Strategic Weapons: An Introduction*. Rev. ed. New York: Crane Russak, 1982.

Potter, William C., ed., *Verification and Salt: The Challenge of Strategic Deception.* Boulder CO: Westview, 1980.

Prados, John. *The Soviet Estimate: U.S. Intelligence Analysis and Russian Military Strength.* New York: Dial, 1982.

Pringle, Peter, and Arkin, William, *S.I.O.P.: The Secret U.S. Plan for Nuclear War.* Norton, 1983.

Rosefield, Steven. *False Science: Underestimating the Soviet Arms Buildup: An Appraisal of the CIA's Direct Costing Effort, 1960-80.* New Brunswick: Transaction, 1982.

Royal United Service Institute for Defense Studies, ed. *Nuclear Attack—Civil Defense: Aspects of Civil Defense in the Nuclear Age.* New York: Pergamon, 1983.

Scheer, Robert. *With Enough Shovels: Reagan, Bush, and Nuclear War.* New York: Random House, 1982.

Schwartz, David N. *Nato's Nuclear Dilemmas.* Washington DC: Brookings Institution, 1983.

Scott, Harriet Fast, and Scott, William F. *The Soviet Control Structure: Capabilities for Wartime Survival.* New York: National Strategy Information Center.

Scoville, Herbert, Jr. *MX: Prescription for Disaster.* Cambridge: MIT Press, 1981.

Snow, Donald M. *Nuclear Strategy in a Dynamic World: American Policy in the 1980s.* University of Alabama Press, 1981.

Speed, Roger D. *Strategic Deterrence in the 1980s.* Stanford CA: Hoover Institution Press, 1979.

Steinbruner, John D., and Sigal, Leon V., eds. *Alliance Security: NATO and the No-First-Use Question.* Washington DC: Brookings Institution, 1983.

Stockholm International Peace Research Institute (SIPRI). *Strategic Disarmament, Verification and National Security.* New York: Crane Russak, 1977.

Talbott, Strobe. *Endgame: The Inside Story of Salt.* New York: Harper & Row, 1979.

Tammen, Ronald. *MIRV and the Arms Race.* New York: Praeger, 1973.

Thompson, E.P. *Beyond the Cold War: A New Approach to the Arms Race and Nuclear Annihilation.* New York: Pantheon, 1982.

Thompson, W. Scott, ed. *National Security in the 1980's: From Weakness to Strength.* San Francisco: Institute for Contemporary Studies, 1980.

Weston, Burns, ed. *Toward Nuclear Disarmament and Global Security.* Boulder CO: Westview, 1984.

Wieseltier, Leon. *Nuclear War, Nuclear Peace.* New York: Holt, Rinehart & Winston, 1983.

Yager, Joseph A., ed. *Nonproliferation and U.S. Foreign Policy.* Washington DC: Brookings Institution, 1980.

Zuckerman, Solly. *Nuclear Illusions and Reality.* London: Collins, 1982.

World Order

Angell, Robert C. *The Quest for World Order.* Ann Arbor: University of Michigan Press, 1979.

Aron, Raymond. *Peace & War: A Theory of International Relations.* New York: Doubleday, 1966.

Bull, Hedley. *The Anarchial Society: A Study of Order in World Politics.* New York: Columbia University Press, 1977.

Clark, Grenville, and Sohn, Louis. *World Peace Through World Law*. 3rd ed., enlarged. Cambridge MA: Harvard University Press, 1966.

Claude, Inis L., Jr. *Swords into Plowshares: The Problems and Progress of International Organizations*. 3rd ed., rev. New York: Random House, 1964.

Cleveland, Harland. *The Third Try at World Order*. New York: Aspen Instituyte for Humanistic Studies, 1977.

Etzioni, Amatai. *The Hard Way to Peace: A New Strategy*. New York: Collier, 1962.

Falk, Richard, and Mendlovitz, Saul, eds. *Regional Politics and World Order*. San Francisco CA: Freeman, 1973.

_____, and _____, eds. *Toward a Just World Order*. Boulder CO: Westview, 1982.

_____; Kratochwil, Friederick; and _____, eds. *A Just World Order and International Law*. Boulder CO: Westview, 1981.

_____; Kim, Samuel; McNemar, Daniel; and _____, eds. *United Nations and a Just World Order*. Boulder CO: Westview, 1981.

Haas, Ernst B. *Beyond the Nation-State: Functionalism and International Organization*. Stanford CA: Stanford University Press, 1964.

Herz, John. *The Nation-State and the Crisis of World Politics*. New York: McKay, 1976.

Hoffman, Stanley. *Primacy or World Order: American Foreign Policy Since the Cold War*. New York: McGraw-Hill, 1978.

_____. *Studies Beyond Borders: On the Limits and Possibilities of Ethical International Politics*. Syracuse NY: Syracuse University Press, 1981.

Independent Commission on International Development Issues, Willy Brandt, Chair. *North-South: A Program of Survival*. Cambridge MA: MIT Press, 1980.

Institute of Philosophy, Academy of Sciences of the U.S.S.R. *Problems of War and Peace*. Trans. Bryan Bean. Moscow: Progress, 1972.

Jacobson, Harold. *Networks of Interdependence: International Organizations and the Global Political System*. New York: Knopf, 1979.

Johansen, Robert C. *The National Interest and the Human Interest*. Princeton NJ: Princeton University Press, 1980.

Kim, Samuel. *China, the United Nations, and World Order*. Princeton NJ: Princeton University Press, 1979.

Lovell, John P. *The Search for Peace: An Appraisal of Alternative Approaches*. Occasional Paper No. 4. Pittsburgh: International Studies Association, 1974.

McGinnis, James B. *Bread and Justice: Toward a New International Economic Order*. New York: Paulist, 1979.

Mansbach, Richard W.; Ferguson, Y.H.; and Lamport, D.E. *The Web of World Politics*. Englewood Cliffs NJ: Prentice-Hall, 1976.

Mische, Gerald, and Mische, Patricia. *Toward a Human World Order*. New York: Paulist, 1977.

Mitrany, David. *A Working Peace System*. London: Royal Institute of International Affairs, 1943.

Nye, Joseph, and Keohane, Robert. *Power and Interdependence*. Boston: Little, Brown, 1977.

Reisman, Michael, and Weston, Burns. *Toward World Order and Human Dignity*. New York: Free Press, 1976.

Rosen, Steven J., and Jones, Walter S. *The Logic of International Relations*. 3rd ed. Cambridge MA: Winthrop, 1980.

Schuman, Frederick L. *International Politics*. 7th ed. New York: McGraw-Hill, 1969.

Sharp, Gene. *Social Power and Political Freedom*. Boston: Porter Sargent, 1980.
Sivard, Ruth Leger. *World Military and Social Expenditures, 1982*. Washington DC: World Priorities, 1982.
Sprout, Harold, and Sprout, Margaret. *Towards a Politics of the Planet Earth*. New York: Van Nostrand Reinhold, 1971.
Stephenson, Carolyn M., ed. *Alternative Methods for International Security*. Washington DC: University Press of America, 1982.
Stockholm International Peace Research Institute. *World Armaments and Disarmament: SIPRI Year Book 1981*. London: Taylor & Francis, 1981.
Streit, Clarence. *Union Now*. Enlarged ed. New York: Harper & Brothers, 1948.
Tinbergen, Jan, coordinator. *RIO Reshaping the International Order*. New York: Dutton, 1976.
Vernon, Raymond. *Sovereignty at Bay*. New York: Basic, 1971.
Wallerstein, Immanuel. *The Modern World System*. New York: Academic Press, 1974.
Waltz, Kenneth. *Man, the State and War*. New York: Columbia University Press, 1959.
_____. *Theory of International Politics*. Reading MA: Addison-Wesley, 1979.
Weston, Burns, et al. *International Law and World Order*. St. Paul MN: West, 1980.
Woito, Robert S. *To End War: A New Approach to International Conflict*. New York: Pilgrim, 1982.
Ziegler, David W. *War, Peace, and International Politics*. 2nd ed. Boston: Little, Brown, 1981.

Conflict Resolution

Bach, George R., and Wyden, Peter. *The Intimate Enemy*. New York: Morrow, 1968.
Boulding, Kenneth E. *Conflict and Defense: A General Theory*. New York: Harper & Row, 1962.
Cohen, Herb. *You Can Negotiate Anything*. New York: Bantam, 1982.
Coleman, J.S. *Community Conflict*. Glencoe IL: Free Press, 1957.
Collins, Randell. *Conflict Sociology*. New York: Academic, 1975.
Cross, Gary P.; Names, Jean H.; and Beck, Darrell. *Conflict and Human Interaction*. Dubuque IA: Kendall-Hunt, 1979.
Deutsch, Morton. *The Resolution of Conflict*. New Haven CT and London: Yale University Press, 1973.
Fisher, Roger, and Ury, William. *Getting to Yes*. Boston: Houghton Mifflin, 1981.
Ginott, Haim C. *Between Parent and Child*. New York: Macmillan, 1961.
Holker, Joyce L., and Wilmof, William W. *Interpersonal Conflict*. Dubuque IA: Brown, 1985.
Kriesberg, Louis. *The Sociology of Social Conflicts*. Englewood Cliffs NJ: Prentice-Hall, 1973.
Likert, Rensis, and Likert, Jane Gibon. *New Ways of Managing Conflict*. New York: McGraw-Hill, 1976.
Oberschall, Anthony. *Social Conflict and Social Movements*. Englewood Cliffs NJ: Prentice-Hall, 1973.
Rapoport, A. *Fights, Games, and Debates*. Ann Arbor: University of Michigan Press, 1960.
Rubin, Jeffrey, and Brown, Bert. *The Social Psychology of Bargaining and Negotiations*. New York: Academic, 1975.

Schelling, T.C. *The Strategy of Conflict.* Cambridge MA: Harvard University Press, 1960.

Simmel, G. *Conflict.* New York: Free Press, 1955.

Swingle, P.G., ed. *The Structure of Conflict.* New York: Academic, 1970.

Wehr, Paul. *Conflict Regulation.* Boulder CO: Westview, 1979.

Weisinger, Hendrie, and Lobsenz, Norman M. *Nobody's Perfect: How to Give Criticism and Get Results.* Los Angeles: Stratford, 1982.

Non-Violence

Bondourant, Joan. *The Conquest of Violence: The Gandhian Philosophy of Conflict.* Berkeley: University of California Press, 1971.

Dellinger, David. *Revolutionary Nonviolence.* Indianapolis: Bobbs-Merrill, 1970.

Easwaran, Eknath. *Gandhi the Man.* Petaluma CA: Nilgir, 1978.

Esty, George, and Hunter, Doris. *Nonviolence.* Waltham MA: Xerox College Publishing, 1971.

Fisher, Louis. *Gandhi, His Life and Message for the World.* New York: Signet, 1954.

Gregg, Richard B. *The Power of Nonviolence.* New York: Schocken, 1959 (1st ed. 1939).

Hunter, Allan A. *Courage in Both Hands.* New York: Ballantine, 1962.

Judson, Stephanie. *A Manual on Nonviolence and Children.* Philadelphia: Friends Peace Committee of Philadelphia Yearly Meeting, 1972.

King, Martin Luther, Jr. *Why We Can't Wait.* New York: Harper and Row, 1963.

Lynd, Alice. *We Won't Go: Personal Accounts of War Objectors.* Boston: Beacon, 1968.

Matthiessen, Peter. *Sal Si Puedes: Cesar Chavez and the New American Revolution.* New York: Random House, 1969.

Meyerding, Jane, ed. *We Are All Part of One Another: A Barbara Deming Reader.* Philadelphia: New Society, 1984.

Muste, A.J. *The Essays of A.J. Muste.* Ed. Nat Hentoff. Indianapolis: Bobbs Merrill, 1967.

Nagler, Michael N. *America Without Violence.* Covelo CA: Island, 1982.

Rabinsky, Leatrice, and Mann, Gertrude. *Journey of Conscience: Young People Respond to the Holocaust.* Cleveland OH: Collins, 1979.

Reardon, Betty. *Discrimination.* New York: Holt, Rinehart & Winston, 1977.

Samuel, Dorothy T. *Safe Passage on City Streets.* Nashville TN: Abingdon, 1975.

Sharpe, Gene. *The Politics of Nonviolent Action.* Boston: Extending Horizons, 1973. (Porter Sargent Publishers, 11 Beacon St., Boston MA 02108.)

Sibley, Mulford Q. *The Quiet Battle: Writings on the Theory and Practice of Nonviolent Resistance.* Boston: Beacon, 1963.

Stadtler, Bea. *The Holocaust.* New York: Berhman, 1973.

Stanford, Barbara, ed. *Peacemaking.* New York: Bantam, 1978.

War Resisters League. *Nonviolent Struggle Around the World.* (1978 Peace Calendar from WRL: 339 Lafayette St., New York NY 10012.)

Woolman, John. *The Journal of John Woolman.* Secaucus NJ: Citadel, 1961.

Index

A

adult education 3, 53, 55, 116, 120, 156
affinity groups 34, 75, 156, 178
ahimsa 48, 79
Alexander the Great 18, 68
American Federation of Teachers 81
American Friends Service Committee 54
American Psychiatric Association 139
Arendt, Hannah 132
Aristotle 123
arms control 12, 45, 60, 61, 63, 176
Association for Curriculum and Development (ASCD) 81

B

Baha'i 62
Belmonte, Thomas 168
Beyond War 53
Boff, Clodivus 49
Bonaparte, Napoleon 18, 68
Boulding, Elise 121, 123, 178
Boulding, Kenneth 41
Brethren 38, 43, 53, 54
Buddhists 10, 38

C

Caldicott, Helen 59
Camera, Don 49
Campaign for Nuclear Disarmament 53

Camus, Albert 2
Center for Peace and Conflict Studies 91
Chamberlain, Neville 45
Chicago Area Faculty for a Freeze 82
Chivian, Eric 140
Christianity 10, 38, 53
civil disobedience 10, 70
Clergy and Laity Concerned 115
Coleman, James 33
community development 34, 43
community education 76, 95, 96, 155
Congress of Industrial Organizations 26
Consortium for Peace Research, Education, and Development (COPRED) 41
Council for Education in World Citizenship 80
Counts, George 23
Cox, Baroness 112
Cromwell, Oliver 10
curve of adoption (s-shaped) 13

D

Day, Dorothy 70, 151
DeBono, Edward 134
De Chardin, Teilhard 62, 177, 184
Declaration of Human Rights 111
defense budget 59
Descartes, Rene 101
deterrence 9, 10, 60
Detroit Council for World Affairs 92
development education 25, 44, 47, 48, 55
Dewey, John 22, 23, 33, 75, 80, 124
Diaz, Jaime 98

229